# The Leadership Revolution in Health Care

## Altering Systems, Changing Behaviors

**Tim Porter-O'Grady, EdD, PhD, FAAN**
Senior Partner
Tim Porter-O'Grady Inc.
Atlanta, Georgia

**Cathleen Krueger Wilson, PhD**
Senior Partner
Specialty Applications
Phoenix, Arizona

**An Aspen Publication®**
Aspen Publishers, Inc.
Gaithersburg, Maryland
1995

Library of Congress Cataloging-in-Publication Data

Porter-O'Grady, Tim.
The leadership revolution in health care: altering systems,
changing behaviors / Tim Porter-O'Grady, Cathleen Krueger Wilson.
p. cm.
Includes bibliographical references and index.
ISBN 0-8342-0633-1 (alk. paper)
1. Health services administration. 2. Leadership.
3. Organizational change. I. Wilson, Cathleen Krueger. II. Title.
[DNLM: 1. Organizational Innovation. 2. Health Care Reform.
3. Leadership. WA525 P849L 1995]
RA971.P67 1995
362.1—dc20
DNLM/DLC
for Library of Congress
95-34808
CIP

Editorial Resources: Lenda P. Hill

Library of Congress Catalog Card Number: 95-34808
ISBN: 0-8342-0633-1

*Printed in the United States of America*

1  2  3  4  5

*To my father, Thomas, who left me a deeper understanding of love; and to Margaret, who lives it every day.*

TPOG

*To Ward, who supports me in every way; and to Ryan Timothy, who teaches me about passion and patience.*

CKW

# Table of Contents

# Introduction

C hange is occurring at a rate that makes it impossible to keep up. In health care, the mechanisms for delivering services and configuring the system are being modified daily. Models for effective provision of health care are emerging in all the localities where health services are provided. New concepts like reengineering, restructuring, service-based approaches, case management, self-managed work teams, whole systems shared governance, patient-centered care, healthy communities, and a host of others confront providers continually and wreak havoc on the current structures and processes in the health delivery system.

The new configurations are having a significant impact on managers and organizational leaders, whose ability to understand and cope with the processes at work is being severely challenged. Old ways of behaving and leading do not seem to be adequate anymore. Job security is perhaps a thing of the past, and role shifting appears to be the best bet for survival in the ever-changing organizations of this new era. What is expected of managers is under revision, and individuals who attempt to function in management roles are often confused and uncertain about what is happening and where the changes are taking them. Uncertainty abounds everywhere.

We are in the midst of a paradigm shift. Everything we have known and come to value and expect in our world is undergoing significant modification. There is nothing in our surroundings and in each individual person that is exempt from dramatic transformation. Driven by technology and the proliferation of information, every aspect of human life is being altered and new kinds of understanding and applications are emerging from the center of the change vortex at a rate that prevents deliberate response. Trying to adapt quickly leaves little time to explore what the changes mean and to discern where they are taking us. Unfortunately, understanding the forces unleashed is a work in progress. The best any of us can do is identify the signposts of the journey and agree to travel together.

In a transformational journey, the rules change. Looking for immediate and sustainable outcomes is inappropriate. Holding on to the assumption that some people know enough to be able to guide us toward a reality only they can understand is simply too risky; no one knows for sure what the new reality will be. The best strategy is to gather together and try to discover jointly the character of the road into the future and the signs we need to be able to read as we proceed. Through dialogue we can begin to see the way more clearly, write the script more accurately, and play our individual roles so as to encourage everyone's movement forward and deepen our mutual understanding.

The specific role of leadership is to facilitate, integrate, and coordinate the structures and processes necessary for progress. No longer constrained by the need to know, parent, control, direct, and supervise the activities of others, leaders are now able to apply a different set of skills to advance understanding, encourage teams to take risks, and develop the relationships between teams and communities.

Using the principles of partnership, equity, accountability, and ownership, leaders are beginning to create a more interactive milieu that balances the roles of providers with the expectations of communities within an environment of fixed resources. Leaders must now be fluid and flexible in style and approach and create the kind of situation that will allow those who do the work of health care to connect in new ways and to interact as necessary to build a truly healthy community. Building a comprehensive continuum of services demands a focus on horizontal relationships rather than vertical structures and challenges status-based and rigidly defined organizational roles.

New structural models are emerging that give form to the point-of-care processes and the empowered relationships needed to make an organization function effectively. Designing an organization around the patient service value chain means pulling down some of the traditional "bricks and mortar" of health care. It means building along the patient pathway and connecting the players together through new information channels. It means making the providers interdependent and accountable for their work, relationships, costs, and outcomes. Indeed, it means forming a nationwide health service community as a foundation for creating healthy communities throughout the country.

New structures, principles, relationships, and behaviors require new approaches and skill foundations for leaders. Leading and managing without relying on the traditional superior-subordinate relationship demands different skills from those most managers now have. It means "seeing" the world of health care work from within the new paradigm and helping others develop new ways of working and relating. It means being able to assess individual strengths, skills, and needs and doing what is necessary to learn to be effective and achieve the outcomes to which a team has committed. It means leaving parenting and status-based behaviors behind. It implies learning how to engage in adult-to-adult interchanges with staff who are viewed as colleagues and team members in a self-managed dynamic. It calls for support, integration, linkage, and risk-taking. It means leaving disciplinary, departmental, compartmental, segregated, and polarized structures and behaviors behind and constructing a framework in which new equity-based values, structures, relationships, and behaviors converge around the communities served by health care providers.

This book addresses the structures and processes that exemplify the new age. It focuses on the context and content of leadership and identifies the foundations of the new role for managers. It takes a developmental and exploratory path and attempts to raise consciousness as it informs and provides new insights and tools for responding to new models.

The authors assume that the greatest transition in structure and roles will occur in the move from hospital to health system. There are many who disparage the tactic of focusing upon the hospital as the point of demarcation. Regardless of personal perspective, hospital-related structures and services make up the vast majority of functions and costs engendered in the health system, even today. It is there where many of the major changes will have to unfold. Although transformation is occurring in all health care settings, if hospitals cannot make the transition to integrated health service models, it will not matter what other settings can. Conceptually, discussion has eclipsed current reality in health care. We dream of the day the health system is no longer hospital centered and reflects the continuum of care. We are, however, a long way from that reality. Although Americans desire to arrive quickly where they want to be, much of the work will require effort, strategy, and time.

This book is basically a toolbox for leaders in all settings in the health system. It is intended to challenge thinking and provide new insights and techniques for transforming managers and organizations. It is far from comprehensive in scope and content. Only when it is used with other sources will its real value be appreciated. Readers should employ it as a foundation for thinking and acting and as a guide directing them toward deeper inquiry. By drawing on as many resources as possible, they will enhance their ability to help others achieve success in the new world of health service delivery.

There is a further challenge the authors make: readers should try to ensure that they and their teams engage in a process of continuous learning. Remaining open to discovery and discourse will prevent the fears and challenges of change from becoming overwhelming. It is through our willingness to explore, discover, and deepen our understanding that we offer the best we have and truly contribute to building healthier people and healthy communities.

*Tim Porter-O'Grady*
*Cathleen Krueger Wilson*

# Chapter 1

# Transitions and Transformations: Leadership in an Emerging New World

The times they are a changin'.
Bob Dylan

The world is the midst of a major social transformation. The changes that are unfolding are of global significance. The problem, however, is that the majority of people are focused on their own lives and work and thus fail to realize that most of what is influencing what they do is going on outside their field of vision.

Often a person's view of the world is a reflection of the person's position. From his or her vantage point, the viewer "sees" a change within a context that may distort the real meaning of the change. The true nature of the

> **Change is a way of life. It is unrelenting and permanent.**

change is obscured by the location of the viewer, and its real content may be missed because of the difficulty for the viewer of seeing it outside of his or her own situation. Although not a great problem for the individual, the position-fixed view of a current change may cause the viewer to totally miss the real meaning of the change.[1]

## A PARADIGM SHIFT

Civilization is moving from the industrial age into a new era characterized by an entirely different set of principles and values. The emerging age does not look like anything experienced to date, and our ability to understand it is compromised by our inability to recognize what is occurring. In addition, the rate of change is so rapid that there is no time to grasp all the facets and implications of the changes

1

quickly enough to fully comprehend what is happening to each of us. As a result, the changes are difficult to personalize.[2]

The comprehensiveness of the changes also creates serious concerns with regard to our ability to incorporate them into our lives and to manage them. Their scope is beyond our ability to conceptualize. Even what we know is no longer adequate to define what is happening. The transformation is so radical that we do not have the language or concepts to articulate it in any way that is meaningful to us. In a curious way, even what we know seems to get in the way of a full understanding of what is happening.[3]

One of our major problems is that what we have learned and the way we have learned it now act as impediments to our understanding of the transformation. The content of the transformation involves the very frameworks we employ for gaining and evaluating knowledge. Much of our context for learning and the content of our curricula reflects industrial ways of learning and of knowing. Newtonian physics, one of the major theoretical frameworks of the industrial age, described the more linear relationships between elements in the universe and their action upon each other. This framework was reflected in our thinking about values, relationships, work, and social structures. Many of the processes we view as fundamental to our thinking and acting are no longer fully valid as we move toward a new paradigm for understanding how the universe works and changes. The incongruity between what we have come to accept and what we now need to know raises concerns in our minds about the future of our society, values, roles, beliefs, and relationships and causes us all to wonder whether we will be able to survive the changes we are currently confronting.[4]

> *A paradigm shift changes our reality forever. We can never be the same.*

There are many signs that the stability of the globe is threatened:

- The decline of nation states has been balanced by the emergence of regional power alliances that compete collectively for the markets and resources of the globe.
- Small local wars and ethnic conflicts often defy the ability of great powers to deal with them and can have a significant enough impact to halt regional progress.
- Current economic vitality is sometimes threatened by past national behaviors. Debt and economic constraints are causing once rich nations to address their domestic economic concerns, often at the expense of their international political influence.

- Communication technology is making it easier for people to know more about what is going on across the globe than across the street. The extent and complexity of available information can prevent the information from being utilized effectively.
- Quantum mechanics theory has changed our notion of how the universe operates, how change occurs, and how we think and act. The very foundations of our learning and understanding are challenged in ways we never anticipated.
- The globalization of business and the broader range of competition has caused a restructuring of the workplace. Business leaders have responded to the challenge by tightening resources, downsizing, and retraining employees for different roles in the workplace.[5]

These examples merely represent the complex array of changes constituting the current paradigm shift. The main difficulty, however, is not the breadth of the changes but the willingness of people to undertake the activities necessary to deal with the changes successfully. Despite their recognition that certain changes are imminent, people often find it hard to conceive the changes in ways in which their personal meaning can be articulated and acted upon.

> **The breadth of the changes experienced today is a sign that we are moving into a new era.**

Even when changes can be described, they are often not personalized to the point that their impact is immediately felt. The world is full of stories of people who saw changes approaching that would dramatically affect their lives, yet still waited until the changes came crashing in before attempting to clarify what their impact would be. It must be noted that the current transformation is so substantial and so radical that it cannot be even comprehended by any single person.

## TECHNOLOGY: WRITING A NEW SCRIPT

Much of the current transformation is due to the rapid development of new technology and the impact of this technology on the very way we live our lives. A good example is the computer chip. The computer chip, much like the printing press at the end of the middle ages, is an invention that has the obvious ability to revolutionize our society for many decades if not longer.[6]

Communication technology has been able to connect people in ways never anticipated and with an ease that boggles the imagination. There is no boundary or

> *The computer chip is the printing press of the new age. It is changing our reality and forcing us into a new paradigm.*

border that can keep individuals from accessing each other and engaging in a dialogue on any issue under the sun. They can generate and transfer amounts of data limited only by their ability to locate the data.[7]

When the attempted coup occurred in the Soviet Union in 1991, there was a major effort to control the press and the communication systems of the country. One thing the coup leaders did not take into account was the burgeoning array of fax machines and modems in a growing number of small businesses, local press offices, schools, universities, and private homes. This alternative information network was able to provide information to other nations regarding activities and events during the period of the coup. Also providing important information were satellite transmissions by international television networks. In short, communication technology probably altered the outcome of the coup and contributed to the fall of the Soviet empire.[8]

> *Communication technology will make strangers of neighbors and neighbors of strangers. We can now know more about what is going on across the globe than we do about what is going on across the street.*

Business systems, health care equipment, radio and television, home appliances, and computers have made our lives easier and better. High technology is now so pervasive that we could barely survive without it. Although we all take it for granted, many adults are still suspicious of its role in their lives. They still do not fully trust technology and are uncertain about its significance. In many ways, they see it as an intrusion whose presence they have not yet fully accommodated.

On the other hand, the younger generation has embraced technology wholeheartedly. For the most part, they were born into a world permeated with technology and they accept it as a fundamental part of their life experience. Often, their introduction to technology was through Nintendo™ and other games that caused them to view it as interactive, fun, and rewarding. To them, technology is neither friend nor foe. Instead it is simply an essential feature of their lives. Unlike many of us over the age of 40, they do not experience it as an addendum or a mere convenience.

Technology can provide virtually instantaneous access to almost any information. And not only can vast quantities of data be accessed, they can be integrated to create almost any picture someone may want to present. One problem associated with such ease of access is that more information is readily available than any one person can ever use. Indeed, so much information is available that people sometimes fail to access relevant information because they are unaware of its existence. In addition to this problem, which might be called information overload, there is the problem that the producer or sender of information may design it in a way that does not meet the receiver's needs. Furthermore, not only might the receiver not want the information received or not want it in the form received, but he or she might be unclear about what information is needed or what form it should be in.

> *Our children are now alien to us. They are already conversant with the technology the rest of us do not trust and are not comfortable with.*

For example, an organization might attempt to design a system for providing accurate and valuable information only to find that the information is inadequate in content or form. The organization might then try to produce more information to compensate, with the result that too much is available in the wrong format, creating further frustration among the receivers.

Technology, of course, is changing the way in which health care is provided. Increasingly, health care technology is making interventions less intensive and less invasive. One result is that treatment of major health problems is no longer restricted to hospitals. Many types of equipment can be taken anywhere and applied wherever the health professional or patient may be, eliminating the need for institutional structures and creating more flexibility in the use of technology. Surgical services in most hospitals have felt the greatest impact of the increasing portability and flexibility of equipment, both in how they provide services and

> *There are those who suggest that we are experiencing information overload. It is not the quantity of information but the prevalence of misinformation that is the problem. If you are getting the right information, you can never get enough of it.*

the quantity of services they provide. Technological improvements and refinements make it unnecessary for patients to have to endure a hospital stay, and they also allow providers to offer services in less intensive and less expensive settings.

Other kinds of technology will further reduce the need for institutional models of health service delivery. Biological, chemical, pharmacologic, radiologic, dietetic, and physiologic research will continue to have an impact on how care is provided. A stronger focus on accountability and lifestyle issues is changing the relationship between consumers and providers and thereby helping to create healthier and longer lived populations (a development having serious social implications).[9]

Much of the potential for applying technology that already exists has not been addressed. Future technologies will yield approaches that have not even been conceived. All technologies will affect our notion of what health care is and how best to provide and integrate it. Current approaches to the delivery of services are seriously challenged by the conception and application of technology. Assumptions about current service rituals will simply dissipate in the face of the reality of emerging technologies, which will enhance our ability to get well and to stay well.

## THE ECONOMIC IMPERATIVE

There is nothing that has a greater impact on American health care than economics. Although the role that economics plays in health care is complex, there is no doubt that we are spending too much for the health care we are getting. Without any improvement in the net health of the nation, health care costs continue to spiral up above every other economic indicator used to judge the strength of our economy.

Americans have watched their health care industry grow from a 100-billion-dollar industry in 1965 to a 1.2 trillion-dollar industry in 1994. Despite the increased application of high-technology services to acute care cases, the public tends not to perceive the greater application of such services as a major factor in improving health overall. Indeed, some suggest that the longevity of Americans and their relatively good health have more to do with excellent sewage systems, comprehensive immunization programs, and decent public health services.

Many current technologies are used to treat only a few people. The problem is that as technologies become more sophisticated, they tend to become more specialized. This means that a large portion of our technology dollar is devoted to the provision of high-tech services to only a small percentage of the population. This small percentage in essence hold the rest of society hostage to their high-intensity and high-tech needs.

What is worse is that the health care system mostly caters to individuals who are sick. Indeed, it depends on sickness for its viability. The rewards, mostly in the form of insurance benefits, are centered around sickness and virtually none pertain to health maintenance. Almost all employer-based benefit plans pay 100 percent of treatment costs in the event of sickness and only a fraction of that amount for sickness prevention.

Physicians, the largest beneficiaries, next to hospitals, of the focus on sickness, have done little to alter the situation. They are paid handsomely for their treatment of sick people and are paid relatively little for helping healthy people maintain their health. One consequence is that there is a growing number of specialists and a narrowing of their specializations (there is now a specialized physician for almost every part of the human body). Another consequence is that American medical care has become fragmented, organ based, procedure based, functional, and interventionist.

> *Social policy in America is driven by economic realities reflecting our national roots as an "economic" rather than "social" democracy.*

It has also become less beneficial to the greater population and the process of first resort for a smaller margin of very ill persons who are frequently there because the health of their lives was compromised long before they got sick or their chances of survival at all was compromised from the very onset of their life.

When comparative research is undertaken, the level of satisfaction with the current approach to health care in America is shown to be relatively low. In Canada–United States comparisons done by Louis Harris and Associates, Canadians claimed to be much more satisfied with the health care they get than Americans.[10] The Canadian system places a greater emphasis on health and on community and preventive services than the U.S. system. Compulsory immunizations and other health services are required in the schools as part of preventive strategy. While not without its own problems, a stronger, more integrated approach to the delivery of services is evident in Canada.

In the United States, there is a great commitment to high-tech, high-intensity sickness services and a willingness to expend substantial resources for very sick people and only few resources to keep healthy people from getting sick. Many of the illnesses that demand high-tech intervention are preventable simply through lifestyle changes. The 1994 data from the National Center for Health Statistics show that heart disease, cancer, injuries, stroke, and lung disease are the highest causes of death over the past decade. Indeed the Agency for Health Care Policy and Research reports that about $30 billion is spent on the treatment of those five diseases alone. The General Accounting Office 1994 data show that by the year

2000 about 17 percent of the gross domestic product will be spent on health care. (Note that a dollar spent on health care does not add value to the general economy since it is being used to pay for the treatment of an individual whose productivity is impaired.) At this rate, health care services will eat up 32 percent of the gross domestic product by the year 2030. Moderating the growth of health care is no longer optional. Regardless of what comes out of Washington, the health care system simply has no choice but to alter the way it provides health services.

As noted, a good portion of the economy is tied up in paying for health care services. Therefore, the political leadership has a powerful influence on what happens within the system. If a general commitment to reform is lacking, the probability that costs will continue to slow is extremely low. A new way of looking at service provision and accounting for health care services will have to emerge if the system is to remain viable and not dramatically hurt the economy. Fortunately, many health care leaders are already aware of the need to retool the system and make it leaner and more efficient. Much of the current dialogue relates to reconfiguring the context of health care provision and the kind and quality of services in a way that better meets consumer demands for health care services (see Exhibit 1-1). Leaders recognize that it is not in the best interest of the nation to have health care costs rise at a rate some 10 percentage points higher than the other economic indices, as has occurred on average over the last two decades. Controlling costs and capping expenditures requires that everyone begin to ask the serious questions regarding health care: what do we provide? how much does it cost? and what is the natural benefit that accrues to the delivery of health care services in the current structure?

## BUILDING INTEGRATION

Voluntary efforts alone will not be able to address all of the issues that affect how much health care costs and what is provided. Recently public attention and

**Exhibit 1-1** Steps Toward Creating a Lean Health Care System

- Moving away from hospital "centrism"
- Organizing along the continuum of care
- Building partnership with all providers
- Defining clinical pathways for delivering services
- Moving providers to the point of care
- Streamlining systems to support the provider
- Reducing the management structure and numbers

political pressure has caused hospitals and others to keep the rate of health cost increases down to a bare minimum (around 5 percent on average this past few years). However, it is debatable how long this low rate can be sustained when the public is no longer pressuring hospitals and others to keep a lid on their costs. There is no longer interest in *expanding* the health sector of the economy. Instead there is increasing interest in *creating a more effective system.* The main task of American health planning is how to make better use of the dollars allocated to health while providing adequate access for the 38-50 million Americans who do not have health insurance.

## HEALTH CARE AND SOCIAL CONDITIONS

Health care should not be viewed as isolated from other social realities. It is important to realize that violence, education, family dynamics, and social commitment, for example, have an effect on who ends up in the health care system. Unaddressed social concerns will always have some impact. Simply pursuing health care reform and service changes will not result in sufficient improvement. Since the demand for certain services is partially determined by social conditions, neglect of social problems will cause the health care system to be overloaded again. Addressing the social problems that generate physical illnesses is as essential as reforming the health care system. The following are among the issues that call for a response.

> **Health care should not be viewed as separate from the other services of society. If it is, the other elements of the social system break down, threatening the integrity of the social system.**

### Family Dynamics

The change in the American family is dramatic. By the year 2000, about 40 percent of the children in America will be born into single-parent families. There is no existing service model that can accommodate that reality. Traditional two-parent family values and expectations simply do not appear valid to those whose experience does not support them. Adapting to the growing prevalence of single-parent families means acknowledging the extent of the change and asking a different set of questions about what this prevalence implies. It means adopting a new social paradigm and finding solutions that have a positive instead of negative impact on society.

## The Aging of America

It is a given that older Americans are aging better than any previous generation. In fact, they are living better than at any time in the nation's history. Because of retirement entitlements, they have access to resources that keep them independent and active much longer than they used to be. They have fewer catastrophic illnesses and more chronic illnesses (illnesses associated with living longer). They are also growing in numbers.

The aging of America—the increase in the number of the elderly as a proportion of the entire population—will have a dramatic impact on the social landscape in the near future. Addressing the specific needs of the elderly and designing appropriate cost-effective services is important for the long-term viability of our society. The challenge will be to reduce the demand for high-intensity services while providing the elderly with adequate health care.

## Violence

There is no doubt that Americans have not dealt well with violence and its impact on society. The conflict that arises between individual rights and the social good places community leaders into the middle of the fray over what should prevail in the next stage of our development as a nation.

New information on the nature and extent of violence has altered our definition of it and our view of the impact it has on our personal and social existence. Certainly there is no other industrialized nation that confronts the intensity of violence that is present in the United States. Although the aggregated data show that crime overall has decreased in America, the incidence of the more violent crimes has increased. The other great concern is that there is a greater concentration of violent crime among the younger and more disenfranchised segments of our society. The relationship between the quality of parenting and the incidence of violence is just now being investigated. Ultimately, violence has a dramatic impact on the use of health resources, especially high-intensity services.

## Drug Use

There is nothing more devastating to a society than the influx of drugs. Little can do more than drug use to destroy mind and body and alter the life of an individual in fundamental ways. Furthermore, drug use is especially common among those who are in a position to contribute most to society. Although the drug trade is operated by the so-called underworld, it draws into its net every level of society and leaves nobody exempt from its destructiveness. Needless to say, ultimately all drug users end up in the health care system, using its resources to return them to health or treat their spiraling medical conditions until they die.

The children of drug users are also seriously affected by drug-related problems. Each of them requires substantial health care resources and thus reduces the amount that can be spent on drug prevention and education. Drugs can disadvantage a child before it even has awareness. The child's birth is a painful and lonely experience, and it is unable to understand or cope with a loss it has no control over. It usually suffers from physical and mental disabilities that it will often never be able to overcome. And what kind of a home will it grow up in? The home will probably include a parent who is an abuser and who is unable to rear the child in a way that can access the best in the child and provide it with hope and the opportunities that can help it get past life's limitations. There are precious few children who are able to confront their drug-related disabilities and overcome the overwhelming obstacles that their environment forces upon them. Each year the number of drug users increases, and virtually everyone is acquainted with people who have had to face drug problems at some level.

## Automobile Accidents

The fastest growing cause of death among young people is automobile accidents (and a growing number of these accidents are related to alcohol or drug abuse). Those who die in automobile accidents are of course irretrievably lost; those who survive often require the investment of huge resources for treatment and rehabilitation. Although many recover from the accident trauma after extensive therapeutic work, most do not—they, like those who are killed outright, have their lives taken away before they had time to live them. As in the case of other illnesses, much of the tragedy could be avoided if people's behavior was more responsible and reflected a higher level of understanding.

## AIDS

There is nothing that has greater potential to deplete the resources of the health care system than AIDS. Although largely restricted to a small segment of American society, AIDS is a considerable health concern. In fact, AIDS is the single largest killer of American males between the ages of 17 and 44. A major education and consciousness-raising program in the gay community has already reduced the incidence of AIDS there. Increasingly education about AIDS has paid off in a substantial way within this community. Recent data, however, suggest that a reduction in educational activities among younger gays has resulted in a growing incidence of HIV infection among very young gay men. HIV infection among women, homeless persons, and drug users is also on the increase. It must be remembered that what emerges at the fringes of society eventually strikes at its heart. This is especially true of infectious diseases. AIDS is exceptionally egalitarian. It has no respect for lifestyle, sex, race, age, or culture and therefore has the potential to overwhelm American society just as it has overwhelmed Kenya and Thailand and other east African and Asian nations. Because of the intensity of the illness and the substantial resources that must be devoted to caring for the sick, health care systems are often forced to limit what they do for persons with AIDS.

The issues described above will have a major impact on how American society responds to its own paradigm shift. In other words, the level of health of the American populace will be influenced more by our response to social issues than by anything that the health care system can do alone to reform its service delivery structure. The time when it was possible to concentrate on one component of society without paying attention to related social issues and structures is long since past. There is simply no way that health care can resolve its difficulties with regard to cost, service, and outcomes without concomitantly addressing the issues that impact use of the system.

### HEALTH CARE REFORM

Washington will not direct health care reform no matter how the new reforms get implemented. Transformation of the system is already well underway. Many localities of America are designing approaches to health care delivery that will serve as classic prototypes for the future delivery of health services.

> *All change is local. Washington will not direct health care transformation. It is in local settings that new models of health service will be created.*

Culture drives design, and this is no less true for the current thrust at reforming the way care gets delivered and the relationship of the players who deliver it. Since local forces determine the design of services, there will be as many models as there are places in which care is provided (see Exhibit 1-2). One of the major strengths of the United States is the degree of creativity Americans bring to their institutions and business ar-

**Exhibit 1-2** Priorities for Transformation

1. Integrating the health professions
2. Building structure around the continuum of care
3. Building services around patient populations
4. Constructing good information architecture
5. Building partnerships with providers along the patient pathway
6. Developing links to subscriber and/or payor networks

rangements. Any effort to constrain them has always met with a new challenge to the constraints and mechanisms for continuing to thrive despite the constraints.

## CHANGE PRIORITIES

The most government can do in the new environment is to provide a context that serves as a baseline for the system in its attempt to meet community needs with some level of accountability. One of the problems with strictly private sector–driven reform is that accountability is not always a constituent of the forces stimulating the health care marketplace. Because revenues drive the service structure in the private sector, the ethics of economics often take priority over the ethics of service integrity. When service providers can select their markets because of their profitability exclusive of genuine community needs, there is a risk that those who require services but cannot access them or pay for them may not get them. In market-based approaches to health care, the ability to select the best market or subscribers to health care often reduces the effort to take on risk that operates just beyond good financial return. Initial efforts at managed care and provider-driven structures exemplify this reality to a high degree. Choosing "good" plans and subscribers with relatively low risk limits resource use and maximizes profitability yet still fails to address the real health needs of the community. Although this is a great short-term strategy, it creates more problems in the long term than it ever addresses in the short term.

Health is also a public good. Society is enhanced by the health of its members. There is some level of responsibility in the public sector for ensuring the viability and health of society. In addition, there are entitlements related to health care for which the public sector has accepted responsibility. The government at various levels in American society has become the purchaser of nearly half the health care services in the country. Since the services are paid for with public dollars, the issues of value and outcome become of serious concern, especially because broad-based research indicates that there may be a stronger relationship between health and good sewage systems and public health programs than between health and the activities of the current health care delivery system. Indeed, the more sophisticated technology becomes, the fewer people in the society it benefits. In America it is easier to get a coronary artery bypass graft than educational and preventive services that would help avoid the need for the procedure. The graft is paid for in full, the preventive services are rarely even available. It is a significant fact that less than 26 percent of people at any given time use over 90 percent of the technology resources of health care. Nearly 70 percent of the health care dollar spent on those over the age of 70 goes to provide care to those in the last few months of life. This is scandalous, but since no formal decisions exist to determine how dollars should be used, they are used for whatever can be paid for whether it should be provided or not.[11]

The prevailing medical model of health care is fraught with serious problems. Medical intervention is situational and depends on the patient undergoing a discernible change before a physician is accessed. Because medicine is disease based, medical treatment frequently is only instituted once the disease process becomes critical. There is little in the medical approach that facilitates those activities that might lead to early identification and treatment of problems that need not become serious. In many ways, the medical model depends for its success on the degree of intensity of intervention. Since high-tech procedures often get paid for at a higher rate than low-intensity services, there is a built-in in- centive to undertake the more intense processes that involve more complex thera- peutics and more services and more cost. Indeed, it could be said that physicians are forced by the model to depend on the high-tech processes to feed their prac- tices and reward their efforts.[12]

> **So many in the health system are benefited by illness that it is enormously challenging to shift to a health focus. Economic realities are forcing the change where good sense could not.**

On the other hand, there is little that is glamorous and exciting about practices whose role it is to keep people healthy and prevent the need for high-tech interven- tions. The physicians oriented toward prevention are not the highly skilled, techni- cally proficient specialists who do miraculous things with their talented hands and brilliant maneuverings and thereby acquire glowing reputations.

In the future, there will be a growing need for primary and preventive care ser- vices (see Exhibit 1-3). Since the health care system will use a subscriber-based approach, it is imperative that a significant increase in primary care services occur in places the services are not already available. It is estimated that 44-55 percent of medical services provided in managed care will need to be primary care related. Since over 80 percent of physicians are specialists, many new physicians will need to be quickly prepared for primary care roles or current specialists will need to refocus so that they can provide primary care services too.

## NEW MANAGER CHALLENGES

The need for primary care providers will outstrip the supply in the transformed system. The task of preparing enough providers is a critical issue that influences discussion about the role of these providers. The use of extenders and nurse practitioners will certainly go far to address immediate and long-term needs for primary care services. The focus of the reformed system will be on treatments that do not use high-intensity, high-cost services. Because the system will be subscriber based and capitated, it must be cost- and service-effective, which means services must be provided that will help to keep costs down.

Much of the debate in Washington regarding health care reform has centered on the funding of health care, and little attention has been paid to the specifics of how it should be provided. The exploration of possible ways to configure health care services and pay for them is based on experiments that are already unfolding in the private sector. It is fairly certain that the service models that prevail will be generated by organizations already designing some kind of response to the vagaries of an altered approach to health care delivery.

The emerging service models reflect certain principles that characterize the changes experienced in all the areas of our society. Retooling and restructuring organizations to be lean and efficient has become the current organizational man-

**Exhibit 1-3** Future Characteristics of Primary Care Systems

- There will be a more diverse work force.
- Health services will be wide ranging.
- Service delivery will not be hospital focused.
- There will be multiple providers.
- Heavy dependence on information systems will emerge.
- Rules will be service and culture specific.
- Practitioners will be mobile and interdependent.

tra in a wide variety of American industries. It reflects the paradigm shift identified earlier in this chapter that is calling organizations to reinvent their systems to reflect the changing social milieu more accurately.

To make the shift to a point-of-service design for the health care workplace requires focusing on what health care is and the obligations of the health care system in relationship to it. The problem is that no one can agree on what a healthy society is. The political debate regarding the public obligation to create a healthy society and the government's role in health care is fraught with all kinds of political partisanship. At the same time, the health care marketplace must respond to the incentives and challenges pushing to make necessary changes. These changes must take into account a number of prevailing realities that need to be addressed while those in positions of power discuss what strategy is best and what should be done to improve the health of the American people without breaking the bank.

**Capitation**

For two decades now there has been a major effort to control the spiraling rate of growth in health care expenditures. The goal has not been to reduce this rate below the rate of growth in the rest of the economy but instead to match the increases in cost as indicated in gross domestic product data. The attempt to hold back the rate for most of that period bore little fruit. Health care costs rose an average of 10 percentage points higher than any of the other components of the domestic market basket. It is only in the past few years that costs have matched the normative increases in the domestic economy. The decrease in the rate of growth has been attributed to downsizing and belt-tightening efforts of hospitals as they awaited the results of potential health care reform legislation.

Whatever happens in the health care industry in America, there will certainly be no return to the cost-paid days of the past. Whatever formulas emerge and are revised through the coming years, there will forever be a cap on the costs of providing health care services. The price-fixing process will give health care providers only the room to move that lies between their prices and their cost of doing business. Managers will have to learn how to put together high-quality, consumer-satisfying services in a way that keeps the expense of delivery down.

**Medical Separatism**

For the past century, the practice of medicine has remained relatively free of broad-based accountability. The individual rights of physicians have been ratified by permissive state practice acts, and the physician-patient relationship has been held inviolable. A whole body of law has arisen that protects physicians, and the only way to break through their legal shield was to file suits claiming incompetence or neglect.

In the past two decades, external control derived from the funding of health care has begun to break through some of the barriers. The need to understand just what care was being provided and what was being paid for has driven the health care system to get clearer about what occurs in the clinical process and the relationship of physician activity to the activity of other care providers. Comparative studies measuring physician practices have pointed out clinical discrepancies between the practices of different physicians. Increased attention has been devoted to pricing and to the relationship between the prices of procedures and the costs physicians incur in performing those procedures. This has resulted in a whole new area of study that looks carefully at what is done and considers whether it can be done differently, with special attention paid to the relationship between cost, price, and outcome. Although somewhat "noisy," this area of study has introduced a higher level of accountability into the practice of medicine than has ever existed before.

## Managed Care

In an effort to get better control over both care and costs, newer approaches to organizing care delivery and health services have emerged in the last three decades. The prepaid, subscriber-based medical delivery approach grew significantly as a result of the belief that it would improve the quality of services and reduce the cost of delivering them. Pulling physicians and other providers into a managed care system and predetermining by contract or by employment how much they would be paid seemed to offer employers and others a chance to get needed services at a reasonable cost. Initially there was great interest and substantial cost savings, but eventually the rate of growth in cost and the rate of growth of service use have almost paralleled the rates for fee-for-service medicine.

The accelerating demand for services that consumers felt they had already paid for and the continuation of the existing medical model approach to delivery pushed costs upward in managed care systems. Consumers also felt that they should have access to the same range of services in managed care systems as they might in other models. In order to appear attractive and to draw consumers into their market, managed care providers have been forced to offer roughly the same services at the same price as nonaligned providers. Questions about the quality and breadth of services available have made many potential customers wary of joining such systems.

Today, however, all health care providers now realize that capitation makes managed care no longer a choice but a requisite for survival. All of them will ultimately be managed care providers. As benefits and service frameworks get better defined, the captitated environment will make all providers abide by the same rules and force them to configure their service structures to respond to the capitated marketplace. This will radically alter the way in which organizations are designed and the way in which care is provided.

## The Quality Movement

There is nothing in the past decade that has had a greater impact on the American workplace than the rise of the quality movement. Deming and others have made Americans aware of the fact that we now live on a global stage and that nothing that we do exists in isolation. Once thought to have the premier economy of the world because of the variety and quality of its goods, America has discovered that others can produce goods and services with even greater variety and quality. The resulting panic has caused Americans to embrace the quality movement, with some remarkable outcomes. How we work, what we produce, and how we manage costs have all come under close scrutiny. Those who have instituted the process-engineering, quality improvement, team-based systems have experienced dramatic increases in the quality and marketability of their products and services.

Health care organizations have just come to the doorway of the quality initiative in the past few years, and its promise has not yet been realized. Quality improvement calls for the commitment and integration of all the players. Unfortunately, getting board members, physicians, administrators, nurses, and other providers in the same room and "singing off the same sheet of music" has proven harder to do than first imagined. Leaders have also been called upon to change roles and behaviors as well as organizational structures, and these changes have proven hard to accomplish as well. Both the efforts and the outcomes have been scattered, and impact on health care is still spotty. Increasingly, however, leaders are realizing that such efforts are really not optional and are taking on the obligation of moving their organizations into the center of the change process.

## Care Delivery Re-engineering

In preparation for a new approach to health care delivery, major efforts are underway to look carefully at how care delivery is organized and clinical relationships are structured. It is clear that the "old" way of delivering services is no longer viable. Because of the compartmentalizing of health care services in non-aligned departments, integration of patient care is virtually impossible in the more traditional hospitals and health care institutions. Efficiencies are viewed in the context of worker needs more than in the context of patient care.

It is clear that departmental structures do not always serve the best interests of patients, nor are they particularly efficient for the providers. Therefore, there is much exploration of alternative designs that better support the provision of satisfying services and the achievement of cost-efficient outcomes. This means that old ways of working and old types of relationships that are entrenched in ritual and routine will be challenged. Roles will be closely examined and functions will be assessed to determine their contribution to specified care outcomes. Certain roles will not survive the analysis and will disappear. Organizations will become leaner and will be structured around core activities. Differently prepared workers will work in closely aligned groups. The design of administrative models and the formation of service systems will change the very nature of health care services.

## PERSONAL ACCOUNTABILITY

Whether the challenge of the times can be met will depend on people's willingness to accept new notions of health service and to experiment with new processes and new forms. They must also exhibit fluidity and flexibility in their roles and relationships. They must realize that the changes are comprehensive and substantive and that there is no way to protect themselves from the changes as they unfold. Indeed, they must adapt their roles and behavior to the changes if they are to thrive in the current environment.[13]

> *Accountability is always personal. It resides in the role and can never be delegated away. Evidence of its effectiveness is found only in the outcomes to which it is directed.*

There is an increasing need for individuals to accept that they are accountable for their response to changes. Many people still do not realize that the transformation involves them personally and are not yet ready to do the challenging work of switching to the new paradigm. Some workers still express the view that the organization owes them a position whether or not they adapt their skills and behaviors to facilitate the organization's adjustment to new demands and opportunity. It is forgotten that the choice to stay with an organization is always the individual's and that the viability of any employee-employer relationship depends on how the employer and the organization respond to the external demands for creativity and change and the internal demands for adjustments. The obligation to learn and grow is unceasing. Those who forget this eventually experience the consequences.

Anyone today who is simply trying to save his or her job has already lost it. The environment is calling for changes in roles and creating opportunities for different kinds of work and workers. Current workers must pay attention to the opportunities as they arise and make a significant commitment to learn and adapt in ways that will maintain their value as employees. Security cannot be ensured any other way.[14]

Opportunities do not await readiness; they have their own timetable. The good strategist sees opportunities approaching and anticipates them. There is rarely time to adapt and prepare all the variables to accommodate an opportunity. What usually happens is that the opportunity creates demands where they did not formerly exist. It requires people to stretch their readiness and skills to the limit, challenging them to adapt old processes to new realities.

> *Change never asks for permission. Opportunity never waits for readiness.*

In this time of great transformation, there is little point in railing against the speed and character of change. Individuals must realize that by the time they recognize the characteristics of a given change, it has already been unfolding for some time. Further, they must realize that the course of transformation is continuous and unrelenting. Although individuals cannot prevent change or control its pace, they can influence its course and content. The achievement of the benefits of change depends on people's commitment to its outcomes.

In health care, there are many who have become accustomed to the steady and slow impact of change in their day-to-day work activities. Indeed, they have become attached to their rituals and routines, and the suggestion that they alter what they do or how they do it creates great discomfort (see Exhibit 1-4). Somehow the past pace of change seduced them into believing that there would never be any great need to work in a fundamentally different way. The design and role of leadership helped foster such a belief, since management assumed full responsibility for making decisions and directing the staff. Now that many decisions require active participation by employees in the change itself, some employees feel confused and discontented; they might not understand the need to change or be particularly skilled in dealing with change.

In the past, organizations could accommodate a number of people who were not always on board or willing to support the goals and activities of the organization. Because hospitals were growing and the demand for technically proficient workers was intense, the opportunity to survive without "buying in" was much greater. The transformation of health care and the service structure, along with new financial constraints and the continuation of capped costs, put an entirely different spin on employment and obligation. The lean and focused organization of today can only survive if

**Exhibit 1-4** Future Role Challenges

- Increased intensity of work
- Accelerating uncertainty
- Personal confusion
- Job insecurity
- Constraining resources
- Renunciation of rituals and routines

all of its players are committed to and invested in the changes that will affect what they do and how they do it. A passive relationship with their roles and their work-places will not see people through the transforming processes currently underway. If someone does not demonstrate an active commitment, there may be good reason to ask if the person's role is necessary or contributes to the vitality of the organization.

Throughout the country every health care service is closely examining its role to determine how best to configure it and how to provide care effectively and efficiently. The attempt to improve health care services will not be successful without the inclusion and active participation of staff.

The closer decisions get to the point-of-service structures and designs for care, the more critical is the involvement of the people who provide the services. A refusal to get involved on the basis that there is no reason to be involved, that there is not enough time, or that such involvement is not part of the job description is shortsightedness at best and possible grounds for termination of employment at worst. Because of the nature of the changes and the impact on everyone's roles, there is simply no alternative to committing fully to dealing with the changes. The notion of personal obligation, ownership, and involvement in decisions that affect what one does is foreign, to a variable extent, in a large number of settings. Indeed, passivity is often expected and change strategies are modified accordingly. Organizational leaders, by expecting passivity or even fostering it, often wind up contributing to the failure of their own strategy for change.

> *All staff are stakeholders and investors in the life of the organization. Ownership is not optional. There is no room for those who choose to remain renters in the system. Buy-in is essential from all the players.*

Managers designing programs for staff, teaching them what they must do, and then implementing the planned changes is a recipe for failure. Absent are consensus strategies, the investment of the players, the involvement of workers at the point of service, and the ownership by workers of the implementation processes. Gone are the days when management could determine what is good for the staff and then mold them according to its image of what they should be. Increasingly organizations depend on well-prepared staff to get invested and involved in the design and execution processes related to changes and facilitate their implementation so that there will be sufficient buy-in to make the changes sustainable.

As Alvin Toffler has so eloquently pointed out, organizations in the 1990s must realize that they will be increasingly dependent on their technical and professional staff for success.[15] Whoever works at the point of service will have the greatest influence over what occurs there. Therefore, it is imperative for leaders to use strategies that get the employees who will be impacted by processes of decision making and program design to become invested in these processes. As an organization becomes more decentralized and positions itself closer to the market and the consumers of services, it simply will not be able to afford processes that lack the investment of those upon whom the processes depend for success (see Exhibit 1-5). The growing importance of worker involvement and investment means that the content of the leadership role is going to have to change substantially.

## CHANGING THE SERVICE CULTURE

It is imperative that the truth about the requirement of investment in transformation be told early in the transformation process. The people at the point-of-service have the right and the obligation to fully understand the implications of a major change early in the change process. Truthtelling will help ensure that the process is not "held hostage" by those who have no intention of making it work. For too long

**Exhibit 1-5** Point-of-Service Changes

- Services are designed around the patient.
- Providers are configured around the patient pathway.
- Outcomes delineate the effectiveness of services.
- Structure becomes fluid to support work.
- Service settings are designed to fit the service culture.
- Physicians join the clinical team as equal partners.

in organizations the 5-10 percent of those who actively oppose innovation have articulated their feelings with great energy and determination. Opponents of a change typically find something wrong with the change, reasons not to make the change, problems with moving in the new direction, or difficulties with the new demands the change will create. They even sometimes feel that they speak for the entire staff when they speak out against the vagaries of the change process. Although they constitute only a small segment of the staff, they often articulate their concerns at a volume and intensity that belies the strength of their numbers. Legitimate concerns must always have a hearing, but individuals who are simply reacting against a change irrespective of its merits cannot and should not impede the change process. It is in the face of this kind of resistance that the leadership must tell the truth regarding the need to change and express the expectation that everyone will commit to the change process and to its outcome. For those who wish to sustain negativity or fail to embrace the process, the issue changes from one of participation to one of fit.

Individuals have the right to make decisions about their personal response to change. They own their own lives and have the right to determine what they will do with their lives. No organization has the right to impede their pursuit of their goals. The reverse, however, is also true. Any member of an organization who chooses not to act in concert with the decisions of peers or

> *Organizations are often held hostage by those who have no intention of changing. Responding to the noise they make takes up precious time that could otherwise be spent making the necessary changes.*

the organization must not try to prevent the organization from undertaking the strategies and changes it has deemed to be in its interest. One question that emerges when opposition is continuous is this: does the individual really view him- or herself as a member of the organization? If the individual cannot commit to the change process, perhaps his or her relationship with the organization should be cut short. The organization is not obliged to pander to the pleasure of individual members. And a single member does not have the right to constrain the journey of the whole group simply because he or she does not like the journey and does not want anyone else to like it either.

The point of these remarks is not to denigrate advocacy and expression of opinion. Advocacy, however, should play its role during the process of deliberation, when plans for change are just taking form. Advocacy of certain plans as opposed to others is different from active opposition to the change process. The advocate is deeply involved in the change dynamic and acts out of a commitment to change, not in reaction to it. Advocacy is always proactive and reflects a deeply felt investment. Reaction, on the other hand, is a sign of lack of commitment, investment, and sense of ownership. The transforming organization needs advocates but could do without individuals who merely react against or resist change.

## PRINCIPLES OF THE NEW AGE

The conditions of survival in the new age differ from those in the industrial age. The industrial age was much more deterministic, individualistic, and linear in its patterns of function. The workplaces, with their assembly lines and functional determinants of work, reflected the age. The breaking down of elements into their component parts and the structuring of work around the components were essential features of the industrial model of work.

> *The new leader is an advocate of those with whom he or she works. The advocacy is about learning and changing. The leader models the changes and challenges others to succeed.*

The move away from Newtonian physics and linear relationships and the corresponding emergence of quantum mechanics is one of the important changes that form the backdrop of the new age. Interest in the whole versus the parts; integration of functions, components, and parts; and a focus on outcomes of process represent a fundamentally different view of the world and of work and workers. The application of processes and structures based on "new age" thinking is forcing organizations to assess critically what they do, how they do it, and who does what. Indeed it is changing the whole framework for thinking about how organizations operate.

When an organization's leadership looks at the outcomes of its efforts and uses them to evaluate processes, it places all processes in jeopardy. No work or activity is exempt from review and no job is safe from scrutiny; all are judged with regard to their contribution to the outcomes.

Motivating the examination of activities and jobs is the need to change quickly the way work gets done. Organizational designs, work methodologies, processes that support desirable outcomes, the quality of the processes themselves, and the quality of the products or services are all involved as elements in the creation of a new context for work. The result: exceptional organizational "noise" and the trauma of uncertainty, the fluidity of systems structure, shifting performance expectations, the loss of jobs, and the creation of new roles. In fact, life in the organization becomes almost untenable.

Because of the intensity of the transformation, it is impossible to anticipate just what will happen over time. Long-term strategic positioning and planning becomes virtually impossible (see Exhibit 1-6). Plans for the organization are undermined by the fact that the world keeps changing.[16] Even as a plan is being devised, the reality it is a response to is being replaced by another reality. Those who plan for change can no longer anticipate it and can vouch only for plans with an extremely short time frame.

This era of transformation requires the players to live the script as they write it. They must recognize that whatever they put in place to respond to changes must be fluid in design because future changes are inevitably imbedded in present ones. Living out changes as they are being identified is extremely hard for a people who like to know clearly what they are doing and where they are going in virtually all the activities of their lives.

When the long-term future is unclear, it is appropriate to develop a different process that helps leaders to discover the correctness of or need to modify the activities they are currently facilitating in their response to the new reality. Long-term vision is not sufficient since any vision will only be partially correct. What leaders need is a template, a set of principles that elucidate the relationship between what they are undertaking and the underlying values guiding their activities. The use of principles helps leaders identify the key renewable characteristics of their efforts and determine how well these efforts reflect the principles of the time.

Using principles that exemplify the context and content of change requires a different set of processes for leaders.

Instead of making unilateral and solitary decisions, leaders must generate an understanding of their vision of the future in a way that represents the consensus of

**Exhibit 1-6** The New Rules

- Long-term planning is futile.
- Discernment is more important.
- Nothing is permanent.
- Read the signposts of change.
- Address the market forces.
- Link with others along the service continuum.
- Share risk rather than control relationships.

> *We must learn to write the script as we live it and live the script as we write it.*

the participants who will construct and live out the responses to future demands. Their role, in other words, is basically to translate the vision and the accompanying principles rather than try to define them for others. To succeed, they must have a clear notion of just what the principles are.

The character of the new age is represented by a set of principles that exemplify the age rather than define it. Since the new age is unfolding, in essence being born, it is hard to devise parameters that define it clearly. In addition, leaders can put form to specific changes only when they are discerned by enough people to know these changes are having an impact on the way they live and work. There are four basic principles that appear to define the emerging age and determine the way in which organizations will operate within it. They can be identified as the principles of partnership, accountability, equity, and ownership.

**Partnership**

Political, social, and economic partnerships are the models of the new age. Old notions of nationalism and the rigid borders that define nations are quickly lessening in importance and losing their exclusionary function. Because of the emergence of a global economy, nations are forming economic coalitions that strengthen their global economic viability. Isolationism and exclusionary processes now detract from rather than contribute to the political and economic health of nations. The competitive model of trade now operating in a number of arenas in the world is forcing nations to relate differently to each other in the international marketplace. Where once only a few major economic powers existed, there are now many, and they are increasing their strength and significance by joining efforts to create economic and, to some degree, political alliances that expand their reach and enhance their economic and financial health.

Clearly, creating and managing partnerships can be risky and even dangerous. The world consists of more or less homogenous nation states, and history is filled with conflict and ethnic and religious animosity. Getting past old relationships, historical prejudices, and feelings of hostility generated by wars and other regional and national conflicts requires painstaking work and mind-bending patience. However, the rewards are significant. Those that can form the effective partnerships are well positioned to take advantage of economic opportunities and achieve greater prosperity.

Partnerships are arising at all levels of society in both the public and private sectors. Companies and major enterprises are merging, purchasing, or contracting with other entities to extend their relationships and enhance their effectiveness within their markets. Larger entities are redesigning themselves to be lean but also broad as a way of increasing their competitiveness. Smaller entities are amalgamating to form coalitions and extend their influence and augment their marketability.

Partnership requires the replacement of hierarchical systems with clearly identified horizontal structures. Increasingly work structures are centered around the point of service or around products, and old management systems are being replaced with structures that support decision making and policy formation in the places where the services are provided or products are produced (see Exhibit 1-7). Self-directed work teams, integrative work arrangements, and multidisciplinary models of organization all demonstrate the value of partnership in the performance of work. Large numbers of management levels and roles disappear as worker decision making becomes the strategy of choice in quality-driven organizations.[17]

The work of building partnerships and making them sustainable is challenging for the leadership of an organization. New management and organizational processes and new work structures must emerge to support the new models of relationship and obligation. The role of the leader changes dramatically and tests the tolerance and talents of the person assuming the role. Partnership demands dialogue about the relationship between the players and the way the work gets identified and done. It demands a willingness and ability to lay process and relationship problems on the table, engage in detailed analysis, and find workable solutions. The organization becomes a permanent learning center where creativity, problem solving, solution seeking, relationship building, quality enhancing, process improving, and opportunity seeking constitute the content of the learning curriculum. Development and training are continuous and unrelenting. Structure is forever fluid, and work roles and content are flexible. Changes are made in work processes based on the product or outcome of the work.

**Exhibit 1-7** Partnership Requisites

- Horizontal, not vertical, relationships
- Building roles, not job function
- Growing a network of partners
- Adult-to-adult interactions
- Creating balance between partners
- Leading partners, not subordinates

> *The new means of control in health care organizations is not ownership. Instead it is the agreement of the parties to share risk and to venture together.*

Partnership creates a significantly different context for the organization and affects its operational structure. No longer can command and control systems permeate the organization. Empowerment is not simply a concept but a modus operandi. Further, partnership demands that all the players be connected in a way that facilitates achievement of the best outcomes. There can be no ascendant players who captain all efforts and bend them to their wishes and will. In health care work especially, different roles must take precedence at different times, depending on need. No one individual can know or control all the elements required for a successful outcome. The key players must learn to accept the role of partner and assume accountability for their activities. Here again history and previous expectations ensure the transition to partnership will require strong leadership and exceptional skill and patience.

In health care, partnering will mean the termination of segmentation and compartmentalization of roles and functions. It will mean the end of departmentalization of work and disciplines. The destruction of barriers to the integration of providers and the building of clinically integrated delivery systems are key first-stage tasks. Anything that keeps the players from accessing each other and obstructs the establishment of sustainable relationships will not survive the move toward partnership models of organization.

## Accountability

There is perhaps no greater transition than that from responsibility to accountability. In the industrial model of organization, control is maintained through the subordination of some individuals to other individuals. The former are responsible to the latter for the work they do, and the subordinate-superior relationship partially defines the character and content of the work.

The role of the manager is to make it safe for the staff to risk. No change can be sustained without risk. In the industrial model, satisfaction of the "boss" is the paramount consideration. If the boss is satisfied with the performance of the employee, all is well. The determinant of success is the impression in the boss's mind regarding the value of the work and the worker. Whole systems of management have been built around that construct.

The only problem is that there is no necessary relationship between the satisfaction felt by a superior and product-, service-, or outcome-based notions of value.

The control of work and workers has been located in the wrong place in the traditional industrial model.

Performance, outcome, and consumer satisfaction data are becoming increasingly available, which means that assessment of work and workers will be less and less dependent on personal judgment. Furthermore, successful outcomes now depend more on the knowledge of the workers than on the skills of the managers. This is a result of the fact that work is technologically based to a greater extent than ever before. The increasing importance of the knowledge worker has done more to change the character of the workplace than almost any single factor. Since the use of technology is so widespread, the capabilities of technologists and their relationships with other workers are much more critical to the success of work efforts than their relationships with managers.

Managers can no longer be familiar enough with all of the components of work to manage from a broad base of expertise. They are increasingly dependent on the competence and skill of workers and are less able to determine just what constitutes competence. Their lack of expertise regarding the functional roles of those with whom they work changes the character of their relationships with these individuals and demands modification of their own role.

In an organizational system that focuses on the quality of service and the outcomes of work, responsibility models do not work well. Since responsibility is a construct in which authority is retained by the organization rather than transferred to the worker, it is not suitable for work in the new paradigm. Accountability, on the other hand, is imbedded in a role and can never be delegated away (see Exhibit 1-8). People are always accountable for something, not to someone. In the industrial model, a worker is responsible to someone for the performance of work; in the new paradigm, the worker is accountable for specific required outcomes. Responsibility, then, is about jobs and their location and status in the structure, and accountability is about roles, their relationship, and the outcomes they are intended to achieve. In the case of accountability, an individual given a particular role must understand what is expected of any person in the role and must prove, through his or her performance and the resulting outcomes, that the role and the role holder are both valuable.

> *Responsibility relates to processes. Accountability is all about outcomes.*

Accountability focuses the organization and all its members on the purposes and the outcomes of their collective activities. Accountability models reflect the understanding that no one person alone fully controls the results of work. The relationship, interaction, and integration of processes have a much larger impact on the activities and the quality of the results. On the other hand, systems theory

**Exhibit 1-8** Accountability Basics

- Accountability is about outcomes, not processes.
- Accountability is individually defined.
- Accountability is inherent in the role, not delegated.
- Accountability must be clear to all those in related roles.
- Accountability is the foundation for evaluation.

teaches that the effectiveness of an enterprise depends on the contribution of every player. Any breakdown in one place affects the whole system. Accountability models take this into account by making accountability for the relationship of the members and the results of their performance a central feature.

Accountability relates to partnership in a direct way. Any partnership demands clarity of role, function, and contribution and a mutual understanding of the purpose and direction of the partnership. Clarifying the accountability of the various parties is critical to the success of the partnership and the achievement of its purpose. Obviously dialogue; negotiation; and clarification of role, function, and relationship are essential for success. Reducing the amount of guesswork and the number of assumptions, and any element that affects the nature or products of the partnership is always subject to review and renegotiation. Evaluation of the results of the partnership focuses on how it is working, how it affects the parties to it, and how successful the products of the partnership appear to all who are invested in it. If the partnership does not achieve the results it is committed to, then the process and the con-

> *In accountability approaches to work, competence is evidenced not by what a person brings to the work, but instead by the results of the application of the person's skills.*

tent of the roles and relationships are subject to further discussion or refinement. The outcomes always indicate the value and effectiveness of the process.

The current focus on outcome in the debate on health care reform creates a question as to whether outcome or process should be the driving force in the evaluation of quality. The truth is that it should not be one or the other. The viability of each depends on the strength of their relationship. The role of quality is to strengthen that relationship—to ensure that the process actually leads to the intended outcome. Accountability is attached to the outcome because that is the sole validator of work and action. If the outcome is not achieved by the process, the

> *Accountability is not found in what one has or is; it is instead found in what one does with it.*

integrity of the relationship is immediately put into question. Trying to make an either/or argument regarding the interaction of process and outcome is a waste of energy.

Accountability demands clarity as regards the expectations for a given role. Critical for the effectiveness of accountability is an understanding of the role's content by all who are in some way connected with the role. Without this understanding, vagueness and ambiguity might prevent the performance of an individual in the role from being judged satisfactory or unsatisfactory. The effectiveness of the person's performance in the role is basically determined by the outcome of that performance. If the performance does not achieve what was expected, it is suspect. However, the outcome can be used to judge the performance only if there is a close relationship between the process and the outcome.

**Equity**

The purpose of the entire reform process is to redefine the delivery system in order to address the health issues more effectively and efficiently. While reform is currently being driven more by cost-control issues than by any other factor, no one factor can be modified without implicating all of health service delivery.

Health care reform must concentrate on reconfiguring service around the point of care and along the care continuum. There is no point in looking only at the events of care and making improvements there. Besides being very expensive, this strategy never gets at the substantive issues of health and

> *Accountability requires ownership. It is not possible to be accountable for what one does not own.*

illness. Refocusing on the continuum calls for a complete retooling of the delivery system and all of the relationships it comprises (see Figure 1-1). Retooling the system requires a detailed analysis of what goes on at the point of service and how the system is structured to support it.[18]

If leaders look critically at the point of service in a continuum health system, they will see that the cost, quality, and service relationship and its efficacy depend essentially on those who provide services and on the places where they get provided. Toffler suggests that leaders will gradually realize that the people who do the work of the organization actually drive it. They will also realize that the design and structure of organizations will have to empower those who provide services and ensure that the care delivered along the continuum is cost-effective and competent. Although expectations will be additionally clarified, accountability will be mainly consigned to the point-of-care workers.

> *Vertical structures define the status of jobs. Horizontal structures define the relationship of roles. Equity is about roles, not jobs.*

Inevitably, these workers will be more decentralized, independent, and continuum based. The viability of the organization, the cost-effectiveness of services, and the efficacy of care will depend on the competence of the workers, the integrity of the worker-organization relationship, and the freedom of workers to make decisions without the supervision of managers. Continuum service structures will be highly decentralized and team based, health care services will be rendered in a wide variety of settings, and consumers will have a great influence on the kind and content of the services offered. Control in this environment will be exerted by both providers and consumers.

Hierarchical structures and status-based relationships will not fare well. Having echelons of decision makers in a point-of-care-based organization does not make sense. Yet the old industrial model of health care provision is hierarchical in nature. As the point of service becomes the critical construct for care delivery, redesigning care around the point of service will be essential. It is thus imperative to

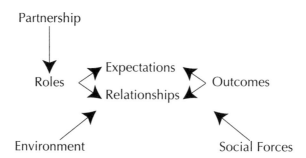

**Figure 1-1** Creating Equity

treat all roles as fundamentally equal and to allow all the individuals filling the roles to participate fully in decisions about their clinical work, the structures and processes that support it, and the character of their partnerships with each other. This simply cannot occur if decrees descend from the top of the organization. Indeed, much of the redesigning of the structure must proceed from the center of the organization. The object is to reconfigure the organization around the point of service and build the necessary supporting systems. Recognizing that all those involved in constructing the service framework and carrying out the clinical work are partners and stakeholders is a good beginning place for creating equity. Embracing team-based, inclusive processes of planning, structuring, delivering, and evaluating work is essential for shaping an effective health care organization.

> *We are watching the end of the age of the job. Now work will be reflected in role relationships and characterized by flexibility of content.*

Equity is more than a belief or a concept. It is represented in the way in which an organization does its work and sustains the relationships between the individuals who contribute to its outcomes and thus its success. Equity is about value. Each role will make a different contribution to obtaining outcomes. While they are different, each individual contributes a specific element or action on which the outcomes of work depend. If not, it is appropriate to ask about the value and appropriateness of the role itself. The structures and processes of the organization and the expectations regarding involvement, investment, and commitment reflect the organization's dedication to equity as an ideal. Equity is enhanced by inclusive decision-making processes that ask not only for participation but for ownership. The degree of organizational commitment to equity is evidenced by the extent to which decisions are kept at the point of service instead of being handed down by administrators and managers.

## Ownership

Refusing to take the journey into the new paradigm is no longer an option. Anyone deciding not to go is simply out of luck. Transformations do not wait for permission. Indeed, at the point a transformation is recognized to exist, it has already been at work for some time.

Because individuals and organizations are unsure and insecure with regard to what they are becoming and what they are leaving behind, they tend to panic. For

> *The time has come where the "renter" role or "job" attitude must go. Each person must express ownership of that part of the work that is his or hers. Our limited resources will not support any other behavior.*

an organization, this panic can result in necessary but precipitous action intended to protect its viability and focus its resources on its core activities. In addition, the roles and functions of workers are modified accordingly. This means that anyone considered peripheral, marginal, or nonessential is at great risk. The level of risk has little to do with the worker's self-perception of value. Value at a time of transformation is determined by circumstances far beyond the control of any single individual. Much of the impact of a major change is random and unexpected. Modifications in role and function are simply reflective of the organization's perception of the likely consequences of the change.

It is necessary for an organization to redesign itself in line with the character of the change. Those parts of the organization that do not appear to fit the emerging reality are simply cut away. Longevity, competence, and status combined may not be enough to save a worker from termination of employment.

Who will survive the dramatic actions taken in response to the transformation? Is it fair to drop off workers who have been a part of the organization for many years? The answers to these questions depend on the individual organization. Certainly the processes of restructuring call all the players back to a reality often forgotten. There is no security in one's job, only in one's heart. The organization cannot provide opportunities for success or longevity beyond its locus of control. Work is always a quid pro quo arrangement. The responsibility for an individual's career belongs to the individual (see Exhibit 1-9).

If events create a situation in which an individual is no longer appropriate for the work to be done, the individual is obliged to make decisions responding to his or her personal circumstance.[19] The organization will need to retain just those workers who can commit to the work in a new way and who understand and accept that the content of work will be different, the context will also be different, and the continuum of care model will shortly become the prevailing model of service delivery. However the organization changes, it must demand commitment and ownership on the part of all stakeholders. There simply is no room for those who, because of the nature of their roles, do not contribute any longer to its success.

There are those who suggest that firing workers who will have trouble adjusting to change is neither merciful nor just. In the view of some, institutions and organi-

**Exhibit 1-9** Ownership Requisites

- Point-of-service locus of control
- Empowerment of staff
- Staff decision-making skills
- Self-directed staff behavior
- Commitment to the purpose of the work

zations have an obligation not to use workers for their own ends and then discard them when the times require cost reductions. It is true that organizations do have a responsibility to be judicious and not cavalier in making decisions that negatively affect the lives of their employees. Care and caution must be used in planning and implementing role and job changes. Workers should be included in discussions about the issues surrounding downsizing and the modification of work processes. No organization has the right to capriciously or arbitrarily make important decisions that will impact its workers.

Responding to change, however, is a two-way street. No worker should assume that a current job or a current job design is permanent and unchanging. Workers have an obligation to pay attention to modifications in the way work is done, technological shifts in function, and environmental changes affecting them and their workplace. Workers must be prepared to focus on their careers and on job change and personal growth and must also recognize that this focus will be demanded in any job they may hold. It is easy to enumerate an organization's responsibilities toward its workers. It is often just as easy to forget that workers are responsible for their own lives and must respond to the circumstances of the time.

*Ownership* refers to the personal commitment an individual makes to both career and work. Investing in the mission and purposes of the organization of which the worker is a member is a minimal form of commitment. Full participation in the creative processes of the organization and the strategic changes it makes as it responds to the marketplace is characteristic of the engaged worker. Such participation demonstrates the kind of ownership of work that is likely to result in a substantial contribution to the future success of the organization.[20]

There is no room for the naysayer, the fault finder, the doom and gloomer, the opportunity buster, and others of like character. Once the organization's direction has been determined by the players and the elements of the change process have been identified, the issue is no longer whether the change process should get underway but whether the players of the organization can act in concert to meet the demands of the situation. Their ability to act in concert is a key indicator of real ownership.

Ownership does not mean just going along with the change process. Rather, it is acting in a way that facilitates the achievement of goals and the effective use of resources. Owners are stakeholders of the processes that advance the work of the organization and enhance the organization's own commitment to providing high-quality services and improving the outcomes of care and service delivery.

Absent the identification of ownership, the locus of control for certain events or processes may remain unknown. In this type of situation, there is an increased need for adequate preparation for continuous change. Note that there should always be a living dynamic between the organization and the individual. The individual has a need, for example, to be recognized, and the organization has a need to ensure its own success. The failure of either to respond to the needs of the other creates a critical condition in the organizational system. Engendering the necessary sensitivity requires the leadership and the staff to engage in a dialogue about the nature of the unfolding changes and the appropriate responses to them. One result of this kind of dialogue is that specific role modifications would be anticipated and their necessity would be understood. There should be few surprises.

Ownership also means that the organization recognizes its own need for independent, articulate, and invested workers. Never should it casually bring on board those who are unable to demonstrate the enthusiasm, energy, and tenacity required to identify what is needed and to work with the team when expectations are only partially clear. The organization must commit to its workers as strongly as the workers commit to it.

The interdependence between worker and organization will become more critical as the differentiation in the system and the potential for conflict accelerate. Both must anticipate the points of convergence in their relationship and the

> *Few men desire liberty; most men wish only for a just master.*    Sallust

points of departure—which demand much dialogue and interaction if the relationship is not to be damaged. As long as both engage in the necessary dialogue, the relationship will be strong and partnership secure. If neither are open to changes in their relationship or to discover the possibilities that partnering provides them, the partnership will falter.

Ownership is based on the organization's and worker's trust that each is fully committed to their relationship and to the organization's purpose, which is to provide health care services in an effective and meaningful way. The worker's obligation is to act in his or her role in a way that contributes to achieving the desired outcomes no matter how much the role may change. Indeed, it is expected that both the worker and organization will contribute to creating the best response to the changes confronting

> *Ownership represents a reciprocity or a quid pro quo between all the stakeholders that evidences the mutual investment each has made to the other and to the work they do together.*

them. This type of joint endeavor represents the highest form of ownership for both the organization and worker and it is essential for their survival in the emerging health care environment.

## CONFRONTING THE FUTURE

The challenges and opportunities enumerated in this chapter provide a backdrop to the work of transforming the health care system so it is able to provide the highest quality care to the American people. The reforms that are occurring represent the ongoing struggle to create a more effective and efficient health care system.

The transformation process is a grand experiment in which many models of and approaches to health care delivery will be tested. The leaders of organizations must be responsive to changes in the industry and society at large and provide a safe place to test new approaches to delivering services and new ways of configuring the relationship between provider and consumer in order to create an environment that supports innovation. Health care workers will have to accept new roles and to demonstrate increased fluidity and flexibility.

The challenges that lie ahead will require new management and leadership skills and processes. The old industrial styles of leading and the old service provision structures will not work in the new horizontal and decentralized service settings. Providers must be given a stronger role in the running of the organization and leaders will need to be more supportive and facilitative than in the past. Radically new skills and talents and new organizational approaches to accommodate emerging systems and relationships will be required of leaders. In addition, if the new approaches are to work effectively and the relationships between the players are to be configured appropriately, new models of integration will have to be designed.

> *The notion of entitlement is the most poisonous of all. It nullifies potential and destroys initiative.*

The purpose of this book is to explore both appropriate leadership behaviors and new structures that support the principles of partnership, accountability, equity, and ownership. These behaviors and structures, which constitute a departure from older models, are intended to provide a framework that supports a focus on the point of service as a means of improving health care organizations. The challenge for leaders will be to apply them and be willing to accept risk in order to create a system that delivers health care services in a meaningful and efficient way.

## REFERENCES

1. H. Andrews et al., *Organizational Transformation in Health Care: A Work in Progress* (San Francisco: Jossey-Bass, 1994).
2. W. Arnold and J. Plas, *The Human Touch* (New York: Wiley, 1993).
3. P.E. Barrentine, *When the Canary Stops Singing: Women's Perspectives on Transforming Business* (San Francisco: Berrett-Koehler, 1993).
4. M. Wheatley, *Leadership and the New Science* (San Francisco: Berrett-Koehler, 1992).
5. G. Hall, J. Rosenthal, and J. Wade, "How To Make Engineering Really Work," *Harvard Business Review* 71, no. 6 (1993):119–133.
6. D. Tapscott and A. Caston, *Paradigm Shift: The New Promise of Information Technology* (San Francisco: Jossey-Bass, 1993).
7. E. Baig, "The Information Society," bonus, *Business Week* (May 18, 1994):122–133.
8. H. Cleveland, *Birth of a New World* (San Francisco: Jossey-Bass, 1993).
9. G. Stokes, *On Being Old: The Psychology of Later Life* (Bristol, Pa.: Taylor & Francis, 1992).
10. Andrews et al., *Organizational Transformation in Health Care.*
11. T. Cole and M. Winkler, *The Oxford Book of Aging* (London: Oxford University Press, 1994).
12. P. Starr, *The Logic of Health Care Reform* (Knoxville, Tenn.: Whittle Direct Books, 1992).
13. W. Bergquist, *The Postmodern Organization: Mastering the Art of Irreversible Change* (San Fransisco: Jossey-Bass, 1993).
14. W. Bridges, *JobShift* (New York: Addison-Wesley, 1994).
15. A. Toffler, *Powershift* (New York: Bantam, 1990).
16. H. Mintzberg, *The Rise and Fall of Strategic Planning* (New York: The Free Press, 1994).
17. F. Adams and G. Hansen, *Putting Democracy to Work* (San Francisco: Berrett-Koehler, 1993).
18. T. Davenport and N. Nohria, "Case Management and the Integration of Labor," *Sloan Management Review,* 35, no. 2 (1994):11–23.
19. L. Sayles, *The Working Leader* (New York: The Free Press, 1993).
20. P. Block, *Stewardship: Choosing Service Over Self-Interest* (San Francisco: Berrett-Koehler, 1993).

# Chapter 2

# When Management Skills Become Obsolete

The values that have been labeled feminine—compassion,
cooperation, patience—are very badly needed in giving birth to and
nurturing a new era in human history.

Rollo May

## SIGN UP FOR SOARING OR SCRUB THE TRIP NOW!

The challenges of the age are at once exciting and intimidating. More to the
point, it is a difficult time to be a leader in health care or any other industry. Business trends are transforming the management map permanently. Commanding
and controlling everyone and everything is becoming increasingly counterproductive. The health care environment demands that leaders understand what the transformation of health care means to their current management paradigms and behaviors and then accommodate that awareness through changes in behavior.

Health care leaders, in response to greater competition and new demands for
cost-effectiveness and quality, are flattening their organizations so that they re-
semble the "shamrock" organization described by Charles Handy. In such organizations, the three leavers or core components include a central core of workers, a
secondary set of subcontractors, and a loose group of temporary and part-time
workers. Leaders will no longer have a vertical set of relationships with which to
manage the delivery of services. Instead, new organizational structures are rob-
bing leaders of the vertical fast track and replacing it with a horizontal one. Focal
management activities are centered on integrating the work of these core components into cross-functional and multidisciplinary units, reflecting the continuum
of health care services. What once were considered "soft" business skills, such as
interpersonal and participative competencies, have now become prescriptions for
leader success.[1]

39

Leaders' responses to the challenges facing them are a reflection of individual management mindmaps determined by unique personality attributes, life experiences, learnings, and present position in the organization. A management mindmap is a cognitive structure that guides present and future action. The problem is a leader's individual mindmap is always limited by its uniqueness, yet the extensiveness, complexity, and speed of contemporary change make it impossible for one person to comprehend and respond to it.

A successful adaptation to transformative change demands profound shifts on the part of any individual occupying a leadership role. Leaders must set a direction crafted from a diversity of views in order to obtain the commitment and the consequent actions needed to realize that commitment. This is a more profound change than it appears on the surface. Most of today's health care leaders have thrived and indeed have been rewarded richly for practicing in a self-directed, compartmentalized, controlling, and independent manner. Now success will depend upon the degree to which leaders can successfully link with many others in the delivery of services at a cognitive, interpersonal, relational, and motivational level. This kind of leadership has no room for carefully crafted organizational personas but requires a new level of authenticity from everyone. The "come-to-the-party skills" include telling the truth without denial or oversimplification, teaching on the run while making risky decisions, being a learner in the organization, helping people to take risks, and being less arrogant.[2]

> *No longer can a single view of the world set a direction for an organization.*

There is no longer a choice between changing or maintaining the status quo. Those who cry that the new order does not value managers fail to recognize that many accepted management practices are now largely obsolete—part of the history of health care management rather than its future. In order to effectively lead the reform of the health care system, those in leadership roles must be willing to accept personal responsibility for examining their own management practices. This means unbundling and sorting through their management mindmaps and discarding outdated information as well as past practices that have become ineffective. Leaders will

> *Bureaucracy demands that reality be divided up into neat little boxes. But patient needs do not fit into neat boxes.*

have to know themselves intimately and thoroughly, which may require learning at hyperspeed. They will have to be aware not only of what they know but also what they do not understand.

Some individuals will not be able to take on the necessary work, for personal or professional reasons. Others may not be able to do the work. In both cases, the individual and the leadership role no longer make a good fit, and a career change will be necessary. For those who commit to transformation, the journey will be challenging.

Adjusting to the coming changes will not be easy, and health care leaders recognize this. The explosion of management literature, on-line educational services, and management conferences reflects the market demand for learning about new management practices. Unfortunately, there is a certain amount of "hype" in the presentation of educational opportunities bombarding contemporary managers. Each new theory of management is claimed to be the one and only true theory.

The environment also does not allow managers to take the time needed for complete learning. Any student of psychology knows that behavioral change and its requisite learning calls for an environment that is free of distraction, includes support for gaining new skills and mistake making, and provides ample time to practice and fine-tune. This is hardly the learning environment of today's leaders.

Instead, health care managers tend to be harried, hassled, and sometimes anxious. They have had their responsibilities increased without concomitant support and have seen their ranks diminished through multiple reorganizations. As new organizational structures unfold through reengineering, restructuring, or downsizing, managers are trying to pack in as much information about new management practices as they can. They do this in the shortest amount of time possible while implementing drastic changes in their home organizations.

Unfortunately, managers' awareness of the need to practice differently is coming at the same time as their recognition that new management practices were desperately needed in the organization yesterday. Once managers were considered sources of knowledge—the organizational experts. Now organizations are restructuring in such a way that the expertise of providers is at the center and the expertise of managers is being challenged and may even be obsolete. It is hard to admit not knowing when they have always had the answers.

Additional obstacles to authentic personal transformation include the social and environmental demands outlined in Chapter 1. Leaders, to some degree, personally experience the difficulties that are creating the demand to reform the health care system. They may be sole supporters, live in dual-career families, or struggle as single parents. Along with the rest of Americans, they are working harder than ever to respond to the alarming increases in the cost of living while facing unprecedented levels of job insecurity.

Wise health care leaders are aware of the personal and professional complexity of the transformative journey they need to embark upon. To learn in the midst of drastic change demands stretching the limits of self-awareness and avoiding the condition that William James described as "Zerrissenheit" or "torn to pieces–hood." Wise leaders will appreciate the opportunity to learn from the complexity of change, will continually look for opportunities to stay centered, and will act upon their understanding of change.

## THE NEW BUSINESS PARADIGM: DEMANDS FOR LEADERSHIP

The new organizational paradigm demands leaders who do not impose their concepts on health care delivery systems and processes. The increasingly sophisticated health care work force demand leaders who liberate current organizational practices from outdated systems and structures that limit contributions to quality, reduce empowerment, and fail to dignify a person's work.

We must remember that people labor to survive, work to contribute, and act to gain meaning in life. In Edward Lawler's view, the ultimate competitive advantage for any organization will be the leader's ability to organize and manage people. In a successful health care organization, providers will understand their place in the whole continuum of health care delivery and act upon that understanding. They will receive immediate information on how their work influences quality and productivity and will use that information as they participate in the design of the delivery system itself and of their work within the system. They will also be amply rewarded for their contributions to business results.[3] In this high-involvement organization, the leader supports the providers through the application of cognitive, interpersonal, participative, and leadership competencies.

### Principles of the New Paradigm

The particular tenets of this new paradigm strongly suggest major shifts in accepted management practices.[4]

1. *Continuous acknowledgment of their own and others' inner wisdom is the hallmark of successful leaders.* Leaders operating in the new paradigm will seek to stimulate the contributions of the whole person to the delivery of care and will recognize the authority and control of health care professionals over their work. Acting upon this recognition will require new *participative and interpersonal competencies.* Participative acts transform not only the social system but the participants as well, and therefore productive health care organizations can become vehicles for creating a life of meaning not only for patients and families but also for providers.

2. *Leaders must recognize and act on their recognition of the interconnectedness of everyone to everything.* Simply put, my output is your input, which then becomes your output. Successful leaders will abstain from the temptation to fragment problems into pieces. A good example is some of the continuous quality improvement (CQI) training being offered to organizations today. The statistical methodologies being applied in CQI are widespread but of questionable value. Statistical models are based on assumptions of predictability and repeatability of findings and thus are less useful when applied to the social systems of health care. The ever popular fishbone diagram can perpetuate linear thinking and fragmented problem solving in the context of intolerance of mistakes.

It may be that the statistical methods of CQI, derived from mechanical and electrical systems, have outlived their usefulness. Linear thinking will not enable health care leaders to produce the innovations needed to solve critical systemic problems such as a decline in organizational productivity or resolve new ethical issues such as those related to access to care. Breaking things into pieces will not produce integrated systems of people, processes, and services along the continuum of care. The problems and issues that arise will be successfully addressed only by leaders who develop those *cognitive competencies* that stimulate systems thinking—by the individuals most affected by the problems and issues, as well as by themselves. For example, some contemporary approaches to work redesign aimed at breaking down departmental walls and creating a seamless delivery system may look successful in the short term. However, they will ultimately fail if the fragmented thinking and processes that created the original boundaries are not also addressed effectively.

> *In work, there is always a choice: to do it willingly and with joy or to do it unwillingly with resentment.*

Self-management and servanthood are the new success behaviors for health care organizations. Designing and implementing the delivery of care needs to be a collective effort. Human resource professionals will be challenged to create team-based pay systems and substitute them for traditional individual evaluations and performance incentives. The contemporary focus on individual performance does not recognize our interconnectedness and encourages people to solve problems in isolation. Leaders in the health care workplace must actively search for opportunities to engender connection, creativity, compassion, and intuition through the application of *participative and interpersonal competencies.* The freedom to use these highest of human resources must be accompanied by a willingness on the part of people to take responsibility and accept accountability for their actions.

The competitive nature of the health care environment has raised performance levels in regard to speed (shortened lengths of stay), quality, cost-effectiveness, and innovation. It is no longer acceptable to bring a patient into the hospital for a 5- to 7-day stay for gallbladder surgery and spend the first two days doing preoperative testing, providing patient education, and getting permissions signed while telling the patient that he or she should pay for it because it is part of quality care.

The information explosion has also made it possible for providers to have direct access to information, reducing the number of specialists who transform and check data checked by someone else. The new health care leader will be facilitating the access of all needed information at the point of service.[5]

Recognizing and acting on the recognition of interconnectedness means providing leadership in both the process and content of patient care delivery and actively searching for connections rather than working alone.

3. *The clockwork view of the world must be rejected.* This view has led to the creation of health care organizations where people are forced to function in rigid hierarchies. Such organizations are characterized by top-down directives and the notion that people are replaceable components. They have been successful at keeping people from having a larger understanding of the business and making them focus on narrowly defined tasks. They have also been able to obtain efficiency through specialization.

However, the competitive arena of health care requires just those characteristics that hierarchies were designed to keep out: flexibility, fluidity, innovation, increased risk-taking, and a tendency toward the use of generalists. The reconfiguration of systems and processes requires leaders who exhibit those *leadership attributes that are transformative* rather than transactional.

For example, servant departments, such as finance and information systems departments, have historically applied distorted versions of participation and empowerment strategies. These strategies have been aimed at curing workers from wrong ideas about what to do. However, the compliance and buck-passing they produce actually decrease quality and productivity levels. Planning for a strategic realignment is replaced by quick fixes. Leaders spend their time dealing with preventable crises.

Tinkering and toying with the design of servant departments will not produce the outcomes required by a provider-driven, high-involvement organization. Such outcomes will only result from the radical transformation of every department based on patient and provider needs. In an international study of management practices conducted jointly by Ernst and Young and the American Quality Foundation, management practices in traditionally layered organizations impacted performance at only one level. The best practices (those that moved an organization up in profitability, productivity, and quality) used large numbers of employees working in independent, cross-functional teams. These teams impacted problem solving across the organization at many levels.[6] In the case of servant departments, transformational leaders will ensure that their organizations are designed in a manner that allows the professionals to define their work based on their needs and the needs of patients.

Health care organizations have grown accustomed to changing largely in reaction to outside forces. In the recent past, they reacted to DRGs, managed care, and the nursing shortage. Now, health care organizations and those who work within them are reacting to alliances, networks, and managed competition. Real change comes from aspirations, imagination, experimentation, and authentic risk-taking rather than from fear.

Authority is important, and the traditional concept of chain of command reinforces that truth. Unfortunately, this concept, a legacy of military and religious institutions, has produced people who are dependent on the approval of others and therefore tend to be reactive. In a top-down system, leaders at all levels of the organization spend significant energy worrying about what the "higher-ups" are planning this week or month. Time is spent trying to figure out what words or phrases carefully dropped at the right time to the right people will guarantee job security. The dependency of providers is reflected in the common practice of shunting problems to the next level in the chain of command rather than solving them when first encountered.

> *Approaching one's work with care and awareness will transform it into an opportunity to learn and grow.*

Health care leaders who do not apply *new leadership competencies* in order to place the main focus on patients and the providers will find themselves maintaining cumbersome, inefficient, and quality-threatening systems to their own detriment. An inefficient organization will eventually attempt to respond to competition and cost constraints by downsizing its work force. The positions eradicated will include a significant number of management positions. The repeated use of downsizing has already become normal, creating work forces so demoralized that transformative change would be extremely difficult to implement.

The reactiveness of organizations and their leaders is one of the biggest obstacles to continuous learning and change. Reactive leaders become fixated on problem solving and neglect the creation of systems and processes using collective experience and thinking. Overemphasis on competition also keeps the focus on short-term solutions and quick fixes. Short-termism is at a dangerously high level in work redesign projects today.

Many management practices are rapidly becoming obsolete as new integrated systems of providers and payors are being put together. Enough time must be set aside for the individuals to make the transition to their new role accountabilities. There are no rules for ensuring the transition. It is simply a voyage of personal and organizational discovery. The necessary personal and organizational transformation demanded by the new organizational paradigm will occur only in organizations in which leaders have repatterned systems and processes to allow awareness, choice, freedom, growth, and intention to operate.

## CORE COMPETENCIES FOR THE REINVENTED HEALTH CARE LEADER

Among the stories involving the goddess Copper Woman is one that speaks to the challenges of transformation confronted by health care leaders. Copper Woman warned her people that their world would certainly change. *In fact, the change would be so great that for the leaders knowing would not be the same as doing but trying would always be important.*[7] One lesson to be gotten from this story is that we have to stop worrying about things to come and simply face the fact that the next century is already here. It is the time to act.

Health care leaders must not be blinded by past success and limit change to the use of new slogans and fads. The new paradigm challenges leaders to engage in a drastic reconceptualization of their world views and to scrutinize the core values, beliefs, and ideas that have shaped their management practices. Health care leaders must change not only the way they think but also the way they act. Therein lies the "trying" that is critical for true transformation. The core competencies for twenty-first-century health care leaders are summarized in Exhibit 2-1.

### Conceptual Competence

For health care leaders, inquiry becomes action through the application of well-developed conceptual skills. Thinking and acting are not distinct but instead are part of a reflective cycle of leadership activity. As leaders think and act purposefully, an enriched understanding of both past and present will emerge.

Management knowledge is structured by the mindmaps or conceptual schemes possessed by leaders. In fact, all that leaders truly ever possess are their ideas. Command and control or chain of command are only ideas. They exist because people believe them to exist.

Mindmaps are both guides and products. Leaders use them to relate uncertain events to a pre-existing concept or mental model in their action planning. Mindmaps become products as they are changed to fit new experiences (see Exhibit 2-2).

**Exhibit 2-1**  Core Competencies for Twenty-First-Century Leaders

- **Conceptual competencies**
  —Systems thinking
  —Acclimatization to chaos
  —Pattern recognition
  —Synthesis
  —Continuous learning
- **Participation competencies**
  —Involvement
  —Empowerment
  —Accountability
- **Interpersonal competencies**
  —Receptivity and similarity
  —Immediacy and equality
  —Facilitation
  —Coaching
- **Leadership competencies**
  —Technical expertise
  —Transformational style
  —Interactive administering

How leaders act upon their thoughts and lead others to act is the foundation for most organizational activities and processes, including decision making, communication processes, structure design, interpersonal interaction, and consensus building. Health care organizations simply cannot act independently of their members and their members' thoughts. New leaders will be challenged more than ever before to develop conceptual competencies that allow them to understand and manage their own and others' cognitions and behaviors. Most leaders in health care today do not possess these competencies.[8]

**Exhibit 2-2**  Conceptual Competencies

- To recognize the primacy of the whole
- To define the self in terms of relationships
- To become acclimatized to chaos
- To develop the ability to recognize patterns
- To develop synthesizing ability
- To engage in continuous and interactive learning

For example, suppose the providers of oncology services are having a difficult time getting good information about the cost and quality of their services, making it almost impossible for them to compete in the marketplace. In response to their request for better information, the leadership group may favor reconfiguring the information services to form a servant department made up of self-directed work teams, one of which would be assigned to oncology services. Their choice of this response would undoubtedly be based on several implicit cognitive schemas, including beliefs about the health care marketplace and the need for rapid response. The most salient mental map guiding action, however, would be their view of the initial request by the providers as an *opportunity for organizational design.*

In a similar scenario, another leadership group may act quite differently. The response to the request might be to add more information specialists or marketing personnel to the relevant departments. Here the salient mindmap is a *strong respect for the advantages of building the necessary expertise within the individual departments.* Other pertinent beliefs might include the as-

> *Are you thinking or merely rearranging your prejudices?*

sumption that providers cannot possibly define their information needs. The risk here is that the specialist viewpoint will guide action rather than the providers' expressed needs.

Management mindmaps can be both limiting and freeing. The organization of information into a schema or map reduces the time spent in processing information and also reduces ambiguity, thus protecting against the information overload characteristic of today's workplace. Mindmaps also allow for speedier problem solving and provide a basis for decision making.[9]

However, management mindmaps can also be limiting. Here is where some of the personal transformative work of the leader must occur. Outdated or inaccurate management mindmaps can promote stereotypic thinking. Even worse, they may limit the leader's ability to identify cues accurately and may reinforce the status quo rather than lead to the pursuit of needed change. Critical cues are ignored because they do not fit the model. The Swiss are still mourning their rejection of the quartz watch, which gave Japan dominance in the watch marketplace in place of Switzerland. Wise leaders, not wishing to find themselves in the same sad situation, will have the courage to look carefully at their own management mindmaps. Figure 2-1 summarizes the structure of management knowledge in relationship to action.

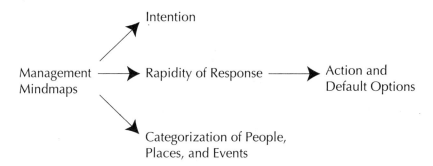

**Figure 2-1** The structure of management knowledge and action.

### Conceptual Competencies and Organization Design

In the new health care paradigm, the successful leader will restructure or rearrange systems and processes to meet current realities. The questions asked by the leader will reflect deep thought. The organizational structure will be examined from many different angles. Why was it chosen in the first place? If the present structure is not effective, what is the best way to redesign it? What prevented recognition that the structure was ineffective?

The decisions about organizational structure will flow from newly conceptualized ideas about organizations and ongoing learning about people and their relationships.[10] These concepts will be operationalized by the new leaders in making organizational design decisions, in helping individuals and groups to succeed in new organizational structures, and in implementing structural changes. The application of new management mindmaps will also lead to an increased willingness to work together and communicate openly and a reluctance to leave the organization.

### Systems Thinking

Systems thinking is the most noteworthy of the conceptual competencies demanded of the reinvented health care leader. A leader who is a systems thinker does not simply look at care delivery as a group of services configured along the continuum of health and illness but sees it as the product of their interactions. Such a leader will view him- or herself as accountable for managing interactions rather than controlling people. Problems are not seen in isolation but as part of a larger universe of problems. For example, a problem in the timing of medication administration is obviously due to a fault in the medication delivery system. But this system is affected by the budget of the pharmacy department and its vendor contracts, which are influenced by the system of departmentalization within the organization. The number of departments and the layers of managers flow from the organizational structure and the predominant executive mindmaps, which in turn are tied to past practices of health care reimbursement and medical specialization. Cutting across all of the systems are differences in the medications different practitioners prefer to prescribe.

There are three basic premises of systems thinking that must be adopted by the new health care leader: (1) the whole has primacy over the parts, (2) the power of language derives from the fact that our statements reflect our conceptual schemes, and (3) the self must be reconceptualized as fundamentally dependent on its relationships to others.[11]

> *There must be time set aside for groups to see, own, build, and maintain connections.*

The notion that the parts of a whole are primary and the whole is secondary must be discarded. Leaders must review their language and thought patterns, discarding whatever causes them to see things in parts.

Leaders must also recognize that the power of language is due to the fact that words and sentences are overt symbols of our conceptual schemes.

Finally, the concept of self will be redefined in terms of relationships and connections. The self only exists because of its relationships to others (e.g., a person is a coach because he or she interacts with others in a mentoring, tutoring, or counseling manner). This means that there is no such thing as individual action.

### Acclimatization to Chaos and Uncertainty

Contemporary leaders struggle with a conceptual confusion about order. Managers have been taught to equate control with order. However, chaos theory suggests that the pursuit of a stable environment is futile. Creative or transformative solutions will remain unattainable unless leaders can convince people to walk through the fires of confusion, uncertainty, and overwhelmedness.[12] Only then will views about order versus chaos be changed. Leaders must partner with chaos, so to speak. This means developing the conceptual skills to generate new information. Conceptually adept leaders are skillful and insightful questioners. They synthesize related information and reap meaning from fear and confusion. The challenge inherent in reaping meaning from confusion is to allow the flux between organization and disorganization to just happen.

Leaders should abandon the search for certainty before action. Acclimatization to uncertainty becomes easier once it is recognized that certainty is never truly achievable. Effective leaders know that they act in ignorance of the final outcomes of their actions, in ignorance of all of the dynamics of the situation, and in the absence of a complete action plan.[13]

The new business paradigm will challenge leaders to establish in their minds a risk-certainty threshold that will be modified as factors change. The steps in thinking that incorporates uncertainty look something like this:

1. *Openness to surprises as opportunities for new ideas.* This prevents the automatic application of old mental maps in a defensive response to problematic situations.

2. *Taking advantage of pre-existing information.* This includes looking at the present situation and testing it against what is already known while recognizing that the pre-existing information may be outdated, erroneous, or incomplete.

3. *Developing hypotheses about actions and their varying levels of risk and uncertainty.* Primary and default options are explored.

4. *Taking action.* Action is taken on the basis of an incomplete and tentative understanding of the situation. Feedback is used to adopt and change mental models that apply to the situation.[14]

### *Pattern Recognition*

Reliance on outdated management mindmaps leads to "pattern blindness," which is often disguised as problem solving. This type of entrenched thinking sounds the death knell for health care organizations wishing to compete successfully in the new health care marketplace. The ability to recognize patterns is a critical conceptual skill, since it allows leaders to take effective action rather than remain paralyzed by confusion. They can avoid "paralysis by analysis" by identifying a few simple basic patterns. For example, reengineering in the hospital setting means devising patterns of care delivery that place the patient at the center. Every action, structure, and process is examined for patterns that represent a true patient focus.

> *Systems are grown and nourished rather than designed and implemented.*

The recognition of patterns also means seeing organizations as cognitive systems. Part of the leadership role is to create systems that take into account the thinking, learning, and self-managing patterns of organizational staff.

Conceptually adept leaders will seize upon opportunities to help people conceptualize what is happening and why. They will then use that understanding to propel individuals and groups to determine what works best in their own work environments. This approach has no room for the laying on of someone else's template of change and hoping for some of the same outcomes.

Degrees of managerial expertise can be looked upon as differences in pattern recognition. Compare, for example, the skills of a novice chess player to the championship skills of a Bobby Fischer. The novice has a limited number of stored patterns. The expert has sharply honed conceptual skills. These allow the expert to read a few basic patterns quickly, determine a multiplicity of potential chess moves for each pattern, and continually invent new moves.

### Synthesis

Leaders need to become expert in systems thinking, which means, among other things, acquiring the ability to synthesize parts into a whole. Analysis gives us only partial knowledge. Analysis might tell us, for example, that the medication administration system is working or not working. Synthesis presents us with the larger picture.[15]

Health care leaders can no longer rely on overly simple or narrowly focused responses to situations. Instead, solutions must come from multiple directions and must integrate multiple viewpoints. Transformed leaders who apply their proficiency in conceptual synthesis will comfortably discard previous role specializations. They will no longer spend their energy handling only those problems that fall into their particular department or area of expertise. Synthesis precludes acting in one's own interests or working around others in order to shift accountability or promote individual viewpoints. Instead, the synthesizing leader will develop, maintain, and support integration. The new management role will encompass risk sharing, networking, actualizing, value clarifying, culture changing, and consolidation.[16] These activities will be a requirement for success as teams become increasingly multidisciplinary and multilayered.

### Continuous Learning

Health care organizations are filled with "brain dead" workers and managers who have been socialized over time to stop thinking. A meal for a diabetic who has ordered three entrees is served anyway because the person delivering the tray did not think about what he or she observed. A leader directs a group on what the "right" action is, seemingly oblivious to the verbal and nonverbal cues of employees that suggest the action is problematic. People stop asking why because they are never assisted in honestly exploring possible answers.

The new business paradigm has as its central theme that people are valuable and their potential for growth should be supported. In fact, an extremely important role of the new leader is to manage people's potential. The new leader must have the competencies needed to create a safe environment in which people can think and learn.

Much has been said about creating a "learning organization." What does this involve? What competencies are needed? The "learning" mindmap, including notions about what teaching is and is not, must be purposefully altered. Learning should no longer be seen as a means of advancement but as a life-long journey. It results not only from studying new ideas but also from interacting and sometimes aggressively clashing with the ideas of others. Teaching sometimes merely involves creating an environment in which collisions can occur without detriment.

> *How are you at supporting the thinking of others?*

In the reformed health care system, providers will be required to be productive and competent members of an integrated system. Leaders will be held accountable for ensuring that provider competence will flow from a holistic orientation rather than from specialization.[17] Developing a holistic orientation in work teams requires a different kind of learning and therefore a different way of leading.

Unfortunately, those in leadership roles are products of professional programs that rely heavily on passive learning and memorization. These teaching-learning methodologies have naturally been carried over into the workplace. The popularity of inservices and long orientations is testimony to the pre-dominance of passive learning in contemporary health care organizations. Even attempts to teach by bringing in

> *I don't know how to help you learn. They didn't teach it at my school.*

popular trainers have sometimes failed. Although the training stimulates excitement, trainees find it difficult to operationalize what they have learned in their own work settings.

Leaders who are competent in continuous learning will invest in *integrated learning* for themselves and for those whom they lead. Integrated learning is based on the idea that the learner must combine thoughts, feelings, feedback, and experiences; any one factor by itself could be an impediment to real understanding. For example, a person may truly think that he or she is facilitating a meeting when the person's real motive is to control the agenda to further his or her own interests.

The person could attend a class where the top ten facilitation concepts were presented and still think that he or she was a great facilitator. Why? Without the opportunity to practice facilitating a meeting, receive feedback, and see others facilitating differently, the person would lack the kind of experience and feedback needed to achieve an understanding of high-quality facilitation.

There are certain prerequisites for continuous learning. The leader's behavior reflects a *commitment* to spend the necessary time to unlearn something or to learn something new. The leader's conversations with others demonstrate the *courage* to explore the emotions associated with learning or unlearning. The leader encourages individuals and groups to invest the personal *energy* to master new thinking. The leader holds everyone *accountable* for what they choose not to learn.

In short, learning must become a part of the very fabric of how work is performed for everyone in the organization. The expectation that this will occur is expressed daily through the leader's interactions with others. A commitment to learning means no excuses for not learning are accepted.

The leader must show a willingness to hear and to understand the truth about what people are thinking. The leader "faces the music" and is prepared to hear the undiscussable become discussed. He or she asks not only what is happening but why people think that it is happening.

Every organization has its share of undiscussables—issues people are afraid to air because they fear punishment or disfavor. Some organizations live with problems for years because people have tacitly agreed not to discuss them.

Fear is a major impediment to learning and should be dealt with as soon as possible. Fear comes from two major sources. First, when given the opportunity, most human beings will work very hard to avoid discomfort and pain. Taking this notion to the limit, one could argue that mental illness is really an individual's fear reaction to a perceived threat.[18]

Health care organizations and the people who lead them can sometimes demonstrate symptoms of mental illness, such as the denial of ineffective practices in the face of reality, depression and its paralyzing inaction, paranoia and its accompanying distrust, and the splitting off of the real self from the persona shown at work. Interactive learning might help individuals see that their view of themselves as not having enough time for their duties may be, at a personal level, an excuse for inaction.

Through a series of experiential exercises involving dyads and larger groups, leaders would be challenged to think about time in an integrated way. The questions explored could be many. What do I think about the time I have to do my job? What was I taught about time as a child? In school? Does my concept of time fit with the realities of today's workplace or is it outdated? What are the skills that I am using to manage my time? Am I a skillful prioritizer? On the other hand, are my activities so prioritized that I cannot flow with unplanned events? What keeps me from doing something about this? Learning activities that focus upon these kinds of questions are very different from traditional courses on time management.

At the organizational level, perceptions of insufficient time may signal collusion. Organizational collusion is evidenced when people say that they believe one thing and then act differently under stress. In the case of insufficient time, a management group may say that they want to grow as a team but there is never enough time. There may be an implicit agreement to continue to be terribly busy in order to avoid conflict, cover incompetencies, dodge the painful truth, or provide ongoing justification for leader job security.

In such a situation, a series of interactive learning sessions may help the management team to identify their defensive reasoning and their false explanations for not having enough time. Feelings associated with taking the time to do something might be explored through the posing of questions. If I take the time to say to my colleagues what I really think, will I be rejected? What will my boss say if she learns that I really do not know how to do a certain part of my job well? What are the policies, behaviors, and practices that perpetuate insufficiency of time? What could they be replaced with that would support taking extra time as well as accepting the consequences for taking or not taking extra time?

In this scenario, leaders are contributing to an environment conducive to learning by personal example. However, a further reform is necessary before people believe that it is safe to think and learn. Leaders must reconceive the purpose and practice of morale building. They have traditionally been taught to "buffer" their employees from tough facts or uncomfortable feelings in order to protect them and maintain productivity. This may be one reason human resource departments have grown in size and have intensified their dedication to addressing employee morale issues. Unfortunately, buffering tends to create a culture in which people cover up what they really feel and are more likely to talk to "objective outsiders" instead of their managers.

> *People who think are more self-directed than those who let the waves of the workday wash over them.*

Learning and understanding require real dialogue between everyone involved—dialogue during which judgment is suspended. Both positive and negative thoughts are listened to in order to uncover the multiple meanings at play in the situation. People are guided to a common view about what is happening now, which then can be collectively acted upon.

Dialogue takes more time than a short staff meeting can provide. Individuals must be coached to say what they really think. Leaders need to ask questions,

**Exhibit 2-3** The Skills of Continuous Learning

- Involving oneself in active rather than passive learning experiences
- Asking why and discussing the undiscussables—even if the undiscussable is the leader
- Accepting the consequences of learning and of failure to understand
- Facilitating real dialogue between all parties

prepare for hearing hard truths, and say what they really think. Partnership in dialogue leads to several important outcomes: critical thinking, learning from mistakes, and consistent actions in both stressful and nonstressful situations. The skills and tasks necessary for creating a continuous learning environment are summarized in Exhibit 2-3.

People who think are more self-directed than those who let the waves of the workday wash over them. Real learning produces greater innovation and more creative solutions. Self-examination leads to improved productivity and quality. The application of continuous learning competencies is sure to engender the internalization rather than memorization of information as well as cause insightful action.

**Participation Competence**

Health care leaders must become adept at gaining the full involvement of people in their work. The participation competencies (Exhibit 2-4) include the fostering of communication skills and purposeful behaviors that promote the prac-

**Exhibit 2-4** Participation Competencies

- To use nondirective and less analytic processes in decision making
- To consistently reinforce, through role-modeling dialogue and teaching, the value and legitimacy of worker involvement
- To identify opportunities for shared decision making, collaborative projects, and relevant training
- To create an environment in which people fully accept that shared decision making is preferable to individual decision making
- To articulate the benefits of high worker involvement and publication of the benefits among all constituencies
- To promote an understanding of the developmental nature of the transformation

tice of enlightened self-interest. Personal and organizational goals must be designed in such a way that both individual and organizational needs are integrated in a meaningful fashion. People do not get involved in activities that have no meaning for them. Leaders must set the time aside to have the kinds of conversations that lead to high involvement.

Take, for example, the work restructuring that is occurring in most contemporary health care organizations. Why are some leaders so successful in involving workers in redesigning their own work while others find themselves confronting anger and resistance? Most likely, the former have spent time informing workers about the economic and technological trends forecast for their service areas and, through individual and group dialogue, have helped them understand how the acquisition of additional skills through cross-training would contribute to their marketability as workers and to their efficiency on the job. Leaders' participation competencies are evident in an organization where there is real, early, and full involvement of people in making decisions about their work.

A high regard for participation is reflected in the choice of a management style that emphasizes collective decision making and deliberate involvement. Whether or not a leader embraces participation is determined by several factors. To what degree does the leader believe that participation truly results in organizational effectiveness? Repeatedly, research has demonstrated that participation improves the quality of information processing and thinking as well as the effectiveness of decisions and their implementation.[19] What has the leader's past experiences with participative structures been? Were they real or fraudulent structures? How does the leader view power? If the leader expects loss of power as a result of instituting participative structures, then he or she will not be inclined to embrace a high-involvement management style. Does the organizational culture embrace participation? Is the philosophy that is espoused reflected in the actions of leaders in the organization?

Leaders who want to increase worker involvement need to spend significant time learning the potential value and the potential problems associated with participative structures and processes *before* their implementation. Doing this homework reflects an awareness of the personal and the organizational damage that could result if participative structures are poorly designed or implemented. The leaders themselves are highly involved in leading the change process.[20]

Participative structures in one area of the organization will usually cause conflict with other areas not ready or willing to engender the same degree of involvement. Leaders who have mastered participation anticipate this problem and will factor into the design of participative structures the monitoring of interfaces and boundaries for potential conflict.

Mastering participation also means recognizing the drastic shifts required of individuals and groups and consistently applying effective interventions. For ex-

> *Are you really tapping all of the talent in your organization?*

ample, one common problem associated with the transformation to shared governance is avoidance. Leaders who have not mastered participation will be thrown off guard when staff attempt to shift work right back to them. They will be frustrated when staff sometimes attack them in order to take the focus off themselves or the work itself. In such a situation, competent leaders will pace the development and the implementation of shared governance structures so that the natural frustration and anxiety accompanying the transformation will not move to a higher level than people can tolerate.[21]

### Empowerment and Accountability

Involvement and empowerment necessarily coexist. The leader who possesses a high-involvement management style must have empowerment skills as well. Adept leaders make use of an internal empowerment blueprint that guides them in the building of high-involvement structures and processes.

Without this kind of blueprint, the organization is at risk for developing what has been described as the "aimless empowerment syndrome." Authority is given to workers but it is so ill defined that there is little accountability for performance.[22] Furthermore, leaders do not really understand why they are sharing decision making. The absence of shared leadership behaviors in the management group is never confronted. Consequently, collaboration is inconsistent. Staff are given authority for decisions that do not belong to them, and changes made by staff are not maintained over the long term because of inadequate systems or processes. All this adds up to a high potential for failure.

Empowerment blueprints used by competent leaders clearly outline leadership expectations, zones of authority, performance expectations, and resource planning and acquisition. Accountability for what is to be done and how it is to be done is clearly communicated to everyone. There are standards for new behaviors and timetables for their acquisition. Resources are accessed and made readily available. In sum, empowerment is individually placed and organizationally reinforced. Empowerment processes cannot be allowed to blow in the wind but must be adeptly guided and sometimes directed by the competent leader.

## Interpersonal Competence

Clearly, the new health care organization obligates leaders to finely tune all interpersonal skills. People skills have always been essential ingredients for success. However, new relationships require additional interpersonal skills (see Exhibit 2-5).

**Exhibit 2-5** Interpersonal Competencies

---

- To engender receptivity, similarity, immediacy, and equality in communication
- To structure groups through processes in order to accomplish objectives
- To acquire expertise in group or team dynamics
- To guide performance improvement through counseling, mentoring, and tutoring
- To solve performance problems while maintaining positive relationships

---

### Communication

To function in a facilitative role, a leader must be a masterful communicator. Relational communication comprises those types of verbal and nonverbal messages through which persons define their relationships (and themselves). In the new health care organization, leader communication can no longer be dominated by task-oriented and position power messages. Leader communication that emphasizes receptivity, similarity, immediacy, and equality is crucial for encouraging high levels of participation among workers.

*Receptivity* is evidenced when leaders communicate in words and action an openness to exploring work issues, even if they are personally uncomfortable with exploration of such issues. When teaching or coaching individuals and groups, leaders share *similar experiences* as a way of modeling and providing encouragement. *Immediacy* is a strategy employed when a controversial issue causes tempers to rise. The adroit leader will drop the issue for the moment and offer a "timeout" or will facilitate working through the issue. *Equality* messages are intended to communicate that everyone's point of view is equally valuable to explore as input into a decision.[23]

### Facilitation

Facilitation involves easing a group through a logical and satisfying process. A process is satisfying when it follows a sensible set of steps and when it feels psychologically agreeable. The right people are in the right place, and the environment is conducive to the success of participative processes and teams.

Facilitators need to understand how people operate in groups and how to use group dynamics to help teams accomplish their work. Using group dynamics is no easy task, as most groups are made up of people who have varying levels of cognitive complexity and are at different stages of development. The dynamics of most groups thus tend to reflect degrees of comfort with uncertainty stemming from unlike judgments and reasoning.

Facilitating leaders are flexible. They understand the development of teams and recognize that at varying stages of development different things are needed from the leader.

A leader must challenge some of his or her basic assumptions that could interfere with the development of an effective team structure. Does the leader expect people to be logical most of the time? It is not in the nature of groups and individuals to always be logical in their thinking and purposeful in their actions. Subconscious and even unconscious motivations may emerge. Recognizing the irrationality of human beings is freeing. It allows the leader to use the behavior being expressed in the group to garner information and develop an understanding of what is happening rather than reacting.

Does the leader believe that the group, given enough time, will come up with a decision that everyone can easily agree with? Novices to the work of groups may unknowingly encourage groups to avoid conflict or cause them to become paralyzed by discussion in order to find the "perfect solution." In fact, many group decisions require challenging discussions and/or conflict resolution prior to implementation. The key is to find the best balance between those task activities that move a group through its agenda and the maintenance processes that address positive and negative group dynamics. It is the quality of the interaction which is the focus of facilitation skills rather than the persons doing the interacting.

### Coaching

Much has been written about the leader as coach. Being a coach means being skillful at forming relationships with individuals and groups in which counseling, teaching, and mentoring discussions aimed at improving performance play a large role. What is not evident in much of the literature is how difficult the transition is from leader to coach. Employees tend to see managers as evaluators of their performance and controllers of their pay. They may be hesitant to approach a manager for a performance coaching conversation.

On the other hand, the strong tradition and the plethora of regulations and laws surrounding performance discussions contribute to leader anxiety about the boundaries of discussion (i.e., what is acceptable and what is not). What is acceptable to discuss is anything the employee feels is a block to performance. This does not mean that the manager becomes a therapist. Instead, the manager provides resources for counseling when it is mutually agreed that personal issues are affecting performance.

In coaching, the manager should usually avoid expressing an evaluation of the employee's work. On the other hand, it is appropriate to provide information, guidance, examples, role modeling, constructive feedback, and tutoring. The manager may also explore obstacles to advancement or excellent performance.

Occasionally a manager may have to confront an employee with a bad performance evaluation before the disciplinary process is initiated. In such situations, the manager initiates the discussion, clearly states the performance problems, uses the communication skills of participation in order to develop insight into performance obstacles, and helps the employee to accept accountability for improvement.

Through the application of a purposeful coaching process, the leader helps individuals to address those factors that are getting in the way of performance. The two goals are sustained improvement of performance and maintenance of a strong, positive relationship.

## Leadership Competence

Leaders will create the context for new organizational structures to emerge. In order to act as leaders, they must possess not only technical credibility as management specialists but also transformational leadership skills.

### *Technical Credibility*

Health care leaders must possess strong business and technical skills. These will ensure that they have the credibility necessary to create, implement, and sustain new organizational relationships. As the staff become increasingly self-directed, leaders will function as a technical resource for the staff's decision-making activities. Technical support in the form of information about delivery systems, marketing, evaluating cost and quality, and building in controls, is provided to teams as they implement new work relationships.

There are eight major domains of technical competence needed by health care leaders (see Exhibit 2-6). The development of new, integrated health care systems demands a good understanding of *organizational design* as it influences delivery systems. Mastery of *financial management* and *health care economics* is essential

**Exhibit 2-6** Eight Domains of Technical Expertise Required by Leaders

1. Organizational design
2. Financial management
3. Health care economics
4. Business ethics
5. Evaluation methodology
6. Health care jurisprudence
7. Information technology
8. Long-term strategic planning

for examining the cost-effectiveness of decisions. Additionally, these domains of knowledge will guide the assessment and the successful negotiation of managed care contracts.

It will behoove leaders to develop familiarity with health care jurisprudence. Their decision making and problem solving are more likely to reflect current regulatory and legal conditions if they have some background in this area.

A new set of ethical dilemmas, stemming, for example, from advances in technology, increased access to care, and the large-scale redeployment of workers, are confronting the health care leaders. The application of *ethical decision-making frameworks* can assist the leaders in finding a good balance between financial realities and humanistic concerns.

Those health care organizations that will be successful in the marketplace will have leaders who recognize opportunities for the application of *information technology*. Leaders who actively develop their understanding of a wide range of types of information technology will be able to identify opportunities for applying technological solutions to work problems as well as acquiring the human, fiscal, and material resources to implement these solutions. In one organization, for example, a nurse executive identified how cellular phones could reduce staff nurse time at the nursing station.

Another important domain of technical competence is *long-term strategic planning*. Students of the Japanese business practices have all observed how every Japanese business decision is tied to long-term strategies. Compare this with the American obsession with the quarterly profit statement and short-term productivity.

It is easy to become a slave to monthly variance reports. Technical skills that enable the manager to justify short-term variances by reference to long-term objectives will result in more thoughtful decision making and put the organization in a stronger position in the competitive health care marketplace. Armed with long-term strategic planning capabilities, the successful management team will ensure that every activity in the organization is in some way linked to strategic business goals.

### Transformational Leadership

An interesting conclusion of some of the most recent research on transformational leadership is that the implementation of integrated, high-involvement systems is being severely impaired by a profound lack of such leadership.[24] Until the gap between transformational leadership theory and actual leader practices is closed, such systems will be less successful than hoped for and will be decidedly less easy to sell. Leaders who have succeeded over the long term in developing new organizational forms differ from traditional leaders in their leadership style. They are transformational leaders.

Transformational leadership theorists have carved out a domain of leadership competencies that center on leaders' adeptness at transforming themselves, their followers, and their organizations. Such transformations are basically achieved through the application of relationship skills. In mutually empowering relationships, transformational leaders are able to commit people to action, convert followers to leaders, and may even convert leaders into change agents.[25]

Transformational leadership competencies are particularly important in this era of radical and drastic change in health care. For example, the actions of transformational leaders can guide people in times of crisis by arousing intense feelings through ideas and inspiration.[26]

### Interdependent Leadership

A limitation of the transformational leadership model is that it paints the leader as an independent administrator somewhat separate from the group. The transformational leader is described as someone who sets and communicates a transformative vision that motivates everyone. However, the interactive, integrated health care organization of the future requires a leadership style that is much more relational in nature. Health care leaders must step *into* situations in order to understand rather than stepping back. A blending of the transformational style of leadership and a more intense relational style can be found in the work of the interdependent leadership theorists.

> *Interdependent leadership consists in getting what you want through the partnership process.*

The focal concern of the interdependent leader is the involvement and the development of people and the management of their potential so that it becomes fully realized. The interdependent leader sees a new relationship between the purpose of work, the individual, and the organization and seeks to preserve connections, integrate differing views, and foster group learning.[27] Traditional health care organizations have not been structured around connections but around function and role. Those working in health care have naturally developed a skewed notion of leadership, productivity, and people.

The interdependent view of leadership reflects the changing leadership paradigm. Women's ways of knowing and leading are now considered to constitute a model for leadership in business. The principles of interdependent leadership are summarized in Exhibit 2-7.

**Exhibit 2-7**  Principles of Interdependent Leadership

- Goals and plans come from listening to people and synthesizing their ideas.
- Interpersonal mastery is critical.
- Never separate self from others.
- Motivation to act comes from relationships.
- Decisions consider individuals in their contexts and situations.
- Systems thinking ties together relationships and innovation.

*Source:* Reprinted from Lyons, N.P., Visions and Competencies, in *Changing Education: Women as Radicals and Conservators,* by J. Antler and S. Bilken, eds., pp. 204–205, with permission of SUNY Press, © 1990.

Interdependent leaders see responding to and caring about people as a moral imperative. In order to abide by this imperative, leaders must maintain good relationships and try to create a caring environment. This does not mean that leaders focus on relationships to the exclusion of technical competency and business goal setting. Rather, relationships are seen as a vehicle for the achievement of business outcomes.

## CRITICAL TRANSITIONS ON THE TRANSFORMATIONAL JOURNEY

Health care leaders can have a real desire to involve people in new ways but at the same time doubt their capacity to change to a new management style. A leader's personal transformation requires not only considerable courage (courage to unlearn old dependencies) but also the assertion of his or her own learning needs in the face of unprecedented daily work demands. The transformation away from managerial obsolescence begins as the leader acquires new competencies. Their acquisition then propels the individual into both personal and motivational transitions within an organizational context. Each organization moves through change differently. The particular circumstances within an organization will foster a leader's growth or impede it. As increasing numbers of leaders move through these critical transitions, a momentum of change will lead to transformational outcomes for the individual, the group, and the organization. These relationships are shown in Figure 2-2.

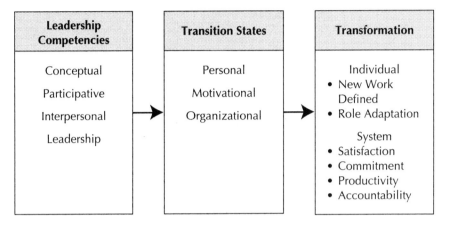

**Figure 2-2** Leader Transitions and Transformations

**Personal Transitions**

There are certain signposts along the journey that indicate a leader has personally invested in the elimination of obsolete practices. Early signs include the expression, through words and behavior, of a willingness to change. For example, the leader might struggle aloud with ideas, comparing and contrasting old ways of doing with new strategies for action. This is quite different from the parroting of ideas expressed by others. A commitment to transitioning at a level of excellence is also evident.

As the leader moves deeper into a personal transition, random acts of courage and risk taking, for self and for others, begin to occur. These acts of courage include active attempts to unlearn old behaviors by confronting traditional structures and processes that impede the development of high-involvement, integrated systems. This means challenging sacred cows and asserting personal authority in the face of hierarchy. The leader will move along a continuum of growth that demands increasing levels of courage and risk taking, as shown in Figure 2-3.

The least amount of risk is associated with actions that are taken within a group context or are aimed at helping to improve existing systems. As the leader acquires the knowledge, skills, and behaviors associated with new competencies, attempts to challenge existing structures become more frequent. Success results in greater

LOW RISK, LOW REWARD

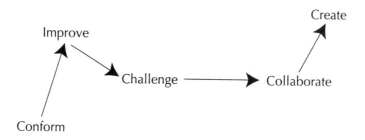

HIGH RISK, HIGH REWARD

**Figure 2-3** Risk and Reward in Transformative Actions

risk taking by the leader, who is also more likely to involve and collaborate with others in challenges. If the outcomes of these challenges are acceptable, individuals and groups are more likely to appreciate the risks and rewards associated with the transformation to new organizational forms and will act accordingly.

**Motivational Transitions**

A transition to a participative managerial style can also be characterized as motivational in nature, since the leader might be deterred by pre-existing discomfort with participation. If the leader's management style is already participative, the transition to an interactive, high-involvement style will be easier. Clearly, it will take motivation and energy to transition from a directive style to a participative one because dramatic conceptual and behavioral changes are required for such a transition.

Motivational challenges are also encountered as the leader strives to develop and exercise new skills and maintain the courage to participate in change in less than ideal circumstances. There are always unanticipated obstacles to change, such as the loss of a beloved leader, the prospect of a merger, or a sudden decline in financial performance. In struggling with their own growth, leaders will prove themselves to be true citizens of their organization.

Organizational citizens are easy to identify. They can be depended upon to exert the energy needed to confront obstacles rather than give up and are consistently conscientious in the pursuit of quality. Their behavior helps foster a contagion of hope for the future.

### Organization and Leader Interactions

The transformative journey of leaders is significantly influenced by the characteristics of the organization itself. The *relational aspects* of the organization will either support or impede the leader who is preparing to embark on a personal change. How is participation really managed? Are empowerment structures real or fraudulent? What are the dynamics of the existing hierarchy? Does the leader carry any baggage and will it prevent him or her from taking the necessary risks? The stress associated with deep personal change is reduced if positive support relationships are present.

Another organizational feature warranting evaluation is the degree to which pattern maintenance exists in the face of change. The individuals selected for leadership positions were selected because they functioned well in the hierarchy. Although a new organization is being planned, do individuals in key positions exhibit a willingness to eliminate the standard operating procedures that they participated in creating? If not, such individuals may not support the leader in the development of new competencies.

The readiness of the organization to transform to a new integrated system will influence the skills selected by leaders for personal development. Degrees of involvement in authentic transformation are illustrated in Figure 2-4. Leadership practices will ensure that the organization either gets stuck at ground zero or accomplishes the transformation successfully.

**GROUND ZERO OR FRAUD** (closed to influence; one-way communication; participation as manipulation)
⇓
**EXPLORATION** (open to influence, dialogue)
⇓
**ALIGNMENT** (partnerships and collaborative processes)
⇓
**CO-CREATION** (authentic invitations to create a new system)
⇓
**TRANSCENDENCE** (reconfiguration of original purpose and even existence)

**Figure 2-4** Degrees of Authentic Change to High-Involvement, Integrated Systems.

*Source:* Reprinted from Pasmore, W. and Fagin, M.R., "Participation, Individual Development and Organizational Change: A Review and Synthesis," *Journal of Management,* Vol. 18, No. 2, p. 388, with permission of JAI Press, Inc., © 1992.

## MAKING THE DECISION

The health care environment is dramatically altering the workplace. It is no longer a place where people can come to merely make a living. Extraordinary actions are required in extraordinary times, and this time is no exception. Health care organizations need competent leaders prepared to take them into the twenty-first century, but the new skills needed are not easily acquired.

Systems and processes once relied upon for success are now beginning to fail or ceasing to produce good results. Gradually, health care leaders have come to recognize that flattened, high-involvement organizations have the potential to thrive in the new environment. For this potential to be realized, however, the leaders must struggle with the possibilities and challenges of new organizational forms and let go of false beliefs about worker competency.

> *Order from the top is being replaced by order from within.*

The joy comes in recognizing that management could actually be fun—that tremendous satisfaction can be derived from helping employees develop and meeting the challenges of resource acquisition. The outcomes that result from individual and organizational transformation are significant. At the individual level, the managing process acquires a new meaning and focus and becomes much more rewarding than controlling others. There is a renewed clarity about what it takes to make the system really work. Success is redefined as managing the potentials of others. At the organizational level, the satisfaction, productivity, and quality gains associated with the new organizational forms are well documented. The only choice left is to take off and soar or to find a new habitat.

### REFERENCES

1. C. Handy, *The Age of Unreason* (Boston: Harvard Business School Press, 1990), 88–117.
2. American Society for Training and Development, Board of Governors, "Executive Development in a Changing World," *Training and Development Journal* 44, no. 6 (1990):23–26.
3. A.J. Vogl, "Bureaucracy Busting: An Interview with Edward Lawler," *Across the Board* 30, no. 2 (1993):23–28.
4. C.K. Wilson, "The New Business Paradigm: Demands for Nursing Leadership," *Aspen's Advisor for Nurse Executives* 9, no. 8 (1994):3–6.
5. Vogl, "Bureaucracy Busting," 24.

6. J. Malone, "Creating an Atmosphere of Complete Employee Involvement in TQM," *Health Care Financial Management* 47, no. 6 (1993):126–128.

7. A. Camaeron, *Daughters of Copper Woman* (Vancouver, B.C.: Pres Gong Publishers, 1981), 53.

8. R.J. Doyle, "Caution: Self-Directed Work Teams," *HRMagazine* 37, no. 6 (1992):153–155.

9. T. Buzan and B. Buzan, *The Mind Map Book* (London, England: BBC Books, 1993), 16–24.

10. H.K. Downey and A.P. Brief, "How Cognitive Structures Affect Organizational Design," in *The Thinking Organization,* edited by H.P. Sims (San Francisco: Jossey-Bass, 1986), 136.

11. P.M. Senge and F. Kaufman, "Communities of Commitment: The Heart of Learning Organizations," *Organizational Dynamics,* Autumn 1993, pp. 5–21.

12. M. Wheatley, "The Learning Organization: From Vision to Reality," *The Systems Thinker* 4, no. 10 (1993):1–4.

13. D.J. Isenberg, "The Structure and Process of Understanding," in *The Thinking Organization,* edited by H.P. Sims (San Francisco: Jossey-Bass, 1986), 102–136.

14. Ibid, 115.

15. R. Ackoff, "From Mechanistic to Systems Thinking," *The Systems Thinker* 5, no. 6 (1994):1–4.

16. A.W. Smith, "Needed: The Integrator Manager," *Personnel* 66, no. 7 (1989):51–56.

17. J.D. Beckman, "Beating the Box," *Health Care Forum Journal,* March–April 1992, pp. 55–58.

18. S. Peck, "Interview with Scott Peck," *Business Ethics,* March–April 1984, pp. 17–19.

19. E.E. Lawler, S.A. Makerman, and G.E. Ledford, *Employee Involvement and Total Quality Management: Practices and Results* (San Francisco: Jossey-Bass, 1992).

20. Ibid., 101–210.

21. W. Pasmore and M.R. Fagin, "Participation, Individual Development and Organizational Change: A Review and Synthesis," *Journal of Management* 18 (1992):375–397.

22. M. Frohman, "The Aimless Empowered," *Industry Week,* April 20, 1992, pp. 64–67.

23. K.G. LaMude and J. Scudder, "Hierarchical Levels and Types of Relational Messages," *Communication Research Reports* 8 (1991):152.

24. D. Collins, R.M. Ross, and T.L. Ross, "Who Wants Participative Management? The Managerial Perspective," *Group and Organizational Studies* 14 (1989): 422–455.

25. W. Brennis, *Why Leaders Can't Lead* (San Francisco: Jossey-Bass, 1985).

26. D.A. Gioia, "The State of the Art in Organizational Social Cognition," in *The Thinking Organization,* edited by H.P. Sims (San Francisco: Jossey-Bass, 1986), 336–357.

27. N.P. Lyons, "Visions and Competencies," in *Changing Education: Women as Radicals and Conservators,* edited by J. Antler and S. Bilken (Albany, NY: SUNY, 1990).

# Chapter 3

# Structuring for Partnership: Defining the New Organization

Time has ceased, space has vanished. We now all live in the global village.

Marshal McLuhan

## REDESIGNING EVERYTHING

Everyone in health care is busy reengineering or, at some level, retooling the workplace. Ostensibly, such activity will make it possible for health care facilities to better provide services and to operate as lean, customer-sensitive organizations that are cost-effective and able to achieve high-quality outcomes. Although providing better services more cost effectively is a tall order, it is the imperative of our time. The "fat" times are long since past. At all levels of society, a recognition of the finiteness of resources is apparent to everyone but the very naive. Yet newer service and relationship models must be consistent and sustainable, and sustainability is a serious problem for many American organizations.[1]

America is addicted to "fashion surfing." Many organizations avidly seek the new, the innovative, the creative, and the different so that they can be on the cutting edge, where there is, they believe, great opportunity to become better earlier and faster. Not much thought goes into fad surfing; in fact, it is a relatively mindless activity and results in outcomes that reflect the superficiality that went into the selection of the fads.[2] Real change is slow, comprehensive, and sustainable. It is built on solid foundations and a set of principles that reflect the character of the time.

Structure is always necessary to sustain an organization.[3] It gives the relationships and activities of a system a context within which to unfold and provides some consistency over time. The replication of function and activity needs to be facilitated in a system, which should not only permit it but support it. The traditional hierarchical structures no longer fit with the emerging emphasis on partner-

70

ship and accountability, especially in point of service-structured organizations. With the first stage of the movement away from vertical structures almost past, newer structures that will support and reinforce partnership-oriented, accountable, and equity-based point-of-care systems are struggling into existence.

These newer structures must be inclusive and operate in a way that does not impede point-of-service decision making and operational independence at the point of service.[4] As outlined in Chapter 1, the health care delivery system will have to be designed around the continuum of care. That means making sure that organizational configurations do not impede the system relationships necessary for point-of-service functioning. Increasingly, health care will be interdependent, multifocal, and noninstitutional. Since the continuum of care will drive the relationships between providers and patients and cost control will be an essential component of organizational effectiveness, all players must be invested in processes that address service and cost issues.

Team-based approaches to clinical care that involve all members in the service relationship must emerge.[5] The old hierarchical, vertically leveled system of organization does not fit well with the character of the relationships that will make the new services in the continuum of care intersect effectively. Further, there is increasing dependence on the knowledge of technical and professional workers for the outcomes of the organization, thus driving the organization to develop stronger, more collateral relationships between them. All people who provide some level of service to the patient have a stake in the cost-services equation. Those not committed to effective service processes are likely to impede them.

A number of current circumstances make it necessary to change organizational relationships, operations, and structure. The trend will be toward more integrated models that are inclusive and interactive and that can break down the artificial barriers and boundaries that currently exist between the various types of clinical staff in health care organizations.

- Professional workers are increasingly important in providing a complex array of services along the continuum of care with a high level of both interaction and independence.
- The decentralization of services requires a different relationship between management and staff, since there is simply no way to hire the number of managers it would require to supervise every worker in every setting where services are rendered.
- Integration must ultimately occur at the service level of the organization. Systems integration is important, but the integration of the work of service providers is absolutely essential.

- Physicians, hospitals, clinical staff, support systems, corporate systems, and the board must interact in a manner that reflects their interdependence. Building a seamless structure requires the organization to understand and articulate its relationship to services along the continuum of care and at every place where critical decision making occurs.
- The organization must have the fewest possible points of decision making in order to prevent decisions being made somewhere other than where their ultimate impact will be felt. The vast majority of decisions should be made at the point of service in order not to violate Taguchi's rule: keep all decisions closest to the place where they have the greatest impact.
- Any effort to maintain paternalistic or maternalistic management-staff relationships will, over the long term, impede the effectiveness of the organization. An immature alliance between the players in the organization analogous to the parent-child relationship will ultimately destroy the trust necessary to maintain mature commitment at every level.
- The structures of the organization are designed to support the activities of the system. Therefore, a structure that does not facilitate the work or essential relationships at the point of service will always act as an impediment. Form must always follow function; otherwise the organization loses sight of its purpose and gets bogged down in its own structure, which eventually becomes an end in itself.

A new set of rules apply to an integrated organizational system in a health care paradigm not characterized by industrial age relationships. No longer can health services be viewed as assembly line activities permeated by compartmentalization and segmentation. Redesigning care requires looking at the whole and then questioning the relationship of the parts that should brace it. This kind of inspection of the whole system and its integrity can help guide the restructuring process toward achievement of a more integrated organizational arrangement.[6]

One drawback of an industrial model system is that its configuration keeps the various key players in the system from having a real relationship with each other. Besides creating artificial barriers between the components of the organization, it ensures that the trust necessary for real partnership never emerges. Creating health-based organizations means creating healthy organizations. Organizations need to be willing to redesign themselves to be more functional with regard to their service frameworks and workplace relationships.[7]

The emerging design of the organization of the future must reflect the principles identified in Chapter 1: partnership at every level, accountability in every role, equity between the players, and ownership and investment by everyone in the organization. As a result, there are some basic tenets that every organization that wants to be truly service based must abide by.

*The leadership at the top of an organization should be very lean.* Having too many people at the top tends to transfer power away from the point of service to the place in the organization that least needs it. An overexpanded leadership insidiously and inexorably draws resources to itself until the key locus of control for direction and decision making is elsewhere than the point of service, reducing the effectiveness and efficiency of service provision.

*The key leader as regards management of the services provided by an organization is the person who coordinates, integrates, and facilitates the activities at the point of service.* This leader, who is poised to contribute substantially to the success of the organization, must have the level of competence that hospital executives had in the past. Every service configuration requires a person whose skills to manage the services are well honed and mature and who can function with little or no supervision.

*The support and consultation roles (e.g., chief financial officer, chief information officer, marketing, and human resources) over time have taken on functions and authority that properly belong to the service leader role.* The more responsibilities and decisions are turned over to those in support and consultation roles, the less likely it is that those decisions will benefit the point of service and the more likely it is that point-of-service leaders will become dependent upon them instead of themselves.

> ### Anything that does not facilitate the exercise of decision making at the point of service will, given enough time, ultimately impede it.

*Accountability should be used to drive an organization toward the fulfillment of its goals.* Responsibility to someone for work performed eventually robs the worker of both commitment and ownership of work, resulting in a "job" mindset. Traditional responsibility and reporting systems have not been able to produce the outcomes that were expected. They eventually collapse and the energy of the organization declines. Accountability systems invest in persons and roles. They define a role in terms of the expectations and possibilities of achievement of someone in the role, not in terms of whom the person is responsible to or reports to. Being clear about the content and expected contribution of a role is infinitely more important than being clear about responsibility and reporting relationships. Responsibility is about process, accountability is about outcomes.

*In the case of most organizations, if integration and linkages are to result in commitment and sustainable efficiency and effectiveness, the entire organizational system must be designed differently.* The disconnects between governance, operations, and service provision inevitably break down the integrity of an organization and impede the dynamics necessary for it to achieve its goals and continue to achieve them. The people in these three compartments of the organization rarely have access to each other, yet they make decisions and undertake activities that suggest they do. The implementation of decisions ends up being subject to the interpretation of people who were not present at the decision making. The decisions often make no sense to them and do not seem to apply to the organizational processes as they actually exist. In the end, the board cannot understand why their mandates are not carried out in the manner they intended (assuming they even know what they wanted), the managers cannot understand why the board is not aware of the constraints that impede implementation ("The board doesn't live in the real world"), and the staff think the board and managers are crazy and go on doing whatever they were doing, temporarily accommodating the "new idea or initiative" while believing that, given sufficient time, it will go away, just as have all the rest. People do only what makes sense to them, not what matters to the other person.

> **Value is imbedded in the fit between process and outcome but is always measured by the results achieved (the outcome).**

> **People only do what makes sense to them, not what matters to the other person.**

*Clarification of expectations and relationships depends on the elimination of processes and structures that allow people to pass their accountability on to others, escape their personal obligations, fail to locate the owners of decisions and processes, and inadequately address relationship issues.* In existing systems there is great opportunity to escape accountability, hide from obligations, and to reject ownership. Although organizations do not desire dysfunctional behavior and relationships, they often make it possible for them to be continued. To find the point of accountability for a process or function in many organizations is impossible; it is often a moving target, and individuals are able to point to someone else until no one is accountable for anything. If role ownership cannot be determined and accountability cannot be affixed, desired outcomes will not be obtained.

> *If role ownership cannot be determined and accountability cannot be affixed, desired outcomes cannot be obtained.*

Current organizational structures make it possible for people to escape or to hide from accountability. Employees can become habituated to avoiding accountability and will react strongly against the demand that they accept their fair share. Some are uncomfortable with the implications of accountability for the way they work and the way they affirm their competence to continue to do their work. In many organizations people have been hired simply because they had the right credentials and have kept their jobs, not because they were committed or competent, but because nobody ever took the trouble to remove them. For one thing, human resource requirements have made it so difficult to fire someone that frequently leaders are reluctant to even try; they simply tolerate the presence of those who fall below their standards. Accountability demands that all people are clear about what is expected of them and strive to perform accordingly. And that is real work for everyone.

## THE NEED FOR A NEW MODEL OF ORGANIZATION

In creating the lean, effective health care organization that focuses on rendering services along the continuum of care, a comprehensive approach to redesign is critical. The health care organization simply cannot stay the same and sustain its effort to provide accountable, high-quality health care. Work reengineering and quality improvement initiatives will be ineffective if the structure militates against such initiatives. Creating a new approach to integrating and arranging the organization to foster point-of-service accountability and decision making will require a makeover of the structure so that it supports the organization, its relationships, and its work.[8]

In a point-of-service design, 90 percent of the decisions are made where the work related to them is done and the decision making includes those who do the work. The organizational systems are configured around the point of service so as to facilitate all the activities of the organization directed toward enhancing point-of-service work (see Exhibit 3-1). A customer and service orientation becomes the backdrop for all the functions and roles of the individuals in the organization. Although the customers may vary, the principle remains the same.

In industrial model organizations, there is a tendency to locate control in the manager's role and create ascending levels of authority up a hierarchical ladder.[9] The person at the top is assumed to have ultimate accountability for everything

**Exhibit 3-1** Rules for Redesigning Organizations

1. Always design around the point of service.
2. Always involve affected people in all planning.
3. Always include a developmental process for everyone.
4. Always ensure that staff leadership is involved in implementation.
5. Always ensure that physicians are involved from the outset.
6. Always remember that relationships are horizontal, not vertical.
7. Always evaluate where people are as you go.
8. Always build a structure that will sustain what you are creating.
9. Always remember that the patient, not the provider, is the center of value.
10. Always incorporate the partners in the redesigning activities.
11. Always remember that you are creating a new health care system.
12. Always keep in mind that there will be challenges along the way.

that goes on "under" him or her. The problem with this approach is that it is impossible for anyone to exercise the kind of control suggested by the model. Lacking familiarity with the range of roles necessary to do the work, the leader depends on the continued support, competence, and compliance of those below. To ensure compliance, the leader is given the power of punishment. The idea is that people will try to avoid being punished and will therefore do what they should—that is, do what they should from the perspective of the leader. There is little ownership, little chance of adult, collegial relationships, and no sustaining belief in the value of the people who do most of the work of the organization.[10] Is it any wonder that organizations only achieve about 20 percent of the goals they set for themselves?

In this time of transformation, when the full resources of every organization must be called into action, it is imperative that there be a switch to a different organizational framework. Vertical and hierarchical structures become less viable at each step of the way toward a truly integrated continuum-of-care health care system (see Table 3-1). Information technology is also making hierarchies archaic.[11] Since information must be accessed by people at the point of service, controlling it at the management level is counterproductive. Among other things, management control of information is an impediment to point-of-service ownership of decisions.

Because hierarchies have been prevalent for so long, changes in normative behaviors do not always lead to the outcomes anyone expects.[12] For example, senior managers want first-line managers to be effective and self-directed. If they are,

**Table 3-1.** Vertical versus Horizontal Integration

| Vertical Integration | Horizontal Integration |
|---|---|
| Internal focus | External focus |
| Departmental design | Service oriented |
| Linear orientation | Systems design |
| Provider based | Patient based |
| Functional focus | Continuum focused |
| Process driven | Outcome driven |

however, senior managers become uncertain of their own role, which might no longer be necessary as currently configured. The transference of power and authority to the first-line role always raises questions about the value and validity of other administrative roles. Therefore, first-line managers frequently are given freedom to do the job but are cautioned not to perform beyond certain boundaries so as not to discomfort or threaten the security of senior managers.

It is obviously a great challenge to create an independent and fully functional service structure. The service leaders in this type of system must be fully competent and be able to manage all the elements of the "business," relate to whatever people are necessary to an effective service partnership, and lead their teams in the direction the data and the service indicators suggest. Accountability for these tasks is fully invested in the service leaders, who now must operate at the same level of skill as senior managers in organization. If such senior managers are still part of the system, the increased independence given to service leaders becomes threatening to them and challenges the value of their role. This is one of the reasons that point-of-service organizations are difficult to design. Effectiveness will fully depend on relationships and roles being altered.

> *Accountability drives all role functions at the point of care. The manager's role is to ensure that nothing impedes its expression there.*

The point-of-service care model suggests that all structures should build on the core services of the organization and that the organization should be designed in a way that supports the work. *Any decision that does not take place at the point of service should facilitate decisions that are made there.* It stands to reason, therefore, that any role that is not directly related to the point of service should be

> *The organization is now more dependent on the knowledge of the worker than on any other factor in the workplace.*

servant to roles that are directly related. Most manager roles in future health care organizations devoted to facilitating the continuum of care will be servant roles. This means that the middle and senior managers will not be the key decision makers but will function as resources for those who are (see Exhibit 3-2). Based on the point-of-service concept, the main task of the managers will be to focus on the resources that support the service functions of the providers. They will be given accountability for the human, fiscal, material, support, and systems resources of the organization. In essence, they will support the staff and provide to them what is necessary for them to do the work of the organization.[13] It is in the distinction between resource providers and service providers that the notion of accountability takes form.

In an effective organization, the locus of control and accountability rests with those who perform the actual work. There will exist ownership, expectations, and a mechanism for measuring whether the activities resulted in intended or desirable outcomes. Workers will have access to information, systems, resources, and support in order to do what they do with excellence. They will also have a sense of ownership and a clear understanding of the contribution their work makes and its value to the customers.

Research has shown that any management style, which removes accountability from those performing the work, will not achieve the best outcomes.[14] Accountability should always be invested in the workers themselves. It should not be delegated or transferred away. If managers attempt to influence or control the ac-

**Exhibit 3-2** New Manager Role

- Accountability based
  —Focus on outcomes, not processes
- Resource oriented
  —Accountable for distribution of human, fiscal, material, support, and systems resources
- Service driven
  —Facilitator, not director
  —Integrator, not controller
  —Coordinator, not custodian

countability that properly belongs to others, they will never attain the outcomes they desire.

Managers and staff must develop a clear understanding of who is accountable for what and must also clearly define the expectations for performance and outcome within the context of the resources available to support the work and the workers. To clarify accountability, it is necessary to identify the differences in content and expectations in the manager role and the staff role. If workers are to be held accountable for what occurs at the point of service, the leadership must stop expecting managers to act as if they were accountable. Distinguishing areas of accountability and the expectations related to them is critical to the success of a service-based enterprise. Delineating what the managers cannot do and should not do and what the staff have the authority to do and must do is a foundation of the more functional emerging relationship between management and staff.[15] Obviously, the same applies to what the managers have the authority to do but the staff do not.

> *If managers attempt to control or influence the accountability of others, they will never attain the outcomes they desire.*

Distinguishing areas of accountability is essential for the new organizational models that include a high degree of point-of-service accountability.[16] It is increasingly evident that a health care organization cannot afford an unlimited number of managers and supervisory activities as it decentralizes along the continuum of care. The cost is untenable, the results are questionable, and manager-staff relationships become progressively nonviable.

In the industrial model, the administrative and control functions are organized around superior-subordinate relationships. It is known how this type of organization works, but what structure and what types of relationships will support the new point-of-service approach to delivering high-quality and cost-effective health care services along the continuum of care?

## ACCOUNTABILITY: THE FOUNDATION OF WHOLE SYSTEMS SHARED GOVERNANCE

Newer approaches to building structure to support and sustain point-of-service organizations must be explored. Any organization has a need to ensure that the obligations of its governance, operations, and service components are met. The point is to build a structure that allows the various components to function effectively and efficiently within a seamless process that facilitates the provision of health care services. In order to foster equity and ownership, all the partners in the process should be involved in a critical way with decisions in each arena of the system. This will also help ensure that the proper information, role, contribution, and relationship are present at every place where decisions affecting the organization and its work are made. The design of the structure and the relationships of the partners should serve to support the point-of-service decision making. Further, the task of the leadership is to remove all impediments that impact the character and quality of point-of-service decisions.

> *The real work of leadership today is to build a seamless relationship between the provider, the patient, the organization, and the community.*

There should be a clear separation between the area of accountability of the management and the area accountability of the clinical and support workers of the organization.[17] The management should not be involved in making decisions for the clinical and service providers but should be accountable for decisions regarding the resources necessary for the delivery of services. Human resource, fiscal, material, support, and systems decisions belong to the managers, and the functions and actions related to them fall into their realm of accountability. However, decisions about the content of work, the quality of work, and the competence of workers do not belong to the managers but belong instead to the service providers. An accountability-based structure would support the differentiation in roles and expectations and incorporate those differences into a supportive organizational design.

There are several reasons it is essential to distinguish between resource leadership and service or clinical leadership roles:

- If accountability and equity are not present in the partnership between the organization and its members, the system continues to be hierarchical and control laden, and the workers never experience ownership. The real owner is still the manager, and partnership and accountability, as they have been described, never fully emerge. The result: the same old parochialism, parentalism, and dependency between management and staff. Nothing really changes.
- Worker accountability is difficult to establish if the staff are subject to an approval mechanism that directs and controls the behavior of others and does not create a situation where performance expectations are both clear

and desirable. The staff must write their own accountability script, not simply have input into the script others write for them who are supposedly acting in their "best interests."

- Managers should be transformed into resource leaders because resource management constitutes their best contribution to the organization.
- Parental type relationships are not appropriate relationships between managers and staff in the workplace. If people in the organization are to ever grow, they must have a different kind of relationship with each other and with the workplace.
- Dependency in the workplace creates relationships that are inherently nonmotivating and impedes workers' chances of becoming stakeholders in the processes that relate to their work.
- Accountability is the foundation of shared governance. Designing an organizational model that features point-of-service decision making requires both a commitment to and an understanding of the principles of accountability.
- Accountability differs from responsibility in its focus on work outcomes rather than work processes.
- Responsibility is linked to processes through the enumeration of job elements and activities to which responsibility can be attached. Placing focus on results makes this emphasis on activities untenable.
- Responsibility is always delegated by those in positions of power, and any person given responsibility for a set of job activities must perform them to the satisfaction of the delegator in order to remain in the job.
- Responsibility implies that someone (the delegatee) reports to another person (the delegator) regarding functions and activities. The delegatee receives the permission needed to perform the specific functions and activities from the delegator.
- Accountability, on the other hand, is specific to a given role, is never externally generated, and can never be assigned.
- Accountability is defined by outcome expectations instead of process requirements (i.e., persons are held accountable for the achievement of expected outcomes).
- The definition of activities intended to achieve specified outcomes should include the role the accountable person plays in the performance of those activities. Further, the person is accountable for the completion of the activities and for meeting all other expectations regarding the exercise of the role.
- In accountability-based organizations, it is essential to make clear the performance expectations imbedded in roles so that those who occupy the roles know what is required of them.

- Clarity, definitiveness, ownership, and outcome expectations all exemplify accountability.

Accountability must be further refined in organizations so that there is no confusion over its content. A hierarchical framework for relationships and decision making is inconsistent with the building of partnerships and with accountability-based approaches. Partnerships are based on equity and on clarity regarding the content of each partner's accountability. Clarity about the obligations and goals of a partnership is also fundamental. Distinguishing the expectations for each role in the partnership requires that each partner be aware of what he or she brings to the partnership to make it work and to achieve the purposes for which it was created. [18]

> *Responsibility is about parental relationships and is associated with vertical communication. Accountability reflects an adult-to-adult set of interactions and is associated with horizontal communication.*

This clarity and differentiation are critical for building accountability in organizational partnerships at every level. In point-of-service designs it is also important to keep decision making close to the point of service and to ensure that decisions that belong there do not migrate elsewhere. It is even more important to distinguish between the accountability expectations of the two key roles in that setting—the role of manager and the role of clinical provider. If accountability is to be properly positioned and focused at the point of service, it has to be clear who owns what in the exercise of their roles.

## STRUCTURAL COMPONENTS OF THE WHOLE SYSTEMS ORGANIZATION

Retooling an organizational system around the point of service and building a service-based system requires the components of the system to be well defined and integrated. There are three main components in a health care organizational system that must be delineated: service, operations, and governance. If decision making at the point of service is to be effective, if the organization is to be able to sustain a rate of point-of-service decision making of 90 percent, and if the structure is to counteract the temptation to push decisions upward in the system, a whole new approach to structuring the organization and its functional relationships must emerge. The vertically linear and compartmentalized approach of department-based systems is no longer a viable option because it creates a lack of linkage and mutual understanding at the various levels of the organization. Building a seamless structure that relates the various components of the care system along the continuum of services requires a very different approach. Enumerating the expectations of each category of organizational function within the service, operations, and governance components is an essential first step.

Workers in service-based systems need more than simply to be empowered. They need to be free to make accountable decisions that others can depend on to be competently made and effective.[19] In a continuum of care-based service setting, there is simply no way that enough supervisors, directors, and other translators of the mission and direction can be employed to address each contingency. Interdependence in relationship and independence of role will be essential elements of work in health care systems, and the organizational structure must change to support these elements.

## Service

The core of any health care organization is patient care. The ultimate purpose of the activities of the person in the organization is to provide high-quality services to those who need them. The service structure in the point-of-service organization lies at the center of the organizational structure. It is within this structure that the relationship between providers and patients is defined and supported. The service structure either enhances or reduces the effectiveness of the relationship between work and worker.[20]

> *The service continuum is the core of the new delivery system. It is important to configure the delivery system around the continuum.*

In a subscriber-based, capitated continuum-of-care system, the configuration of the service component of the organization is considerably different from the configuration in other systems. Because the system requires better integration of service providers, easier access to a variety of services along the continuum, expenditure of the fewest number of resources, and assurance of service excellence, design of the service component can no longer exemplify the assembly-line approach to providing services.

Several realities of services-based design need to be considered:

- The service continuum demands more lateral connections in the organization beyond its vertical linkages.
- Providers must have much easier access to each other in a service-based structure and therefore need to be positioned as close to each other as possible.
- Team-based activities tend to increase in a service-based organization because of the necessity to integrate clinical services to better address patient needs.
- Physicians must be partnered more fully with teams in continuum-of-service structures and become increasingly dependent on other health care professionals for patient care management at various points along the continuum.
- The relationships between the health care professions must be more clearly defined, and the contributions of each and expectations for each must be better enumerated.
- Flexible and fluid structures and processes must be developed to support the interdependence and mobility of the team members as they fulfill their obligations at various points along the continuum of care.
- Critical patient pathways must be clarified continuously in order to maintain the highest level of function for patients. In the subscriber-based approach, illness is to be avoided in order to prevent intense resource use, which quickly eats up capitated dollars and limits the resource flexibility of the organization.
- Providers must know more about the cost-quality relationship than has been expected in the past. Clinical decision making can either threaten or extend the organization's resources.
- Evaluation of outcomes must be part of the evaluation of the services provided. Best practices and the achievement of normative parameters in clinical pathways along the continuum of service are requisites in every service structure.
- In order to follow the real value chain in health care (the patient continuum of service), the design of the work structures of the organization must reflect the service configuration. Structure is built around services, not departments or functions, and gets better defined through clarification of the components of the service continuum. Structuring, staffing, processing, and supporting activities must conform to the service categories.

Structuring around the service continuum demands a new perception of organizational design and integrity (see Exhibit 3-3). Hierarchical, linear designs are rarely appropriate anymore. New health care organizations will utilize structures

**Exhibit 3-3** Features of the Service Continuum

---

- Service centered
- Integrated
- Continuum based
- Linked across services
- Interdisciplinary
- Patient based

---

that support service-based relationships and service realities. Providers will be more self-directed, will have stronger relationships with other care team members, and will focus on keeping the patients from getting ill. They will need, as a consequence, a different kind of organizational structure to support them in their efforts.

### Accountability and Service

Research shows us that effective organizations have few layers (often not more than two) and that most authority is located as close to the point of service as possible.[21] This means that the design of an organization must allow support for activities to be provided close to where the activities occur. In a service-based organization, this is most often in the patient care setting—at the patient's side, in the diagnostic services, or wherever the work of patient care is done. All resources necessary to support point-of-service decision making and control should be provided to the staff. Furthermore, the content of roles and obligations must be as clear as possible.

As layers are removed from the hierarchy, the number of places where decisions can get made diminishes. Although this increases the effectiveness of the decisions and reduces the problems associated with them, it challenges the organization and its leadership to determine who should make specific decisions—or, said another way, who is accountable for what decisions.

As already noted, those who do the work should have accountability for it. That means that the staff must own the processes that define their work, have the competence to do it, and be accountable for the outcomes produced. The organization should be structured so as not to impede staff accountability or transfer accountability to managers or others. The danger to watch out for is captured in this dictum: *given the opportunity, accountability will escape from its proper location and migrate to the furthest point possible in the system.* Outcomes can only be fully achieved by those who have accountability for them. Therefore, the structure and processes of the organization must be configured in such a way that account-ability is never removed from those who own it. That means several things:

- Managers should not assume accountability for outcomes or activities that properly belong to the staff.
- The staff must be accountable for those activities that fall within their area of obligation.
- The organization must not have structures in place that remove accountabil-ity from where it belongs simply out of fear it may not be properly exercised.
- The staff must not have access to a mechanism or structure that allows them to foist on others accountability for activities that are especially demanding.
- Mechanisms need to exist that help the staff develop higher levels of skill in exercising accountability and making the right decisions.
- The role of the managers must be configured to support the staff in exercis-ing accountability and ensure that they have the right information, support, skills, and processes to make the most effective decisions.

It is within this framework that point-of-service, accountability-based organiza-tional structures take form. They must have several characteristics to be effective and support the principles of partnership, equity, accountability, and ownership:

- There should be the fewest possible management levels, certainly no more than three.
- Decision making should occur at the point of service 90 percent of the time.
- Managers should never make decisions for the staff or decisions for which the staff are accountable.
- The organizations should be structured around the service continuum and provide support to service-located and -based decisions. Those in the support roles should never make decisions that belong to those at the point of service.
- Resource information that could affect decisions should be provided to every point where decision making occurs.

### Building Service Structures

An old behavioral rule expresses the value of building appropriate and mean-ingful structures:

> We cannot change behavior by addressing behavior alone. We must also address the structures within which that behavior emerges. If we do not change the structure, we cannot successfully sustain the behavior we want to change.

The challenge for any health care organization is to devise a structure that supports point-of-service decision making, yet remains lean and nonbureaucratic. Further, the structure must support service integrity and provide a broad system of communication that links all entities in the organizational system.

Because health care is reconfiguring along the continuum of services and because services are being structured in a tighter formation, a simple relationship between continuum of service components must be established. It is important for the service providers to be related to other service providers who share responsibility for managing a specific patient population along a defined clinical pathway. Their relationships can be better defined and more completely supported because of their common characteristics. For example, a medical critical care unit, instead of being aligned with other critical care services, would be better aligned with the general medical units with which it is clinically associated. It thus would become a part of the medical continuum of services. Patient flow is determined by the intensity of service needs and the placement of staff along the continuum. Ideally, staff will be able to move along the continuum of services as a result of having the skills to provide a range of services.

> *Bringing workers together in one place is easier than making them work together there.*

Each service category would have the same configuration of related service structures along a horizontal set of relationships and intersections, and each would become a strategic clinical service accountable for the relationships, interactions, and resource needs that drive its operation. The service leader of this continuum would manage all the components of the service, assisted in providing the clinical coordination by staff leaders located in appropriate places along the continuum of care.

Within the service structure, the following activities and processes are essential for clinical success:

- Clinical protocols that define stages of the continuum of care are defined, implemented, and evaluated by the staff of the clinical service.
- Accountability, standards of practice, and quality indices are all defined and implemented within the service continuum by the service providers.
- Service team construction and management reflect the culture of the service and are developed to meet the specific needs of the subscribers being served.
- Case management along the continuum is specifically designed to follow particular patient populations within the context of the care framework of the

> *Service is constructed on a patient-based value stream. It does not simply reflect a cost-driven value system.*

service, individualizing care management unique to service-specific clinical conditions and protocols.

- The service leader must possess the level of competence once expected of vice-presidents. That level of expertise is now demanded at the point of service to ensure resource integrity and organizational and operational effectiveness.

- Staff and clinical teams must be essentially self-directed and have a clear idea of the parameters of their functioning and the impact of their decisions. Since there will not be continuous supervision of function, clarity with regard to accountability and expectations will be essential to the effectiveness of each service provider.

- Clarity with regard to the clinical pathways and resource parameters will be required of each service and its service providers. Success will be reflected in whether value is evident in the activities of the service as it balances cost and quality.

- Services are not institution specific. Rather they are located wherever they best serve patients. Information, communication, and data systems connect the providers to each other and to the organization in such a way that most providers can be highly mobile and immediately responsive to the needs of those they serve (Exhibit 3-4).

- Managers are essentially resource purveyors and translators of the goals and priorities of the organization. They assist in decision making by ensuring the decision makers have access to the correct information so they can arrive at the right decisions.

**Exhibit 3-4** The New Architecture for Health Care

- Mobility of provider, not patient
- Multiple settings for services
- Case management along the continuum
- Information system as new structure
- Lateral integration instead of vertical control
- Systems linkage to sustain service integrity

- All activities and relationships with individual medical staff members and service leaders occur within the context of the service continuum. Consequently, clinical issues and problems in the relationships between physicians and other members of the organization can be dealt with where the problems exist.

The service context becomes the central focus of the work framework for the clinical service it encompasses. All issues and processes are directed to supporting the clinical service along the service continuum. The organization's systems are designed to help the service leadership to become more effective and address its issues within the context of the service. The intent is to restrict problem solving to where the problems occur. If problem solving occurs elsewhere, the point-of-service structures and processes are not working and the outcomes will be negatively affected.

A point-of-service design requires that the service structures support staff in meeting their accountability. This means, essentially, that staff processes for decision making must operate effectively and must constitute the preferred method of staff functioning and outcome achievement (see Exhibit 3-5). It is here that the elements of continuous quality improvement (CQI) become important. Since CQI relates primarily to the process of doing work, its methods and mechanisms become important in efforts to arrive at decisions about work—in deliberation, problem solving, solution seeking, performance improvement, innovation, and creative processing.[22] These methods discipline the staff's deliberations and decision processes, give teams the tools that they need for effective decision making, and help them focus on evaluating their processes and their ability to achieve desirable outcomes.

Through use of CQI processes, the service teams can enhance their effectiveness, build relationships with each other, discipline their thinking and planning, and main-

**Exhibit 3-5** Staff Decision Making

Accountability-based decisions
- Work content
- Performance effectiveness
- Quality of clinical outcomes
Team-based decisions
- Group relationships
- Team effectiveness
- Process assessment and adjustment
- Efficacy of service outcomes

> *Continuous quality improvement disciplines deliberation and action through methodologies that focus on results, not just work processes.*

tain a format to sustain their decision making and productivity improvement. Further, CQI processes can help them define their ownership and accountability and can provide a format for continuous quality improvement and, when used effectively, for validation of their efforts.[23] In a point-of-service organization, there is a continuous focus on ensuring effectiveness at the customer sites of service and a strong commitment to designing systems that do not have any place where clinical decisions can be made except the sites of service. The locus of control for point-of-service decisions never moves from where it belongs—as close to the providers and patients as possible.

## Operations

### *The Operations Framework*

There is a myth afloat that health care systems must be complex and that future corporate or regional health plan structures will demand complex organizational frameworks. The relationship linkages between a multilateral service, it is assumed, will also be highly complicated and elaborate. Nothing is less true. Although there are complex relationships that must be defined, the principles and foundations that set their parameters are simple and straightforward. Complexity in organizations is very often an accommodation to the political discordance between roles and relationships. Many or-

> *Many organizations are held hostage by their attachment to a political structure that is no longer appropriate or viable.*

ganizational designs are more the result of adjustments to the people who hold positions of power than the result of conscientious efforts to find a configuration that facilitates the balanced interactions of entities and the outcomes of work.[24]

Also, designs based on old industrial notions of span of control and the like are simply not tenable in point-of-service organizations. Service leadership should have included within the auspices of particular leadership roles whatever structures and functions are necessary to integrate the organization along its normative continuum of work. For some service structures, that will include many entities;

for others, very few. It is the comprehensiveness and intensity of service that determines the span of leadership any role may need in order to be effective.[25]

### Management Accountability

The notion of accountability affects the role of the manager just as it does the staff. It is important not to hold the managers accountable for activities and functions that do not belong to them. Mintzberg's research and theoretical work points in the direction of focusing the manager on the work that is legitimate to the role and eliminating from the role things that are not appropriate to the leader function.[26]

Management is specifically resource based.[27] When it becomes anything else in the organization, it is an impediment to the effectiveness of decision making and service delivery. The old parental approach to work and relationships in the industrial model of organization has proven, over time, not only to be ineffective but is also essentially dysfunctional. The neurotic parent-child communication and control structure embodies a belief about the players and their relationships that forever keeps them at odds with each other and even builds a structure around their relationships that continues to facilitate the conflict.[28] As more data emerge about effective structuring and relationship building in the workplace, it it becoming increasingly obvious that the old model is no longer viable.

> **Management is concerned with context issues; staff are focused on the content of their work.**

Shifting to a new model, however, requires changing the manager's role (see Exhibit 3-6). The new role should focus on the resources that are directed to supporting the work of the system. As a result, it will have associated with it human, fiscal, material, support, and systems resource accountability. These areas of stewardship form the content of the role.[29] Excluded are those activities and functions that define the work itself, delineate and measure the quality of the work and its outcomes, and define the competencies and relationships necessary to do the work. Those belong specifically and exclusively to the people who provide the services—the staff. The role of the leader in relationship to the staff is to ensure that there is an appropriate context that supports the staff's accountability for their work.[30]

In the industrial model, all responsibilities fall within the purview and control of the manager. The manager's role is to see to it that the organization's goals and objectives are fulfilled and the rules and relationships as described by the organization's leadership are maintained and obeyed. Process and outcome re-

**Exhibit 3-6** Managerial Tasks

- Making it safe for staff to risk
- Connecting staff to resources
- Providing information
- Facilitating problem solving
- Building team skills
- Creating linkages to the system
- Preparing for future changes

sponsibilities are also well within the scope of the role. As indicated previously, this approach to management is hierarchical and parental in nature.

Besides being very ineffective, the approach has not served well those who have used it. The kind of adult-to-adult interchange necessary for truly mature relationships has simply been missing. Now that organizations are becoming increasingly dependent on their technical and professional workers for their success, a different type of interaction will be required. Staff have more control over decisions and more role independence and are consequently demanding respectful and equitable relationships with managers.[31] What staff need from managers is not direction with regard to the content of their roles but the information, tools, and resources necessary to fulfill their work obligations. Increasingly staff are self-managed with regard to their professional team interactions and clinical performance. They still need to find out from managers, however, the implications of their decisions and the parameters that determine just what is or is not possible or consistent with the system's resources. The shift to this new "servant" role for managers and for operations functions in the organization is the source of much conflict in current efforts to create meaningful organizational change.[32]

> *The staff serve the patients; the managers serve the staff.*

> *The manager role is always resource based. All issues that are not resource related are the responsibility of the staff.*

The problem is to make it clear to everyone that hierarchy has no place in a point-of-service organization. It must be accepted by everyone that the role of leadership in such an organization is to ensure that good decisions are made at the point of service by those who own them. Any other assumption ultimately leads to creating impediments to accountability and the achievement of desired outcomes. Some new rules apply:

- No more "mama and papa" roles.
- No more codependency behaviors between managers and staff.
- Everyone must define the content of their own accountability.
- No more parental caretaking and "checking up."
- No more "bossism" and "because I told you to" behavior patterns.
- No more defining for others what their work is.
- Everyone must make the decisions that belong to them.
- No more surrogate peacemaking.
- No more taking on other people's problems.
- No more blame.
- No more turfing up the ladder or down the ladder.
- There must be much more serving, much less directing.

Looking at operations in a new light will mean dramatic alteration in the roles and functions of most managers. Those managers surviving such a shift would have to be committed to a new way of doing business and a nondirective and noncontrolling set of behavioral patterns. Their roles would be initially and primarily developmental, focusing on building the managers' own skills and the skills of the staff, especially those that will allow the staff to work in a more collaborative fashion.

> *Staff, unlike children, do not need raising. The relationship between managers and staff should be an adult one, not a parental one.*

The notion of the servant role in the operations framework can be frightening to leaders currently placed in high-level positions and expected to make decisions for others. The claim that most of those decisions should be at the point of service suggests to many that there may not be a need for as many (if any) positions at the executive level. Further, those who should have the accountability for major decisions may want to shy away from such decisions, recognizing that they may have to confront real issues of competence. Clearly, in these revolutionary circumstances managers and staff must make a commitment to honest self-appraisal and exhibit a willingness to be flexible in making role and career choices.

It is important to keep in mind that organizations are being forced to change because of market, economic, and service changes not necessarily of their own making.[33] There are not a lot of options available that allow an organization to revert to previous behavior or to avoid implementing leadership behaviors and operational roles that are in line with the new organizational paradigm.

Configuring the function, location, and content of the operations role in the new health care system will be a noisy experience. The focus of the process should be on the service continuum and the relationship between service provider and patient and between service provider and the organization.[34] The operations function can assist by creating a fluid balance between those who provide the health services and those who support them. The final configuration should reflect a commitment to a leaner and more effective system.

### Governance

Creating a seamless organization is impossible without dealing with governance issues. It is in the area of governance that some of the real problems exist: compartmental approaches to decision making, the narrow distribution of power, and the lack of accountability.

Boards generally have legal and civil accountability for the activities of the organizations they direct. A board is made up of persons who usually have some stature in the community or some assumed contribution to make to the board. A hospital board also has physician members because of their economic and service relationship to the hospital. This member configuration ostensibly provides diversity and breadth to the board and leads to the making of effective decisions.

Hospital boards have historically been fairly passive in their relationships with the hospitals they direct. More often than admitted, the administration of a hospital constructs the board's agenda and provides the context and information base for its decision making. The administration, by controlling inputs, places the board in the position of having to assume that the administration is operating in the best interests of the hospital. In this situation, the board in effect colludes with the administration in relinquishing its responsibilities and is likely to be unprepared to deal with the stresses the health care system is experiencing during this time of transformation. Board passiveness and ineffectiveness can occur for all or some of the following reasons:

- Board members may have only a limited understanding of the character of health care and the ways in which health care organizations differ from other business establishments.
- The administration may set the agenda for the board and make recommendations regarding membership on the board, thus creating a relationship in which the board depends on the administration instead of the reverse.

- Physician members of the board frequently benefit financially from their relationship to the hospital. As a result, they have a certain bias, which can skew the board's response to critical service and financial issues.
- The board and the health care services of the organization are virtually unconnected except through administrative channels. The assumption is that the administration understands the health care services completely and will adequately represent the service providers to the board.
- Board members are not always clear about the extent of their individual and collective roles. They sometimes do not understand that they have no authority on their own to influence or direct and that it is the board as a whole that wields authority and sets direction for the organization.
- Many boards have audit, review, and process groups that do some of the work of oversight. Often these groups do not know what they are doing or depend heavily on the administration to set their agenda and follow up on their business, which can obstruct the separating of important issues from superfluous ones by board members.
- The competence of board members to make the journey to a health care frame of reference is often suspect. One problem that arises is an overemphasis on the business aspects and a failure to comprehend the unique service characteristics of health care facilities. Board members usually understand finances very well but are less adept with service, care, quality, and ethical issues.

The complexity of hospitals and health care systems frightens most reasonable people (and should frighten them). The issues that health care organizations and providers typically deal with include some of the most fundamental issues of life and death. Thus, the health care arena can test the mettle of the strongest of persons. It is understandable that boards frequently fail to tackle some of the real issues of health care or even sort through them.[35]

### Linking Board Accountability and Provider Accountability

Accountability is fundamental to the functioning of an organization at any level. The problem with accountability is that it cannot be delegated away and that it requires strong relationships between all components of the organizational system. In order for accountability to be effective, the relationships it depends on must be clearly specified.

> *Most boards are not competent to deal with the issues they must confront. The responsibilities of most boards are beyond the ability of most of those who now serve on them.*

The board's accountability is broad based and has been well defined in the literature.[36] However, the radical changes in health care organizations have altered the very notion and character of board accountability as well as board membership, leadership, and relationships.

In a point-of-service organization, the relationship of all the functions is altered. The need for horizontal relationships between equals changes the configuration and "location" of the board. Since the operating structure is no longer hierarchical, putting the board at the top of the system is ruled out.

Since accountability is structured at all levels of the organization and summary accountability is banished as an organizational concept, the board should not be thought of as unilaterally responsible for all the activities of the organization. The board's main objective should be to become more effective in its particular role. To achieve this objective, the board must know what its accountability is as well as its relationship to all the players who make up the organization.[37]

If accountability is to be located at all the decision points of the organization, it should be clear where these points are. The board is obligated to ensure that everyone is aware of his or her accountability and the expectations of the board regarding that accountability. Remember that accountability is about outcomes, not processes. Clarifying accountability thus is essentially a matter of clearly defining the outcomes toward which the activities of the organization are directed. The board must see to it that accountability is clarified, that it has access to all the places where accountability resides, and that issues and problems regarding the integration of the system, community direction, and the mission of the organization are dealt with at the board level.

Increasingly, accountability, in most hospitals, requires a more critical look at membership and the relationship between the board and the organization. The stewardship of the board has much more significance in a point-of-service, accountability-based organization than in previous types of organizations. If the seamless connection necessary to support accountability and point-of-service decision making is to be created, the board's connection to both operations and service must be better.

The traditional distance between the board and the rest of the organization is challenged in an accountability-based configuration. The linkage to every place where accountability exists challenges the distant relationship most boards maintain with the members of the organization. In the industrial model, the separation of the board from operations and service is held sacrosanct and is expected to be preserved at all costs. The administration is delegated the task of operating the organization; if effective, it wins the trust of the board leadership. While this arrangement sounds good, it has several drawbacks. For example, the board, although having no direct role to play in the operation of the organization, is accountable for seeing that operations, service, and governance are linked. Integrating these so that they support each other is a critical board function.

> *A primary role of the board is to see that there is linkage between all the places where accountability resides in the system.*

In shared governance, it is essential that the board be connected to the forums where direction is set based on the organization's mission.[38] It is ridiculous to assume that a board can fully understand the implications of acting on a strategic decision when it has no direct access to the staff whose role it is to translate or undertake strategic action. Conflict often arises between goal definition and goal achievement because those who are required to achieve the goals of the organization are rarely involved in their definition. Staff ownership is missing and therefore commitment to board goals is also missing. In addition, the dialogue regarding direction or strategy would have different content if the staff were included as participants. They would provide a unique perspective on any board decision needing to be implemented at the point of service. The direct linkage between the board and the providers (not just physicians) is as important as the linkage between operations functions and service provision. In a true partnership, all partners must have an opportunity to communicate with each other and to have input into decisions that could affect the likelihood of achieving the outcomes the partnership is intended to achieve.

> *One cannot expect to sustain the results of personal achievement if a sense of ownership is not present in those who do the work.*

If the real goals were good integration and sound outcomes, the old elitist view of board functioning would soon lose its luster and the focus of boards would become more practical and balanced. Each board would play a larger role in decision making and goal setting. To do this, it would need a clear understanding of its accountability and the attendant demands. Rather than being an honorary role or an item to add to one's curriculum vitae, board membership would be a social obligation of some significance. If the board was filled with active, committed members, the results could be a more community-based health care system.

### Board Focus

The board must be clear about its own expectations and obligations before it can redesign and configure its relationships with the rest of the organization.

The board must be clear about what its accountability is and what it is not. In the industrial model (vertical, responsibility based), the ownership framework is essential for understanding the responsibility of the board. In an accountability-based model (horizontal), it is more important to be clear about the accountability of the persons and functions. Unless the members of the organization have a clear understanding of the accountability associated with their roles, they will have little commitment to the achievement of the organizational goals.

The mission, direction, and goals of the system impact accountability. Organizational goals cannot be achieved in isolation, so linkage with the rest of the system is as important as the clarity of goals. Clarity without commitment cannot achieve outcomes; conversely, commitment to an unknown purpose takes the organization nowhere.

One task of the board is to discern the principles and values of the local community. These provide the underpinning for strategy and service decisions. The staff will depend on their understanding of the board-defined principles and values in determining whether the goals and work of the organization are acceptable to the community.

In establishing the goals of the organization, the board does not work in isolation. It is appropriate for the board to view its role over the long term, looking specifically at the relationship of the health care organization to the local community rather than focusing on the functions and roles of the organization. This prevents a narrowing of the perspective of the board and confusion of its role with the activities and roles of others in the organization. It also helps the board focus on outcomes rather than processes. Further, it keeps the board from missing changes in the community that might provide clues to how the organization should change.

The board must realize that it has an obligation to define the parameters of the organization in order to determine the range of activities that best serve the interests of the organization. The parameters may relate to service configuration, finance, capital formation and management, even outreach in meeting community needs. Defining the parameters provides a good database for the providers as they work out their service goals and for managers as they figure out the appropriate distribution of resources.

The board must select leaders who do not apply ego-driven methods or favor unilateral strategies for vision setting, decision making, and relationship building in the organization. Hero models of leadership ultimately cost the organization dearly. The best leaders have the ability to integrate the players, stimulate collective processes, and work toward a mutual vision. They provide the kind of leadership that ensures all the players get to the places they need to be in order to succeed on both a personal and organizational level.

The board should evaluate outcomes, not processes—with the exception of its own processes. The outcomes will always tell whether the processes are good or bad. If the board's agenda is not achieved and the desired outcomes are not attained, the board will know there are process problems that need to be identified and attended to. The board should keep its eye on where the organization is going and how that direction is affecting the actions of the organization. Keeping focused on outcomes ensures that the critical processes for achieving the organization's goals can be facilitated and evaluated.

As multifocal and multiservice systems are constructed from previously independent systems, the role of the board as a culture definer becomes more significant. The integration of various systems into an overarching system is essential to their effectiveness. Political, systems, and operational consolidation must be done with sensitivity to ensure that the new system is viable and provides meaning to all the players now working together. The culture of support, integration, and service focus will demand rigorous efforts to address the issues and concerns that affect service and cost-efficiency in the system.[39]

### The Board's Relationship to the Community

The board's fundamental obligations include nurturing of the relationship of the health care entity with the community of which it is a part. Failure to meet this obligation can have a lasting negative impact. Yet many hospitals located in communities do not perceive themselves and are not perceived as having a relationship with those communities.[40] Unfortunately, a hospital's lack of investment in its community is associated with a lack of awareness of the health and social needs of people the hospital ostensibly serves. The hospital, as a result of this lack of awareness, might appear to local residents as unsupportive only incidentally able to meet community needs.

> *Hospitals are often unaware of the needs of the communities in which they reside. Health care systems simply cannot survive this way.*

As the subscriber-based approach becomes prevalent, it will become increasingly important to define the character of the relationship between a health care system and its community and the way in which it will be developed and sustained by the health care system.[41] The board has a major obligation to link the health care system to the community and to design the service structure of the system so as to ensure that it reflects the linkage to the community. Placing members of the community as representatives in the service components of the organization, and on the board, and in the management leadership is helpful to service integrity. The unique needs of the community—needs that may reflect ethnic, cultural, and gender characteristics—have an impact on the subscriber mix and the service characteristics of the health care system.

Focusing on the community means that community characteristics are reflected in the service and benefit activities of the health care system. For example, a certain caregiving process or procedure may need to be part of the service mix in one community but not a different community with a different culture. The cultural makeup of the community in which a health care organization is located should even be reflected in the diversity of the board's members. The mission and values of the organization and its activity priorities should also be influenced by the cultural makeup of the community.

## SEAMLESS INTEGRATION

A seamless design, where each component of the organization has access to all the others, provides a stronger framework for the dialogue necessary for the development of a good relationship between the community and the organization (Exhibit 3-7). Among other things, it allows ideas for the modification of service structures to accommodate social and cultural characteristics to get an ample hearing. The result is that everyone in the organization feels a greater sense of obligation and commitment to those to whom services are directed.[42]

It is one thing to enumerate the advantages of a seamless structure in a health care organization and quite another to achieve it. Certain expectations and criteria

**Exhibit 3-7** Seamless Health Care Organization Design

- Linkage between all levels of the system
- Communication pathways from board to provider
- Information system support for all parts of the system
- Clinical integration across the continuum of care
- Multifocal decision making and service provision
- Interdisciplinary partnership and integration
- Organizational structure supporting integration

must be met to ensure the collateral and equitable relationships necessary to sustain a seamless structure:

- There must be a thorough commitment to the notions of partnership and empowerment throughout the organization. If such a commitment is lacking somewhere, the type of relationships necessary for success simply cannot be sustained.
- The content of each role and the relationships between players are constantly under revision. Players must be flexible and fluid, since their relationships will be redefined in response to changes in the efficacy of service provision and strategies to increase effectiveness. Active participation from staff in the process of defining interaction and work roles is essential to successful performance.
- There is considerable opportunity for conflict during the development of new relationships and roles. The processes associated with restructuring roles have substantial room for misunderstandings and perceptual difficulties. Besides an openness to dialogue on the part of everyone involved, what is needed is mediation by those skilled in consensus building and conflict resolution.
- Old expectations and patterns of communication and relationship may prevail in some quarters. The desirability of new role definitions and relationships may not be felt equally by all players. Some may lack the skills necessary to dispense with the hierarchy and deal with people to whom they were never previously exposed. Depending on who and where they are in the organization, such individuals may receive various types of help to assist them in dealing with the changes demanded of them.
- Changing the locus of control for certain decisions can cause an intense reaction in some sectors of the organization. The issue of control is one of the most challenging for those engaged in a process of change. The location and ownership of decisions can give rise to all kinds of power-related concerns. Imbedded in them are issues of loss and threat to self-image that may be very difficult to deal with.
- The move to using collective processes for dialogue and decision making is a major functional shift for an organization. When decisions are made by individuals, they are more immediate and usually take less time and there is also a clear point of control. Collective decision making demands a different set of skills, and ownership of the decisions is diffused among the group members. There can be concern that the decisions may take longer and not be as good as those made by selected individuals.
- Building partnerships is a great ideal but is often extremely hard to do. Past assumptions about roles and relationships can impede the change toward

equality, collateral interaction, and greater use of group processes. Time, patience, and skill development are requisites of partnering.

An organization does not become seamless without great difficulty. If the current structure is departmentalized, efforts to create an integrated design configured around the point of service can cause a high level of conflict. Even when an organization is energized to make the switch, there is no guarantee that anyone knows precisely how to implement and sustain the new design.

To date, there is precious little evidence that point-of-service approaches are effective. The models are too new and they completely reorient organizations to a new way of operating. The lack of evidence of effectiveness creates many problems for leaders. Nothing but good sense justifies the efforts at restructuring around the point of service and building the necessary organizational structures. Data of the kind that might support the efforts are simply not yet available (a dearth of relevent data always occurs at the beginning of any change). What is clear, however, is that the current structures and processes are in need of extensive revision. The research on empowered approaches indicates their importance and viability. Even so, making them work requires a willingness to undertake great risk.[43]

The real endorsement comes when an organization commits itself to building a sustainable structure. There are many health systems that like the idea of a point-of-service structure, along with empowerment and service-based decision making, yet never make the commitment to do the hard work. The difficulty is not in the notion but in its implementation. It is easy to find organizations that claim they have a point-of-service structure and are truly service and patient focused; it is not so easy to find organizations that actually have such a structure in place along with service-based processes that are working effectively.[44]

> *It is easier to find organizations that say they have point-of-care systems in place than to find those that really do.*

It must be remembered that a change in the way an organization operates has a personal dimension. When all is said and done, such a change really means a shift in the roles and activities of individuals. Since what people know and do is connected with their sense of self and their notion of personal value, any attempt to change their attitudes and behaviors can easily be perceived as a threat. The best way to overcome their defensiveness is to generate a real commitment to learning—in essence, to build a true learning organization. This kind of organization validates the challenge to and transitions in people's roles and behavior. Indeed, the organization expects a certain amount of defensiveness and builds processes and vehicles for making it safe to act out, experiment, practice, take risks, and engage in dialogue during any change of large magnitude.

No change is sustainable without a transforming structure that gives form and support to the revisions made in the roles of the various members of the organization. Creating a structure ensures that the new order of things is not accidental and that a return or a fallback to old practices and behaviors is not anticipated. It also validates the change itself, since the structure provides a context within which the change can continue to unfold.

Those pursuing point-of-service transformation, quality initiatives, or work redesign sometimes run into the following problem: while the reforms are underway, the structures necessary to make them work and sustain them are simply not present. The ownership expected at the grass roots or the point of service is more talk than substance. The way to restrict decisions to the point of service is to eliminate any other place in the organization where they might be made. This of course takes time, since it requires, in addition to behavioral changes, revisions in structures and operations.

## CONCLUSION

In this chapter we have attempted to justify the building of new structures and relationships in health care organizations. The components of any organization— service, operations, and governance—have been addressed in the context of some newer notions about their relationship to each other and the need for them to be related differently. The value of building a new structure that supports the patient-focused, service-based organization has been discussed.

The challenge is to identify and construct models and practices in harmony with the character and structure of transformed health organizations. The main goal of these organizations is to be more responsive to those they serve and the communities of which they are a part. A subsidiary goal is to change the relationship of those who together provide a continuum of well-integrated health care services into a true partnership. Shared governance is one possible means of sustaining a point-of-service design. The nursing and the patient care–centered context for shared governance helps clinical service providers focus on accountability and establishes a baseline for constructing a whole systems approach to shared governance. The organization then has a framework that sustains the point-of-service design and empowers its stakeholders to invest in efforts to improve the health of the community.

## REFERENCES

1. M. Hammer and J. Champy, *Reengineering the Corporation: A Manifesto for Business Revolution* (New York: Harper Business Books, 1993).
2. D. Beckham, "The Longest Wave—Fad Surfing," *Healthcare Forum Journal* 36, no. 6 (1993):78–82.
3. G. Beneveniste, *The Twenty-First Century Organization* (San Francisco: Jossey-Bass, 1994).
4. T. Atchison, *Turning Health Care Leadership Around: Cultivating, Inspiring, Empowered, and Loyal Followers* (San Francisco: Jossey-Bass, 1990).
5. M. Graham and M. Lebaron, *The Horizontal Revolution: Guiding the Teaming Takeover* (San Francisco: Jossey-Bass, 1994).
6. C. Elliott, "Leadership without Bosses: Shared Leadership in the Creation of a Health Network," *Healthcare Management Forum* 7, no. 1 (1994):38–43.
7. H. Anderson, "Hospitals Seek New Ways To Integrate Health Care," *Hospital and Health Networks* 66, no. 7 (1992):26–36.
8. J. Byrne, "The Horizontal Corporation," *Business Week,* December 20, 1993, pp. 76–81.
9. H. Mintzberg, *Mintzberg on Management* (New York: The Free Press, 1990).
10. C. Argyris, "Good Communication That Blocks Learning," *Harvard Business Review* 72, no. 4 (1994):77–85.
11. E. Baig, "The Information Society," *Business Week: The Information Revolution,* bonus, (1994):122–133.
12. E. Lawler III, *Motivation in Work Organizations* (San Fransisco: Jossey-Bass, 1994).
13. P. Block, *The Empowered Manager* (San Francisco: Jossey-Bass, 1991).
14. P. Block, *Stewardship: Choosing Service over Self-Interest* (San Francisco: Berrett-Koehler, 1993).
15. L. Brown, "Crime and Management," *Harvard Business Review* 69, no. 3 (1991):111–126.
16. T. Peters, *Liberation Management* (New York: Harper & Row, 1992).
17. T. Porter-O'Grady, *Creative Nursing Administration: Participatory Management into the 21st Century* (Gaithersburg, Md.: Aspen Publishers, 1986).
18. T. Porter-O'Grady, "Building Partnerships in Health Care: Creating Whole Systems Change," *Nursing and Health Care* 15, no. 1 (1994):34–38.
19. P. Dupuis and M.E. Connington, *Unit-Based Nursing Quality Assurance* (Gaithersburg, Md.: Aspen Publishers, Inc., 1990).
20. T. Hancock and C. Bezold, "Possible Future, Preferable Futures," *Healthcare Forum* 37, no. 2 (1994):23–29.
21. W. Bennis, *Beyond Bureaucracy* (San Francisco: Jossey-Bass, 1993).
22. P. Scholtes, *The TEAM Handbook* (Madison, Wis.: Joiner Associates, 1992).
23. G. Leavenworth, "Quality Costs Less," *Business and Health* 12, no. 3 (1994):7–11.
24. L. Paine, "Managing for Organizational Integrity," *Harvard Business Review* 72, no. 2 (1994):106–117.

25. R. Rosenfield, "Replacing the Workshop Model," *Topics In Healthcare Management* 20, no. 4 (1994):1–15.

26. H. Mintzberg, "The Manager's Job: Folklore and Fact," *Harvard Business Review* 48, no. 2 (1990):163–176.

27. T.J. Rodgers, W. Taylor, and R. Foreman, *No Excuses Management* (New York: Doubleday Currency, 1993).

28. M. Kets de Vries, *Leaders, Fools, and Imposters* (San Francisco: Jossey-Bass, 1993).

29. L. Sayles, *The Working Leader* (New York: The Free Press, 1993).

30. Paine, "Managing for Organizational Integrity."

31. K. Nair, *A Higher Standard of Leadership* (San Francisco: Berrett-Koehler, 1994).

32. P. Russell and R. Evans, *The Creative Manager* (San Francisco: Jossey-Bass, 1992).

33. C. Bell, *Customers as Partners* (San Francisco: Berrett- Koehler, 1994).

34. J. Womack and Daniel Jones, "From Lean Production to the Lean Enterprise," *Harvard Business Review* 72, no. 2 (1994):93–103.

35. J. Laney, "Ethics in Health Care: What Do We Have To Do? What Should We Do?" *Journal of the Medical Association of Georgia* 79 November 1990:829–833.

36. R. Johnson, "The Purpose of Hospital Governance," *Health Care Management Review* 19, no. 2 (1994):81–88.

37. Ibid.

38. T. Porter-O'Grady, "Whole Systems Shared Governance: Creating the Seamless Organization," *Nursing Economics* 12, no. 4 (1994):187–195.

39. D. Flarey, "The Nurse Executive and the Governing Body," *Journal of Nursing Administration* 21, no. 12 (1991):11–17.

40. J. Patti, K. McDonagh, and T. Porter-O'Grady, "Streetside Support," *Health Progress* 71, no. 5 (1990):60–62.

41. D. Beckham, "Building the High Performance Accountable Health Plan," *Healthcare Forum Journal* 37, no. 4 (1994):60–67.

42. A. Etzioni, *The Spirit of Community* (New York: Crown, 1993).

43. M. Wheatley, *Leadership and the New Science* (San Francisco: Berrett-Koehler, 1992).

44. P. Lathrop, *Restructuring Health Care: The Patient-focused Paradigm* (San Francisco: Jossey-Bass, 1994).

# Chapter 4

# Along the Continuum: Building toward Point-of-Care Health Services

*It is increasingly clear to me that the real issue of effectiveness, of winning in the marketplace, was finding ways to make the company work horizontally.*

Louis Gerstner, IBM

One of the greatest challenges for American organizations is to decentralize power. Both those who hold power and those who might receive it tend to be wary of the implications of decentralization. Such wariness will need to be managed because the time is fast arriving in health care when centralized structures and functions are no longer going to serve organizations well. Meeting the needs of defined subscriber (patient) populations will require a significantly different approach to organizing and managing services.

Organizational effectiveness is now mainly achieved by organizing around smaller units of activity or components of service. In health care, the units of activity might correspond to particular patient populations or service categories. The clinical pathway upon which patients travel also indicates how services are organized. Well-defined units of service in a continuum-based organizational system will not be sufficient for success, however. Linkage to the broader service arena and to the organization will also be essential. Further, information designed to support the work of service units is becoming more important as a means of ensuring their efficacy. Accessibility and ease of relationship between people and processes will influence the efficiency and effectiveness of the service system, as will the information system. The ability to access information and material will be the test of the quality of the relationship between system and provider. The ability to get needs addressed quickly and effectively will be the measure of success used by consumers.

Building horizontal relationships in an organization is fraught with myriad challenges. The very core of the system is at issue, and its reformatting requires the utmost diligence. One of the fundamental problems is that the power structure used to change the system is one of the key parts of the system that needs changing. Reformatting the structure and processes associated with the use of power is both noisy and traumatic.

> *Work is now arranged in horizontal configurations. The challenge of the time is to build relationships, not job categories.*

## RESTRUCTURING FROM THE CENTER OF THE SYSTEM

The role of workers at the "bottom" of the organization can suggest that they are in service to the management of the organization. The way decisions are made, problems solved, resources allocated, and service decisions applied hints at some level of indenture to the management.

In revising the service structure, the method of restructuring should focus at the core of the system and the players located there. In fact, it is essential to see them as constituting the central component of the system if a service orientation is to develop. It is by making the service providers the center of the system and the patients the center of the service providers' attention that the organization will become fully service centered (see Exhibit 4-1). This means increasing the focus of the system on the service role and those who are in it and de-emphasizing the role of management.

## BEGINNING THE CONTINUUM

Accountability for clinical decision making rests with the providers. Regardless of the approach to care delivery, the health care professionals are accountable for

**Exhibit 4-1** "Center Out" Work Design

- Begin at the point of care.
- Involve all people at the center.
- Reject all top-down and bottom-up strategies.
- Define accountability clearly.
- Let staff drive the design.
- Focus on relationship building.

the outcomes of the services provided. In this time of great emphasis on nonprofessional providers and functionaries, it must be recalled that health care professionals have a social obligation to act in the best interests of society, not the organization. The problem is that society does not directly employ or pay the providers. This places providers in an awkward situation, especially when there is conflict between organizational demand and patient need.

Historically, physicians have been able to avoid being caught in the conflict between patients and organizations. They have always had a strong position because of their control over patient admissions and hospital activities. As the control related to patients shifts more to payers and buyers, physicians are experiencing the same challenges and conflicts that other providers have in their more limited roles. Their difficulties in fact are now increasing as financial constraints become more severe.[1] Managed care and other cost-capping methods of organizing payment of care are becoming the rule rather than the exception, and consequently the whole focus of the energies of managers and staff is being altered. In organizing to providing services, no health care service entity is exempt from the vagaries of the radical transformation in the delivery of health care services.

> *The challenge for physicians is to abandon unilateral and ascendant roles. Partnership means forming relationships with other providers and patients.*

The challenge is to organize care so it can be provided efficiently and within predefined cost constraints. This requires providers to think about what they are doing and how they are doing it. It brings them into the center of the dialogue and forces them to confront the issues of cost, service, and quality. The noise that emerges from the dialogue reflects the uncertainties and lack of clarity in the health care system and its inability to define the value and the legitimate outcomes of health care.

Confronting the leaders of health care organizations are questions related to how services are provided, how they are organized, how they are paid for, and what a non-illness-based system would look like. Further questions related to the health of the community and the societal ills impact the delivery of health care services. Making care accessible by keeping the price affordable and offering a full range of convenient services is a challenge that demands a rethinking of the way services are structured, delivered, and paid for.

All change is local. Any workable transformation in health services will be constructed around local populations. Newer models of service must use configura-

> *In a capitated system, health takes on more importance than does illness. Cost savings are generated by reducing sickness-based services, not building on them.*

tions that support a more efficient provider-patient partnership and a more disciplined relationship between clinical processes and anticipated outcomes. They must also use service-based strategies appropriate for the specific populations to which services are directed. One problem is caused by the demand for national standards and a national policy that lays out funding and payment strategies. The conflict is between unique community needs reflecting a wide range of demographic variables affecting the use of health resources and national and state allocations of those resources. This conflict defines the battlefield where the delivery of care gets configured over the long term.

All care must be organized around a legitimate value stream. That value stream, contrary to the view often expressed in the health care business literature, is not the revenue flow. It is, rather, the patient pathway. The financial continuum reflects the patient pathway to the extent that the continuum allocates resources to support it and receives revenues generated by it. It is subordinate to the activities and elements of activities within the patient pathway. Its actions and resource applications are basically responses to the legitimate needs of those served.

All care must be organized around the patient pathway. All structures must support the effective and efficient delivery of services along the pathway. This will require a substantive rethinking of the design and organization of services within the health care system. There are several areas of significant change:

- Currently systems are organized around the physician provider. New systems will have to be organized around patient populations and service pathways.
- Health care services are hospital centric. Future health care will not focus on the treatment of illness.
- The community will become an increasing focus of service; this will tend to decentralize and mobilize care services.
- Current hospital redesign efforts, which focus on departmental decentralization, will be replaced by efforts to structure services around service categories or patient populations.
- Linkage between physicians and other professional providers will not remain poorly defined. The intensity of the linkage will often determine the level of cost and the degree of quality of the services provided.

## ORGANIZING CARE AROUND THE PATIENT

Historically, hospitals were places where physicians could do their work and have the supports necessary to take care of the sick. In a patient-based approach, the focus is not on sickness but on health. The goal is to prevent the use of high-intensity resources, which means preventing illness in cases where that is possible. This requires a shift in the focus of health care services:

- Providers cannot wait for patients to come to them for services. If they do, it will be too late to do anything about what brought them there in the first place.
- The focus can no longer be restricted to diagnosis and treatment; rather it must include assessment and identification of health status, which is a longer term issue.
- Physicians will not be the only key providers making critical decisions about what happens to patients. There will need to be a broader range of professionals assisting patients in making health-generating decisions.
- Health care is now mainly concerned with life management processes instead of illness treatment processes. This necessitates more dynamic and longer term relationships with patients.
- Clinical outcomes are now influenced more by preventive measures than by medical interventions alone.
- Cost structures facilitate the focus on low-intensity services intended to diminish the need for high-cost services later on.
- The contracting for one price for a group of subscribers provides clear parameters within which decisions can be made about how health care gets provided.

When the parameters regarding payment, service, and expectations are laid out in advance, it changes the nature of the relationship between providers and patients. No longer can they avoid the effort it takes to achieve a clear understanding of their mutual obligations. A provider-patient relationship makes the patient part of the organization and increases the obligations he or she has with regard to that relationship. Patients are not mere recipients of service. They, like the other players in the system, are partners in the processes directed toward helping them. They now must take on a more active role in the management of their lives and their health.

The current system does not place accountability on virtually any of the partners in health care. Although there is beginning to be an interest in quality and accountability, only superficial processes now exist to address the related issues.[2] The goal is to develop a format and a set of actions that accelerate the rate at which all the parties, patients and providers alike, accept accountability for meeting their obligations.

Providers have encouragement to accept accountability because the consequences of their actions are direct. Not maintaining an adequate margin between the cost of providing a service and the price paid for the service results in loss of revenue. Not sustaining a level of quality and patient satisfaction with services and their outcomes increases the risk of desertion by patients.

Patients, on the other hand, are partially buffered from the consequences of their behavior. The third-party approach to payment has created a third-party consciousness about life management among patients. Directly connecting actions and consequences will be necessary for ensuring that a patient-based system remains viable. The service continuum must require patient accountability. For example, if a patient acts irresponsibly, the patient could be charged a penalty or an increased share of the cost of service provision based on the degree of risk to health (see Figure 4-1).

Developing a partnership orientation will mean a significant change for providers too. Service delivery and provider-patient relationships will need to be configured differently. Old industrial notions generated in the commercial segment of society do not translate well to the field of health care.[3] Transferring these notions does injustice to what is essentially a unique set of variables. Although some of the notions of customer service are transferable, most are not. The health care field does not have the same quid pro quo arrangements frequently found in business. Although it is essential for health care organizations to operate in a more business-like fashion, that does not entail that they should foster business-type relationships between the players. The locus of control and the social and personal accountabilities of the players call for a different set of relationships and interactions. Attempting to make health care a commodity engenders the very problems that have brought American health care to a crisis. It creates an emphasis on service func-

**Figure 4-1** Health Care Value Equation

> *Generally missing from health care reform is any sense of accountability, both on the part of the health care system and on the part of the individual.*

tionalism, prices, and costs to the exclusion of human accountability and obligations. The result is that accountability is missing where it counts and poor relationships exist between all the elements that might effectively make the health care system work.

Leaders must think critically about what changes are demanded by the switch to a patient-based approach. The obvious first-stage tasks and activities would have to reflect a stronger sensitivity to service-oriented considerations:

- Organizing support structures around service lines and care delivery within the context of service categories
- Changing from a geographic orientation toward allocation of services to a demographic orientation
- Focusing on specific service needs of patients and providing services in a cost-efficient manner
- Examining institutional services and determining the category of care or service level required to offer high-quality, cost-sensitive services
- Changing the focus from processes to outcomes so that attention to quality measures becomes part of the normal work of every provider
- Breaking down the artificial barriers between disciplines and providers and locating them as close to each other as practicable in the places where patients are served

The above tasks constitute the first step in a series of steps needed to turn a hospital-focused system into a health care service continuum.[4] The steps are not an end in themselves. Any activity where the current focus is the hospital is an interim stage in the journey to a continuum-based approach to health care services. Leaders must begin with a broader notion of health care services so that the goal does not become mere redesign of the hospital. Looking beyond the walls of the hospital is the foundation for creating a longer term vision. Following are a few of the key considerations to keep in mind when starting to build a service continuum:

- Think horizontal integration, not vertical integration. The relationships between the partners will determine the effectiveness of the continuum of services.
- Do not seek to own all the elements or components of the service continuum. Ownership creates costs in both support and operation of the service as well as costs due to its conjunction with other owned services.

- Control is no longer found in unilateral ownership or decision making. Instead, control is a function of the character and kind of risk sharing that service partners agree to bear together and is therefore negotiated between the partners.
- Retraining the professionals is essential. All providers, from nurses, physicians, and ancillary professionals to support staff, need a different understanding and a unique set of skills in a health subscribed system.
- All barriers to equity-based clinical relationships will have to be demolished, no matter how much "noise" and pain that might entail. Hierarchy impedes development of the kind of relationships necessary for the continuum of care.
- Departmental, compartmental, and segmented managerial configurations and organizational charts will have to be eliminated in order to facilitate point-of-care leadership.
- Assessment of competence will not be based on what credentials individuals bring to their work but instead on what they do and what they achieve.
- A service continuum is built on the notion that health is the focus of the provider and the patient. Illness-based services must be viewed as a subset of the totality of services in order for a patient-based system to be sustainable.

The above guidelines can serve as a beginning point for thinking about building service structures to reflect the continuum of care. They establish a baseline for considering what cannot be transferred to a continuum-based, point-of-care design. Following are some additional guidelines:

- The organized medical staff and its bylaws obstruct the creation of the kind of partnership needed in the clinical environment. They take the problem-definition and -solving processes away from the point of service, with the result that the chosen solutions are not viewed as appropriate by providers or patients.
- Every discipline is required to identify its frame of reference and social and legal mandates before it defines the nature of its partnership. The organization must accommodate this. The members of the discipline should "sing off the same sheet of music" whenever engaged in a dialogue about their role with others.
- The organization should not attempt to create an amorphous or generic caregiver role. "The broader the base, the lower the mean and the less clear the expectations" should be an emerging tenet for organizations. It is more important to be clear about the expectations for and accountability of each discipline than to eliminate the disciplines.
- The fewer the managers, the better. The effectiveness of an organization is in inverse relation to the levels and number of managers. The higher the ratio of

managers to staff, the more effective and independent the staff; the lower the ratio, the weaker the role of the staff. In a continuum of services, it is untenable to have more managers than absolutely necessary.

It should be evident that activities directed to addressing the above factors take precedence when the organization is preparing for the switch to a point-of-care service continuum. Increasingly, the organization must be able to operate successfully where services are provided and the majority of players make decisions about care. It is these players who must be clearest about parameters, expectations, outcomes, and resource use, and their decisions must take into account the cost and effectiveness of the work they do. The partnership between provider and patient that ultimately determines the viability of the system is forged in this arena. Providers must understand this and be aware of the consequences and implications of what they do.[5]

> *The core relationship in health care is between the patient and the provider. All structures serve to support this relationship.*

The behaviors of a number of players, including the clinical providers, must be changed. Decisions made by providers are often focused on the work and clinical activities within the context of individual clinical events regardless of other circumstances. Patients are given what they need and there is relatively little consideration given to other factors such as cost, choice of materials, long-term need for supplies, and alternatives to conventional approaches. Providers have been cautioned about cost control but cost remains an elusive issue. They rarely make meaningful resource use decisions at the point of service. The role partially engenders this lack of resource sensitivity because the job often requires a provider to go from one critical or clinical event immediately to the next. It will take a considered effort to change the frame of reference for providers so that they balance cost and quality in making decisions about the kind of services to provide to patients (see Exhibit 4-2). Some forethought about cost will need to be incorporated into the role.

## COST AND QUALITY INTERFACE IN A SUBSCRIBER SYSTEM

Providers, in discussion, rarely seem to have an understanding of the intimate relationship between cost and quality in an economically driven social and work system. These elements can no longer be viewed as separate. There is no quality

**Exhibit 4-2** Cost-Quality Balance

---

Focus on cost the first time the relationship is established:
- Price
- Volume
- Services
- Comprehensiveness

Evaluate quality indices for sustained relationships:
- Outcomes
- Value
- Comparative data
- Sustainable service

---

without a cost measure and no valid cost delineation without a quality element. Cost and quality are in fact inherently related and value hangs on the closeness of their relatedness. No provider, therefore, can expect to argue for quality without discussing the cost associated with obtaining the defined level of quality. That notion is both challenging and painful to the majority of providers, since it means they must be available to deal with cost-related issues they were previously exempt from having to handle.

Often the variables affecting the work of the providers were controlled by the managers. The problem is that the wrong people were controlling them. The managers, by and large, did not expend the resources of the organizations; they merely budgeted them. It was the staff who used the resources in the course of doing their work. Any dissonance between what staff was doing and the resources necessary to do it was never personally experienced by the staff because someone else was managing the resources for them. As resources began to be constrained, the staff reacted by seeing it as a threat to their activities. They rarely gave any thought to the possibility that they should either not be doing what they were doing or be doing it differently. Changing their behavior would require more knowledge and a deeper investment than was typical, as well as a desire to see beyond the immediacy of their activities.

*In a subscriber-based approach to service provision, cost and quality must be looked at together. The level of cost should not be set without considering the attendant level of quality and vice versa.*

When an organization reconfigures around the point of service, it automatically removes the insulation protecting the staff from having to deal with the things that most affect their work: structure, power, resources, and relationships. Indeed reorganization strips responsibility for those elements from management and shares it with those who work at the point of service. Further, many managers' roles are removed as well, and there are thus few barriers between the staff and the organization, which, in point-of-care approaches, is redesigned to support the staff's work and their relationship with patients.

Staff and management are not ready for this reality and are in fact reeling from its implications. The rules so well known by all parties are now out of date, whatever new rules emerge must be devised by those who will be most affected by them. Being unprepared to devise new rules (and not especially interested in devising them), the staff feel abandoned by the managers who took care of such things in the past and protected the staff from the vagaries of the marketplace, the organization, and the payers.

No longer is the relationship between provider and patient insulated from all the variables that affect its content and outcomes. All players are in the same game and are required to know all the rules. Indeed, the role of the manager is to make adequate information available to those who will need it so that they may make the wisest choices. The role does not include parental oversight or furnishing approval of the staff's work. Reliance on manager approval suggests that correct decisions might not be made the first time. Either the necessary resources might not be present, the necessary information might not be available, the right person might not be involved, and so on. In any case, inadequate decisions require supervision, possible correction, and final approval. The simple truth is that if the right decision is not made the first time by the players who need to make it, cost is always greater and quality is always reduced. In addition, higher cost and reduction in quality both accelerates the further up in the hierarchy this dysfunctional approval dynamic is forced to operate.

An entrenched system of supervision and approval of managers can present enormous obstacles to an organization trying to create a service-based continuum of care. Several issues come quickly to the forefront:

- The effectiveness of point-of-service decision making is directly related to how few managers there are in the organization.
- The effectiveness of the organization is dependent on how much critical information providers have in making decisions.
- To become truly self-directed, the organization must actually believe that the staff will make the right decisions and take the right actions at least as efficiently as managers have historically done.

- Effective reeningeering requires increasing the number of staff at the point of care and reducing the number of staff and managers who draw resources and decisions away from the point of care.
- Creating a lean organization requires removing from the system roles that are not directly related to or do not influence those who make point-of-care decisions. Whoever is not servicing a patient should be serving someone who is.
- Problems and providers who directly impact patient care must deal with their issues within the context out of which they arose. There should be no other parallel, nonrelated problem-solving process into which the participants can retreat.

> ### Whoever is not servicing a patient should be serving someone who is.

It is clear that the rules of relationship change dramatically in a point-of-care format. The old structures no longer have validity; indeed, they impede the establishment of healthy relationships. This means the organization must become serious about making the requisite shifts to support and sustain the point-of-care continuum. A series of actions will be necessary to undergird the lean structures necessary for creating a continuum of care.

- Management levels should be reduced to no more than three (having only two levels is even more desirable). The proportion of managers to staff should be a third of the proportion most clinical organizations now operate with.
- Most vice-presidential roles should be removed. In place, service or servant titles should be devised that indicate the roles of finance, human resources, marketing, plant services, and other personnel indicating a consulting role.
- Patient care units should be redesigned to reflect the patient pathway rather than the provider departments. Artificial units, such as critical care units, must be disposed of and the services relocated within the continuum of care.
- The skill and knowledge base of point-of-care managers must be increased. These managers now must have the skill base once expected of vice-presidents. They will be facilitating the strategic service units, where 90 percent of decisions and activities occur.
- Organizations with "fat" corporate structures must be pared to the smallest size consistent with integration. The corporate structure of an organization should not be making administrative, market, service, or relational decisions—to do so interferes with the effectiveness of the points of care and the service continuum.

- The medical staff organization must be closely connected with the patient care organization. Unilateral structures and bylaws that operate independent of the relationships necessary to effect integration and point-of-care interaction must be eliminated. Physicians must identify and solve clinical and operational problems at the point of care where they originated, not in an isolated medical staff "silo."
- All appropriate providers must be located within the service continuum. Departmental structures must be eliminated to the fullest extent possible so that all providers are located and relate within services structured at the point of care.
- The foundations for a seamless organizational structure, with no barriers between board and provider and between provider and community, must be installed. Compartmentalization must be eradicated at all levels of the system. Horizontal integration supersedes vertical integration. Relationships, not status, define value.
- Control strategies that attempt to place the locus of control within a single entity must be eliminated in the planning and structuring of a continuum of care system. Risk sharing and agreement constitute the new method of control, with performance and outcome the measure of value.
- Old styles of leadership that are "hero" based or in which execution is unilateral must be excluded. These are management approaches that are not appropriate in horizontal organizations. The new organizational models require considerable dialogue, decision making, and relationship building. Styles of leadership that support these behaviors are mandatory.

## BUILDING TEAMS AT THE POINT OF SERVICE

Before linkages with other providers along the continuum of care can be developed, service mechanisms within each setting must make it possible to build successful service relationships. Staff must be configured in a such a way as to make service connections viable (see Table 4-1). Without team-based behaviors and approaches within each service entity, the relationships necessary to sustain a point-of-care orientation and linkage along the continuum simply cannot grow and the kinds of interactions necessary to construct long-term relationships across service settings never emerge.[6]

> *All team approaches to work depend on intense and viable relationships and on a method for building relationships.*

**Table 4-1** Changes in Work Processes

| *Traditional Approaches* | *Team Approaches* |
|---|---|
| Individual behavior | Group behavior |
| Process focused | Relationship based |
| Job oriented | Outcome oriented |
| Functional focus | Results focus |
| Task specific | Interaction values |
| Indeterminate outcomes | Solution oriented |

## FROM INDIVIDUAL TO GROUP WORK MODELS

All intersections in the workplace build on relationships. Success in a health system always depends on the quality of the relationships established between all the essential players. Teams are simply a gathering of people configured around an essential relationship and a fulfilling common purpose. It is the construction of essential relationships that lies at the heart of an effective continuum of care.

Following are guidelines for engendering the kind of team functioning that will undergird the clinical relationships necessary to facilitate clinical activity along the continuum of care:

> *The challenge in making patient-centered approaches work effectively is getting providers in different disciplines to relate well with each other. The problem has been that they do not want to have a relationship with each other. Providers can barely relate to other providers within their own discipline.*

- The clinical team must reflect the services provided and the culture of the service unit or component.
- Services are multifocal and thus multidisciplinary. The essential players must have a common core around which they are organized.
- All workers are organized around a patient population, pathway, or service. The grouping reflects the relationships that are necessary to address all components of the continuum.
- The roles of each member of the team must be clear to all members. Expectations will be built on the contribution each role is intended to make to the whole.

- Fixed role descriptors must be dispensed with. Each role must be fluid and flexible so that it can easily adapt to changes that occur. Absolute role parameters impede the adaptability necessary to respond to changes in clients, culture, or market.
- Teams will have some ad hoc characteristics as members necessary to specific functions move in or out in response to changes in clients served or clinical needs.
- Teams will be essentially self-directed. Therefore, a significant development cycle will be needed to assist members in moving from more dependency models of organization. All team members must possess the ability to participate fully in the design, implementation, and evaluation of work processes used in the provision of services.
- Accountability is the essence of role definition. It leads to a stronger focus on the contribution of each role to the achievement of results or clinical outcomes. Each team member must be oriented toward the achievement of results more than toward the performance of activities.

> *Team-based approaches facilitate a focus on the continuum of care rather than the events of care. It is a team obligation to link with others in order to close the loops where the continuum is not the central focus of providers.*

Clinical teams must be aware that the linkage between players along the continuum of care may mean the establishment of relationships over which team members may not have absolute control. For one thing, partnerships will be established between providers from separate disciplines, and none of the disciplines involved will be the sole determinant of the character of the relationships. Yet key members do not have the option of deciding not to relate, work, or interact with other providers along the service continuum. Outcomes will depend on the interaction of all the required resources. A partnership makes demands on its members, demands that are unrelenting. All team members must be aware of this reality and accept the rigors necessary to maintain the relationships and functions.

Teams must have several characteristics if they are to be effective. Accidental relationships and unstructured processes are generally not sustainable. The trick with teams is to be able to structure them around some fairly strong concepts without creating rigid parameters that do not allow for the flexibility and responsiveness they will need to adapt to the vagaries of a wide variety of activities.

## A Clearly Defined Purpose

Teams often have a very clear set of functions and activities. The service providers must be aware of the unique needs of the population served and be configured to meet those needs. The team should know from the outset what it does and the purpose toward which its activities are directed. Each member must be aware of the contribution his or her work makes to the agreed activities of the team. One problem is that coworkers often do not share the same understanding of the activities they are jointly engaged in performing. A common understanding can usually be achieved through dialogue. If the purpose of work is unclear, the activities and outcomes of the work will be unclear as well.

## Membership Clarity about Team Goals

Each member of the team must work in concert with other members of the team to ensure that the team's work is contributing to the achievement of its goals. There are basically two kinds of team goals. First, there are goals that relate to the team's own needs and activities or those of the organization or system of which it is a part. These goals keep the team focused on its functions, activities, competence, and development and are essential to the construction and integrity of the team as a functioning unit. (Among the pertinent team activities are those concerned with issues of education, relationship, function, interaction, and effectiveness.)

Second, the team has service or work goals. Service goals take into account the needs of those to whom the team directs its attention. Here again the team has goals that relate to generic work applications, such as the development of protocols, standards, pathways, clinical plans, and so on. The team also has goals that may be patient specific or part of a framework for pursuing the team's purpose. These goals are related to individual team members and their specific activities (clinical and other activities).

Goals of these two types make up the structural framework of the activities of the members of the team. They keep the team integrated and directed toward its purpose and functions. Through the structural impact of its goals, the team can continuously assess its activities and the results of its work.

## A Quality Improvement Process

Every team must be able to evaluate its effectiveness. The activities of a team are always subject to review and adjustment based on the evidence of congruence between what it does and what it achieves. Without a clear foundation for making this comparison, the efficacy of the team's activities cannot be analyzed. In essence, the team works in an information vacuum. The tendency in this situation is to get "stuck" in rituals and routines that may or may not help achieve the purpose and goals of the team. This tendency toward rote work is the single greatest obstacle to true team effectiveness.

Analysis and evaluation of processes and functions is continuous in effective teams. The strategy of quality improvement ensures a strong link between the activities of the team and its attainment of meaningful clinical outcomes. Quality improvement requires the use of tools and techniques that discipline the clinical and critical process of the team. The quality tools that externalize and make objective the dialogue about work activities are essential to good quality review. Each team should be trained in the use of the tools of quality assessment and required to use them regularly in the assessment of their activities and the evaluation of service outcomes.

## An Understanding of Each Member's Specific Contribution

It is imperative that the role of each team member be clear not only to that person but to every other member. This will help the team function in an effective manner. Dialogue and consensus building will be necessary to ensure a common understanding of the function and application of each team member's role. Repeat discussions of the issues involved should be expected. What should not be expected is that every team member will maintain an understanding of every other member's role without evaluation and dialogue. Continuous understanding is impossible without continuous interaction in human work groups.

As discussed in Chapter 7, accountability serves as the baseline for defining functions and activities for each role. From the perspective of the accountability of the role, its contribution can be best delineated and reviewed by all whom the accountability touches and affects. Clarifying these issues ensures that each member is focusing on the work necessary for the smooth and efficient functioning of the team in the course of providing services. There is nothing that will negatively impact team functioning like the lack of clarity regarding role functions and expectations.

## An Understanding of the Character of Team Behaviors

A team does not function like an individual. Facilitators must be sensitive to the construction needs and the developmental issues unique to the team. Working together within the same structural, functional, and service framework requires great patience and good skills. Each member of a team is unique and brings to the team his or her individual personality. In addition, the team as a whole has a personality. Blending and matching individual personalities to create a team personality that supports the team's work takes time, care, and effort. Unilateral and nonrelated activities can have a tremendous impact on the vitality of the team. Again, once the team is constructed, ensuring that it remains effective is a continuous task. Each team has its own personality, and the type of support and guidance it needs will depend on its personality and how it performs its work.

Maintaining good team relationships is a dynamic process. Part of the collective work of the team is the evaluation of the relational character and needs of the members. Each member must be given a hearing and must feel he or she is making a contribution. Each must play a role in the team's discussion and decisions. Without essential buy-in from each player, relationship and function problems always emerge. In clinical teams, there will also be consistent variation in membership depending on the clinical situation and the patient population. Members moving in and out of teams and the forming of ad hoc groups around specific patients create real stress. Constructing a way of dealing with membership variation requires a continuous focus by members on the pertinent issues.

It should be remembered that team functions and activities will change depending on changes in patient needs and in the marketplace. In a changing environment, the vagaries of service provision work against the permanence of structured activities. No person will have a specified set of functions cast in stone. Every role will be subject to adjustment and change depending upon the character and content of the demands made on it. Attachment to specific functions can be poison to a team and damage its ability to respond to the widely disparate needs of the community it serves. The individual team members must be able to adjust functions and activities quickly to match needs. Clearly this kind of responsiveness requires members to develop a different attitude about roles and work. The transition to the new attitude will need attention and discussion by team members.

**Effective Communication Mechanisms**

Good communication does not simply happen; it requires special strategies and skills. Teams, in order to function well, must have a broad-based understanding of effective communication processes. Techniques and processes that foster communication are available to any work group. When a group is being formed, the facilitator can enumerate and experiment with techniques designed to help work through some of the complexities of interacting and dialoguing effectively. Discipline will be required to ensure that the group continues to use processes that maintain effective dialogue and openness among its members.

Developing good group relations and continuous interaction is an extended process. The old industrial, linear, assembly-line approach to jobs was not supportive of healthy dialogue and good interaction. In today's more interactive and relationship-sensitive work frameworks, many of the old behaviors impede the effectiveness of work teams. Interaction problems will not be overcome overnight and will require repeated attention forever. Since human work groups are dynamic, there will be no point at which attending to the nature of the interaction of members can stop. A way of nurturing dialogue and relationships will need to be built into the ongoing activities of the group. Since team effectiveness is partially determined by the quality of group interactions and group dynamics, work cannot continue when issues affecting the relationships and communication of group members are left unaddressed. The skills and techniques of good communication are available to all and simply require discipline and practice to be used effectively. Usually, a facilitator is needed in the initial stages of team formation to assist in developing effective communication skills.

## A Solid Decision-making Framework

Making decisions also demands skill. There are tools that can be learned that help groups process information and lead them toward more effective decisions. Here again acquiring the skills requires discipline.

Although dialogue is essential to good decisions, it must be subjected to rigorous assessment in order to ensure that it is paving the way to meaningful decisions. In many work groups, talk is plentiful but decisions are few. It is not the purpose of a work team to dialogue. Dialogue is merely a means of moving the group toward decisions that will enhance the work of the team.

It is also imperative that the team have a way of structuring decision making so the outcomes are achieved in a timely fashion. The following guidelines will help ensure that decisions are made quickly but with the attention to detail necessary to guarantee their correctness.

- A format is required for laying out the issue in clear enough terms so that all members can understand it enough to discuss it appropriately.
- Techniques of explicating the issue must be available to the team so all the variables affecting the issue are clear to all members.
- A mechanism for ascertaining the level of consensus is needed to ensure that the team's position on the issue can be assessed quickly.
- Experts and ad hoc members should be included in deliberations so that the team is aware of the essential implications prior to committing to a decision.
- The team must possess clear accountability for the decision, which means the decision should not be subject to review and approval by another body once it is made.

- Once agreement has been achieved, all members of the team should understand that their commitment to the decision is essential. Any hint of a lack of commitment must be clarified and dealt with before the decision-making process is brought to a close and the members move on to the implementation of the decision.
- There needs to be a process for evaluating the decision after implementation. Adjustments can be incorporated into the implementation process as long as they do not substantially change the decision without team dialogue.

## A Format for Group Processes

It is important that there be some consistency in how the team does its work. Interaction protocols provide some parameters that guide the team's work. Certain norms must be established that let members know what is expected of them and how they should behave with each other. Formalized acknowledgement of the team's structure and processes tells the members what they need to keep in mind relating to each other.

Of course, the parameters are established by the team in the formative stages of development. They become nonnegotiable once the team has committed to them and adopted them. They can only be changed by a consensus. As with all rules, team members must be informed of the consequences of noncompliance. The application of the team's rules must be fair and consistent. Minus consistency, the rules will fail to achieve their purpose and will lose their meaning.

## Clear Leadership Roles and Processes

All too often in developing self-managed work teams there is a failure to establish clear leadership roles and expectations. Leaders are typically given responsibility for meeting facilitation, project follow-through, and task assignment. The team has a right to evaluate the effectiveness of its leaders in performing the duties they have accepted.

There should also be a process format that allows the team to maintain order during its meetings and interactions. Group process skills can facilitate team activities such as dialoguing and problem solving. The team's facilitator must be sensitive to the personalities and behaviors of each member and respond appropriately. Some team members may be very assertive and communicate their views well. Others may be more reticent and may need to be drawn out. Leaders must be familiar enough with group dynamics that they understand these issues and can handle them.

**Group Ownership of Processes**

In the old workplace, individuals were the source of all interaction and the objects of all blame. If something went wrong, it was assumed some individual had done something wrong. The tendency to lay blame on individuals created all kinds of dysfunctional interactions. In the emerging workplace, it is the process that is the focus of attention. The way work is done, the system that supports work, and the expectations of the work system are all subject to analysis. The team, in other words, concentrates on issues that it can adjust and improve. This does not suggest a lack of personal accountability; in fact, it facilitates accountability. The basic strategy is to revise activities and functions to ensure results are achieved appropriately. Focusing on persons and personalities often deflects attention from the real issues. If the performance is incorrect, the desired outcome not achieved, or the relationship not established, the relevant activities must be looked at critically as a matter of course. All members must be aware that attentiveness to activities is an essential characteristic of team-based approaches. Creating a more objective process of analysis and response is essential to the effectiveness of the team.[7]

Team processes demand a real shift in the organization's focus as well as its structures. Managers can no longer play the supervisory and directing roles demanded in the older management paradigm. This can create a crisis. Most managers are not prepared to perform in the team-based facilitator, coordinator, and integrator roles. They lack the necessary skills. If team-based processes are to work, the managers must go through a developmental process to prepare for their new role. This will be the greatest organizational challenge, and it may mean that some of the people who occupy management positions will not remain in them. As indicated before, the number of managers needed in the point-of-care organization is significantly less. Those who survive should be skilled in team-based approaches to leadership. Some critical elements of the manager's new role are described below:

> *The manager cannot be a parent or an autocrat in team-based approaches. Teams need facilitation, not control.*

- The role of the manager in the team-based organization is to facilitate the processes of the team. The manager must focus on the team's functioning and direct attention to its effectiveness.
- Decisions are made by the team or assigned team members. The effectiveness of the team and its members in making decisions, not the decisions themselves, is the proper focus of the manager.

- The manager is accountable for ensuring that the appropriate context for the team's work exists. This means that barriers to team success are addressed and the skills necessary for good team functioning are available to the team.
- All roles are learning roles in the organization. The manager acts as a role model for the team members by his or her willingness to learn and grow.
- In self-managed work teams, the leaders assume many of the process-oriented functions that once belonged to managers. In an accountability-based design, the manager's main task is to make certain team leaders have what they need to perform in accordance with their roles and the expectations of team members.
- Leading is a dynamic process and leadership skills require constant development. The manager must see to it that opportunities are available for personalized leadership development and growth in a format that staff leaders can access.
- In team-based approaches, the manager's role becomes more systems-oriented and less function-driven. The manager must ensure that what is needed in the learning process, information, finance, and systems components is available to the team members in a format that they can understand and use. Because team members are doing the work, the manager is accountable for the contextual and support or organizational issues that affect the work. They serve as a linkage between the clinical system and the operational system in a way that strengthens the interdependence of the two.

The nature of the horizontal organization also changes the character of team relationships. The teams are not permanently configured, and members do not usually have long-term relationships with other members (see Exhibit 4-3). Although some members may remain on a team for a long period, many or even most will not.

**Exhibit 4-3** Requirements for Team Effectiveness

- Every member knows the central focus.
- Group interaction skills are well developed.
- The focus is on solutions, not problems.
- CQI techniques are used for decision making.
- Each member's accountability is clear.
- All necessary players are members.
- The team has authority for its decisions.
- The desired outcomes of team work are enumerated.

## TEAM EFFECTIVENESS

Clinical teams will need to be much more fluid than in the past, especially in organizations based on the partnering of providers along the continuum of care. Since the continuum of care will define the character of a team more often than not, membership will be determined by the content of the work of the team and by the continuum. Further, members will come from a variety of settings and have a variety of roles along the continuum. The prevalence of horizontal relationships places special demands on the team:

- The team-based approach to clinical service must be supported by all partners along the continuum of care. Most providers currently view team-based clinical processes as essential to the delivery of care services.
- Members must be clear about their specific team obligations at the outset. Team roles and obligations are as much a part of initial contractual negotiations as financial and service issues. Clarity at this stage reduces conflicts between members later in the partnership.
- The accountability of each member must be delineated at the earliest possible time. As the roles of members of the clinical teams get defined, the partnership and functional activities belonging to each member must become clear to all the players. Like any set of expectations, the clearer expectations regarding accountability occur early in the partnership, the fewer problems will emerge later.
- Mechanisms for solution seeking and problem solving must also be developed early in the process. Since a partnership is based on risk sharing instead of outright ownership, mechanisms for resolving service and contract problems need to be identified right away.
- The locus of control for issues that arise from the team's activities should never be taken away from the team for resolution by any parties to the partnership. Solution seeking should be maintained at the service locus of control as much as possible; that is where the work is done and the ownership of it must be located.
- No component of the organization should have corollary decision-making processes in place that address issues properly belonging to the clinical teams. Any dual, duplicating, or second-level decision-making processes will complicate the team's functioning and reduce its effectiveness.
- The management of any aligned or partner organizations must meet regularly to discuss the content and progress of their service relationship. Functional, support, and informational issues affecting the success of the team-

based activities should be dealt with during the meetings in order to make the system work effectively.

Interaction between the partners and the teams is critical for the teams' effective functioning. If team members and the teams themselves are to be self-managed, the necessary supports must be in place.[8] The role of the managers is to see to it that the appropriate context exists and that the required tools, information, and resources are available. The managers must evaluate the needs of the teams in the same way the teams evaluate the needs of their patients. If the managers and teams assess their activities, analyze their results, and adjust their actions to better support those whom they serve, the outcomes of their activities will always be enhanced.[9]

## COLLABORATION: THE KEY TO EFFECTIVE PARTNERSHIPS

A common topic of conversation in health care circles is collaboration. Unfortunately, collaboration itself is not much in evidence except in rare circumstances. Collaboration is not simply cooperation or coordination; it is much more comprehensive. In the case of collaboration, the partners create a structure for their relationship and make a strong commitment to an agreed outcome. To be successful, the relationship demands a major investment on the part of the partners and a virtual identification with each other. The partners consent to interact with each other for a common purpose and to communicate continuously regarding their relationship.

> *Collaboration demands equity. If the partners do not see each other as equal contributors to their mutually defined outcomes, the relationship will be short-lived.*

In a collaborative relationship, there is an agreement to pursue a common purpose.[10] The partners hammer out together the kinds of activities and functions that each will contribute. Issues of power and control are discussed, along with the other issues that could affect the nature of the relationship. Although a collaborative relationship is typically intense, it does allow for the separateness of each partner. Indeed, the recognition of separateness is an essential feature of collaboration. Each partner agrees to contribute special talents and skills to the pursuit of a common purpose in return for the benefits the partners hope to achieve as a result of the other partner's contribution of any special talents and skills. In short, the partners hope to achieve mutual benefits.

> *Collaboration requires a commitment to the relationship between partners. They agree, in essence, to work through any barriers and sustain the relationship despite any impediments.*

Collaboration will change the way the partners work with and relate to each other. In the old model, they would likely compete with each other, unilaterally provide the same services, duplicate functions, and be concerned just with their own interests. Entering into a partnership critically alters their interaction. They acquire a different understanding of their work and their relationship. The horizontal notions of mutuality, value, mission, sharing, and interacting replace the older, unilateral, nonrenewing concepts.[11]

## Barriers to Collaboration

There are many barriers to creating a point-of-service collaboration. Dealing with them will require concerted action on the part of all parties. Commitment to a collaboration is a vital first step toward building the processes associated with making it successful. Honest recognition that there are historic barriers that will have to be honestly confronted is another important step. The barriers should not be thought of as unusual or insurmountable. They are the expected products of long years of competition for resources and patients. Now that competition is being replaced by integration, behaviors associated with it must be confronted directly, and that can be very uncomfortable for everyone. Following is a description of areas in which major obstacles to building the necessary infrastructure for collaboration may arise.

### Past Experience

The past can get in the way of building the future. This is especially true for those who were in direct competition with each other or had a clouded relationship in the past. Old experience, behaviors, and animosities can extend into the partnership and must be anticipated regardless of how petty or ridiculous they may appear to either party. The mythology of old relationships is strong and must be dealt with. Ignoring the past or making light of it can create difficulties later on that may even threaten the partnership.

### Philosophy

There is nothing that means more to an organization and its leaders than its philosophical foundations. A partnership between organizations must be based on common ground—on the commonalities in their belief systems, purposes, and roles in the community. Universal integration of the organizations' philosophies will not be possible. There are cultural and organizational characteristics that give each organization its unique identity. Trying to eliminate them is futile and frankly a waste of time and energy. The goal should be to build a strong relationship on shared values, beliefs, and purposes. After all, each organization supposedly understands the mutual benefits to be obtained through the partnership.

Honoring old differences and seeking out areas of commonality provides a strong framework for building a partnership.

### Ego Needs

One of the most difficult tasks of partnering is dealing with personal issues, including personality conflict. Leaders generally do not have passive personalities, and in the old model highly competitive behavior was honored and promulgated. Those who were aggressive and strongly directed were rewarded and validated. When a partnership is being built, competitive behavior is counterproductive. Collaborative and supportive leadership that seeks consensus through dialogue is essential. The issues of power must be worked out at the outset so that accountability can be clarified and the decision-making and functional roles of the parties can be defined. Personality conflict, divergency of views, and unilateral ownership of tasks and activities can get in the way of this process if not laid on the table and worked through with honesty and commitment. In a perfect world, obstacles such as these would be overcome in this way. In the real world, however, it is often valuable to have a third-party facilitator lead the process and help the involved parties work through the obstacles as they emerge.

### Contribution to the Partnership

Each member of the partnership will bring something different that is essential to achieving outcomes. It is to be expected that the levels of contribution will differ depending on the skills required and the resources available. Each partner will have a different mix of those elements upon which the relationship is to be built. Size, wealth, role, positioning, and need will all influence how much any one party brings to the relationship. While these will affect how the partnership unfolds, they are not the foundation of the value of the partnership. Each member has sought to build a collaborative relationship because there are benefits each hopes to achieve thereby. Ultimately, each sees the partnership as a means of enhancing the provision of services. The construction of the relationship should always be driven by this insight so as to avoid getting stuck on issues of equity, resources, and contribution. If one organization can contribute more, it should. The contribution of each should reflect its involvement, expectations, and resources. These will always be variable and no one should expect it to be otherwise.

## Linkage

In today's health care system, information linkages are essential for a successful collaboration. As indicated in previous chapters, information architecture is rapidly replacing the bricks and mortar architecture of the industrial age. Information linkages along the continuum of care will provide the database upon which a partnership can be evaluated and sustained. It is impossible to maintain the dynamic necessary for a clinical relationship without a connection that defines and exemplifies the work processes of the relationship. Systems must be constructed by the partners that reflect the elements necessary for the ongoing work and the processes associated with their purpose for collaborating.

Collaboration does not mean agreement. People will not agree on every issue; nor should they. Entering a partnership involves making a commitment to work toward mutually beneficial ends together. Problem solving and solution seeking are at the heart of that commitment. Ways are sought to resolve concerns. The expectation is that the differences and disagreements that really matter will be worked on. However, at no point in the collaborative process will all the issues finally be resolved. That *never* happens.

The partner must realize that self-interest is essentially involved in any collaborative process. Thus, there should be no effort undertaken to eliminate or reduce the impact of self-interest—that would be a futile exercise. The interests of each of the parties to the collaborative venture must be enumerated for all so that they can be properly attended to in building the relationship. It is the combination of the various interests that defines the collaboration and gives it a purpose. When all the parties recognize the content of each party's interest in the collaboration, the foundations are secure. Knowing each party's reason for being present helps keep the group focused and aware of the factors that bring them to and keep them at the table.

### The Stages of Collaboration

Generally the first step toward collaboration occurs when an individual recognizes the potential mutual benefits in a specific set of circumstances. The next step occurs when that individual communicates the insight regarding collaboration to another. All collaboration begins with a vision of what could be and moves from vision to actuality through a series of steps that result in an effective operational process (see Exhibit 4-4).

Getting past the barriers to establish trust is perhaps the hardest task for the initiator. The genuineness of the initiator may be questioned, and all the potential collaborators may show deep concern about the changes that will be entailed. Framing the

**Exhibit 4-4** Collaboration along the Continuum

Individual
- Knowledge of the parameters
- Willingness to negotiate roles
- Commitment to the work
- Investment in the outcomes
- Discovery of a quid pro quo
- In it for the long term

Partners
- Mutually agreed relationship
- Continuous dialogue about the issues
- Flexibility in work relationships
- A process for conflict resolution
- A strategy for role clarification
- A mechanism for integrating with others

idea of collaborating in terms that others can understand is an important early step. The goal is to create an interest and motivate potential partners to consider the applicability and advantages of collaboration given their circumstances.

Also important is the ability of the initiator to get powerful people interested enough in the idea to move forward and begin to pull together the resources needed for the initiating effort. The choice of who to approach should be based on several factors: Who will it be possible to interest in the collaborative effort? What resources are necessary to get started? Who is an important stakeholder in the outcome? What kind of players are needed to make the effort work?

Rituals are essential to the success of any collaborative effort. Every person has rituals that have personal meaning. When attempting to influence and get support from key individuals, knowing appropriate social and personal rituals is helpful to stimulate the process and get things moving. Relationships with such individuals can be enhanced by knowing personal habits, such as where they prefer to meet and what they like to eat and drink. All initiators must remember that any coalition is founded on relationships.

The initial steps taken to convene the partners have a large impact on the long-term effectiveness of the partnership. The goal of the first meeting should be to lay the groundwork for a new relationship between players not previously connected to each other, at least not in the same way. Making a good first impression is critical, and there are several rules that, if followed, will lead to a positive first impression.

- *Preparing.* It is important that the initiator of the meeting be clear about the purpose of getting the parties together and of what should be accomplished. The participants need to understand that the meeting is exploratory and relationship enhancing and is intended to introduce concepts and people to each other and create a foundation for further dialogue.
- *Planning.* The initial process should be informal and be designed in a way that facilitates interaction. The agenda should be simple and brief. The time allotted for the meeting should be reasonable—shorter rather than longer. There should be food and beverages, and the atmosphere should be relaxing and professional. The objective is to create an appropriate environment for a safe and productive introduction to the idea of collaboration.
- *Content.* Written support materials should be available to all the parties present. They should present the necessary concepts without being comprehensive or overly specific. After all, if the initiator has all of the details worked out, there is no need for dialogue. The agenda should include introductions and interaction, a presentation of the concepts, a short period of response, a summary of further refinements needed, and an identification of the key players who should be involved in the next step.
- *Initial agreement.* The first session hopefully will result in a decision to explore the implications of collaboration with more intensity. If it does, the individuals responsible for the next step need to be identified, as do the expectations for the next step. Also, the participants must be clear as to the indicators of progress and when the leadership will need to certify the progress of the discussions and any related decisions. This forms the foundation for dialogue concerning collaborative arrangements.
- *Establish the next step.* At the end of the first meeting, the time and content of the next meeting must be established. Everyone should indicate their understanding of what has occurred, what will happen next, and the basic agenda of the next meeting. The facilitator of the present meeting is either reaffirmed or a new facilitator identified so that all participants know who to contact.

## Collaboration, Community, and Team Building

It can never be emphasized enough that building a successful partnership depends on remembering that each collaborator is unique. Each collaborator must attempt to understand the characteristics of the other collaborators and respect the differences that exist.

Creation of a continuum of care has cultural and social implications for the providers. The goal is to serve the local community as much as possible in community and residential settings rather than in health care facilities, and thus the nature of the community has an impact on service delivery.

- The ethnic makeup of the community is a determinant of the range of health care needs. The ethnic background of the providers in the continuum of care is likely to influence the kind of services offered. The community and the providers should engage in dialogue to make certain needs and services are in harmony.
- All of the models for service provision identified early on by parties to the collaboration may turn out to be inappropriate once the planning process begins. Openness to new possibilities that emerge from the interaction of the parties is essential for sustaining the collaboration and making it successful.
- Community members must, at some stage, enter into the planning. Some suggest they should be included at the outset. Though not a bad idea, sometimes initial discussion among providers is necessary to convince them to bring in community members. In any case, the community must eventually participate in building the continuum.
- The continuum must be constructed so that it achieves the purposes for which it was intended. The challenge here is to get all the providers to recognize and accept that their roles must be modified in light of the outcomes that they and the community define collaboratively.
- The community defines the parameters within which services are provided. Unlike the old days, the culture of the patients has a greater impact on service provision than does the culture of the health care facility. Service providers will always have to modify service activities to suit those to whom services are offered.
- In the continuum-of-care approach, modifying lives is more important than simply treating conditions. The point of service may require activities not traditionally considered by providers, which, in the newer framework, become the keystones for the provision of health care services along the patient pathway.
- The effectiveness of the service continuum will be directly related to the degree of community ownership of the processes that determine its health status. The providers must acknowledge that their primary collaboration is with those they serve. The greater the community's investment in the health care processes, the more likely that outcomes desired by both the providers and the community can be achieved.

As indicated in previous chapters, the model of health care service is being inexorably altered. Providers must learn to adapt to an entirely different approach to the delivery of health care services. The relationships between providers are becoming more important, and the intensity and closeness of these relationships need to increase. Clinical models of collaboration, such as rehabilitation and psychiatric team models, can be taken to indicate the kind of framework that must exist all along the continuum. But even those models must evolve further if the continuum-based approach is to work:

- Teams must be configured around the patients and led by the individual most directly related to the focus of the clinical team. This means that not all teams should be led by physicians.
- The character and membership of the team are fluid and may change as patients move along the service continuum.
- The service continuum drives all team activities and is dependent upon the cultural, social, personal, and economic resources of the patients.
- The intensity of the interaction between team members and patients depends on how well the patients are able to use their resources in managing life processes.
- A major portion of every clinical team's work is educational. The ultimate goal of clinical teams is to provide the highest level of independence and health to those the team serves.
- The two indicators of success in the continuum approach are the independent health of the patients and the cost-effectiveness of the services provided.
- The team is forever vigilant regarding the service pathway and its effectiveness. It is committed to adjusting the pathway as the data indicate. Adjustments are immediate and always occur at the point of care.
- The role of the management is to ensure that data are correct and timely and that cost and service information is presented in such a way that it can be understood and used by the clinical and service teams in their deliberations.
- Team members' faithfulness to clinical protocols and service plans is more critical than ever since teams will be increasingly decentralized and members will often be connected only by the information system. The quality of the evaluations of clinical processes will be as good as the data upon which the evaluations depend.
- The information system is the lifeblood of the continuum of care. The leadership is responsible for ensuring the effectiveness of the system, which must be user friendly, comprehensive, and accurate.
- Information must be shared across organizational lines with all members of the clinical team. Access to information must be quick and uncomplicated for the users. Ethical and legal issues must be resolved at the outset of the continuum building process so that impediments to seamlessness along the continuum are removed.

## BUILDING LEADERSHIP

The needs of the continuum change the character of the service environment dramatically. The processes associated with managing and leading the continuum will not be the same as when institutional models for service were prevalent. One common mistake committed by point-of-care and continuum leaders is to try to lead the system in the way they did when services were site specific and located within institutional structures. Although a good portion of illness care services will still be offered within institutions, the goal of health care services will be to reduce the need for such services to the fullest extent possible. The attempt to achieve that goal will create a different dynamic for the delivery and management of services.

Most of the providers will have to work in a self-managed and relatively independent environment. The current behaviors of staff and management are not suitable for the new paradigm. The noisiest of the necessary changes is likely to be the shift in management and staff behaviors to reflect the more decentralized and "adult" work environment.

> *Ultimately, the continuum of care is about building a healthy community. A real partnership between provider and community ensures that the focus of both will be the enhancement of society.*

Those professions and professionals who have claimed independence and a unique set of principles, body of knowledge, and clinical role will now have to prove the validity of their assertions. They will be expected to abstain from dependency behaviors, protective initiatives, and retroactive behaviors. Providers must collaborate, articulate roles and functions, interact as partners, and reach negotiated agreement on roles and performance.[12] Rewards will be increasingly based on results and the contributions made by members of the care team. Professional demands will have to be clearly supported with evidence of their validity. Organizations, other providers, and patients cannot be held hostage by the unilateral demands of any provider whose value to all has not been unequivocally demonstrated.

On the other hand, organizations cannot continue to act as parents or autocrats. Administrative and management goals and desires, like those of the staff, must be subject to exploration through dialogue. The staff should not have to accept demands, rules, notions, or plans that affect what they do without participation in the processes from which they originated. Position or organizational status is no longer a justification for unilateral action. In organizations using a systems model, it is understood that actions undertaken in one place affect the activities throughout the whole. The implications of decisions must be apparent to all whom the decisions will impact. This rule includes absolutely everyone—those in the boardroom and those by the bedside, those in the hospital and those in the community.

Continuum approaches to organization and service have a significant impact upon management and administrative processes, changing the patterns with which leadership was once so familiar. New expectations emerge that demand a significant shift in the role of every leader in health care.

- Decisions about the mission, purposes, and service objective are made by the whole system, not just by those at the "top" of the system.
- The board of trustees are partners in the process and have the task of ensuring that appropriate linkage exists between components of the operational and service system and the community.
- Horizontal integration is more important than vertical integration. Relationships become critical to the viability of the health care system. Building them is the major work of the leadership.
- A health care system should compete, not with other providers or systems, but with itself. It should constantly try to improve its performance in order to ensure that the services it provides are of the highest quality. If it succeeds in offering excellence, it never need worry about competing with other systems.
- The quality of the partnering along the continuum of care is the central focus of the leadership. The extent, quality, effectiveness, satisfaction, and outcomes of the service partnerships are measures of the success of the system. It is these measures that are the central concern of the management process in continuum models and will demand the greatest leadership time and effort.
- The role of the leaders is to nurture the relationships in the system. Continuum of care systems are built on mutual relationships. Offering the kind of support and guidance that will strengthen the relationships is key to the success of the system.
- The leadership is at all times community based and focused. The subscriber approach demands that leaders have a consumer or customer orientation conjoined with a community orientation. Success will be determined by the health and satisfaction of community members, not by how much they have used the services of the system. The goal of the system should be to provide more health and less care.
- Team-based approaches do not require intervention from managers and administrators. The need for intervention represents a failure of leadership.

Self-managed processes require contextual resources, information, support, and tools. It is those elements for which the leaders are accountable. If resources are appropriate, the leaders do not have to worry about the character and quality of the clinical work.

- Public evaluation of the performance of the system becomes a must in patient-based approaches. Patients constitute the market of the health care system and must share in the establishment and evaluation of practices and processes directed to addressing the health of the community.

Patient-based approaches to the delivery of health care services along the continuum of care demand a new mindset, new partners, and new processes. The insightful leader will be busy building the kinds of relationships that facilitate the construction of the continuum of care along the clinical pathway. Taking bed-based care out of prescribed structures and bringing services to the community will necessitate a dismembering of institutional models and a construction of a community-based health care services delivery system.[13] The resources of all the players—providers, board members, administrators, and community members—must be brought to bear.[14] Each player has a role to play in making health care accessible and effective and in increasing the community's health.

The same effort will be needed at the micro level as at the system level. Each member of the clinical team makes the same commitment as the leaders of the community and the health care system. The components of the system must act in concert and form a seamless structure. The leaders of the system must recognize that a change from an institutional to a continuum of service orientation will be required to support an integrated approach to health care delivery. Radical designs must emerge that configure the point-of-care system and sustain the relationships necessary to make it work. Nothing less than transformation is needed. Focusing on the point of care and building the structures and relationships to sustain it will be the main task of the leaders of the system. At the heart of the system will be an effective and well-functioning continuum of partners—providers, patients, and managers—working in concert to address the real issues of health.

## REFERENCES

1. P. Starr, *The Logic of Health Care Reform* (Knoxville, Tenn.: Whittle Direct Books, 1992).

2. J. Heskett et al., "Putting the Service-Profit Chain to Work," *Harvard Business Review* 72(1994):164–173.

3. R. Rosenfield, "Replacing the Workshop Model," *Topics in Healthcare Management* 20, no. 4(1994):1–15.

4. M. McNamee and S. Garland, "A Guide to Health Reform," *U.S. News & World Report* 115, no.12(1993):28–33.

5. D. Beckham, "Building the High Performance Accountable Health Plan," *Healthcare Forum Journal* 37, no. 4(1994):60–67.

6. M. Graham and M. Lebaron, *The Horizontal Revolution: Guiding the Teaming Takeover* (San Francisco: Jossey-Bass, 1994).

7. J. Katzenbach and D. Smith, The Wisdom of Teams (Boston: McKinsey & Co., 1993).

8. J. Mason, "Building the Team During Consolidation," *Seminars for Nurse Managers* 2(1994):213–217.

9. Graham and Lebaron, *The Horizontal Revolution.*

10. H. Coeling and J. Wilcox, "Steps to Collaboration," *Nursing Administration Quarterly* 18, no. 4(1994):44–55.

11. J. Janov, *The Inventive Organization; Hope and Daring at Work* (San Francisco: Jossey-Bass, 1994).

12. J. Goldsmith, "Driving the Nitroglycerin Truck: The Relationship between the Hospital and Physician," *Healthcare Forum Journal* 36, no. 2(1993):36–40.

13. T. Porter-O'Grady, "Building Partnerships in Health Care: Creating Whole Systems Change," *Nursing and Health Care* 15, no. 1(1994):34–38.

14. S. MacStravic "Warfare or Partnership: Which Way for Health Care," *Health Care Management Review* 15, no. 1(1990):37–45.

# Chapter 5

## Whole Systems Shared Governance: Creating a Seamless Organization

> The universe looks more like a great thought than a great machine.
>
> Sir James Jeans

### LAYING THE FOUNDATIONS

Horizontal systems require a different structure to support them. Vertically integrated approaches alone are not suitable for the kind of networks that will emerge in the field of health care. In the business community during the early eighties, controlling all organizational components through ownership was the operational strategy. Unfortunately, the cost of both ownership and operation ate significantly into the profits. Newer models of partnership that depend on the sharing of risk have become common and horizontal relationships are now a priority. The companies that have switched to these models, however, did not realize that a partnership orientation would require substantive changes in the way in which the organizations were structured and in the design of their decision-making frameworks.

Many health care organizations are using the older industrial age notion of ownership and vertical integration to configure themselves in a managed care environment. The problem is they too will become burdened with ownership costs and with the costs of managing and capitalizing a large system. The ownership approach does not allow the flexibility and fluidity needed to respond to service market changes and newer approaches to care delivery. A continuum of services must be able to adjust to payment, demographics, and other unforeseen changes. A large, vertically integrated system is partially immobilized because of its size.

As previously indicated, relationships and structures in the new health care era will be based on the concept of partnership. This means that risk sharing and network arrangements will emerge as the framework of preference. A network arrangement allows the system to create relationships along the continuum as necessary and to sever or change relationships as consumers, payers, or the market adjusts to new opportunities or constraints. Since permanent ownership of the structures and operations of the various partners is lacking, the partners can alter their relationships as conditions demand.

> *The work of the leaders today is to create, instead of vertically integrated organizations, horizontally integrated systems.*

The organizational and decision-making structures must be designed to reflect the system's characteristics—the fact that it is a fast-paced, horizontal, and accountable organizational system. Hierarchical structures are no longer viable. While some organizational leaders deny the need to eliminate hierarchy, point-of-care models require the kinds of relationships inconsistent with hierarchical thinking. In accountability-based models, decision making must be primarily located at the point of care, and the structures of the organization must prevent it from moving elsewhere. The following should be kept in mind:

- Given the opportunity, accountability will tend to escape from its appropriate locus of control and will go to the furthest possible point in the organization.
- In order to accommodate the shift in this accountability locus of control, the organization is always forced to increase the number of roles devoted to dealing with illegitimately located accountability.

> *The object of shared governance is to build a structure that supports the point of care and sustains ownership and accountability there.*

- The more managers an organization has the less it has in accountability.
- The only way to ensure that accountability never escapes from the place it belongs is to remove the places or positions to which it can escape.

Shared governance builds on point-of-care principles. It is imperative that a new type of relationship and a new notion of the stakeholder role serve as the foundations for the emerging structure. Building seamless relationships between all levels of the organization is harder than first imagined. It is not the redesign that is challenging. Rather it is the movement of persons and roles into a new configuration that creates the greatest noise. Often, the roles most in need of change (and possibly elimination) are the ones positioned to have the greatest influence on the organization's ability to transform itself.

Shared governance provides the framework for horizontal integration. The purpose of shared governance is to create a format that is fluid enough to adjust to changes in the marketplace and service arena, yet solid enough to provide a firm context for operating the system and its components in an effective manner. The ultimate goal is to facilitate the achievement of outcomes, not impede their achievement. Further, shared governance helps keep decision making at the point of care, and it is thus appropriate for emerging work models.[1]

New organizational structures must have fluid and permeable parameters. They must be able to change and take new shapes and forms as easily as the staff respond to the changes that occur in the course of doing their work. Every structure should be modifiable to better support work activities. Shared governance allows that sort of modification to happen. It represents a whole systems approach to creating and sustaining a flexible form for work and organizations. Shared governance models are easily adaptable to any changes in the relationships between people and the work they do together.

In the past decade, over 1,000 hospitals in the United States have implemented shared governance in their nursing department.[2] The literature is filled with information regarding its implementation and effectiveness as a means of empowering nurses.[3] Organizations' experience with shared governance demonstrates the value of interdependence and accountability as a basis for constructing a new organizational paradigm.[4]

The goal of implementing shared governance was typically to (1) empower nurses and partner them with each other so they could better confront issues that affect the practice of nursing and (2) create a framework that helps nurses develop partnerships with other decision makers in the health care organization.[5] The ability of nurses to interact with the full range of providers in patient care delivery is necessary if the patient needs are to be fully met. Shared governance also has strengthened the self-image of nurses and has aided them in their push toward equality in decision making and in their rela-

> *Shared governance as an organizational concept was first implemented with nurses. This reflected the notion that change must begin with the largest group closest to the point of service. If change does not happen there, it does not matter where else it takes place.*

tionships with other providers. Shared governance has, in essence, been a tool for facilitating the empowerment and professionalization of nursing. It supports adult, collaborative behavior among the members of any clinical partnership.[6]

## SHARED GOVERNANCE AND EMPOWERMENT

Much of the first-stage work in shared governance has focused on empowerment models for staff at the divisional level and the unit of service.[7] At the service level, the expectation has been that the managers and staff will work to make practice-based decisions collectively and in the interests of those they serve. The second-stage efforts have focused on building an organizational structure to support clinically driven decision making and to strengthen the partnerships between staff members and between each staff member and the organization.[8] Accountability is used as a means of building structure to support practice and of actively involving staff in all decisions that affect their work. Newer models of empowerment have been created that give form to shared leadership and ensure the presence of an ongoing system necessary to maintain empowerment as an organizational constant.[9] Such models have now been in place in many institutions for ten years or more, and a host of new settings are moving to implement shared decision-making models.

> *Empowerment is recognizing the power already inherent in a role and ensuring that it finds the necessary expression wherever and in whatever form required to achieve the defined outcomes of the role. Shared governance is a structural model that provides a sustainable format for an empowered workplace. It creates a framework for ensuring that the processes of empowerment operate effectively throughout a system at every point where work and relationship intersect.*

## BEYOND NURSING: MOVING TOWARD INTEGRATION

Shared governance is, by design and concept, invitational in nature. Because it is dynamic, it cannot be contained in any exclusive framework, nor can it be limited to any specific work group. If it is, it will devolve into parochialism, paternalism, and organizational isolation.[10] It has a natural tendency to spread throughout an organization and empower others and include them in relationship building and decision making (see Table 5-1). The energy currents related to its effectiveness permit no barriers to its reach and inevitably touch the work lives of all the players whose purpose is to facilitate patient care.

Shared governance was first tried in nursing departments, purposely. In a major organizational or social transformation, there are some key principles that guide implementation of change. A major organizational transformation will rarely succeed if it is restricted to the top of an organization or system.[11] It generally will succeed it if begins at the center of the organization—at the places closest to where the work gets done. In a health care organization, a major change must begin in the patient settings. Further, the change will not be successful if the major purveyors of the organization's services (i.e., the nurses) are not fully invested in the change process.[12] Because of their numbers and their proximity to the patients, it is reasonable that structural redesign should begin with nurses and move outward to other parts of the patient care system.

> *Shared governance is inherently invitational. It must have the full and complete investment of all the persons in a system or it simply cannot be sustained.*

The role of professional nurses is important to the management of the continuum of care because of the location of nurses in the delivery system.[13] Further, nurses have a social mandate to ensure the safety of patients in the course of receiving services from health care providers. It is the role of most providers to engage in specific interventions. It is the legal role of the nurse to see to it that the aggregate of activities performed by providers is in the best interest of the patients

**Table 5-1** Comparison of Industrial Model and Shared Governance Characteristics

| *Industrial Model Systems* | *Shared Governance Systems* |
| --- | --- |
| Vertical | Horizontal |
| Highly formal structure | Fluid structure |
| Definitive job functions | Role relationships |
| Hierarchical | Interactive |
| Status roles | Collateral relations |

and that the patient's safety is not jeopardized. All other activities of nursing are incidental to their social mandate to provide care and ensure safety, and it is this mandate that places nurses at the center of the continuum of care and therefore at the center of attempts to effect major transformations. Noting the centrality of nursing is not intended to diminish the contribution of any member of the team.[14]

> *Shared governance facilitates the structuring of the system around the patient, not the provider.*

It simply explains why so much attention is devoted to the role of nurses in the initial stages of change.

The third stage of shared governance involves other service centers and disciplines related to the patient care functions in the health care system. Partners in care include all the professional and technical workers that operate within the patient care continuum. This group, it should be noted, includes physicians, although they have historically been viewed as working independently of or above the functional relationships of the institutional providers. Since partnership is the essential theme of shared leadership and decision making, bringing the physicians into partnership is necessary for creating productive service arrangements, evaluating care, and building effective supporting structures.[15]

## IMPLICATIONS FOR PHYSICIANS

In a health care system, it is impossible to fully integrate without creating partnerships along the continuum of care between all the involved providers, including physicians. Physicians have traditionally been outside of the loop of partnership with other disciplines and providers because of their location at the top of the allopathic "food chain." The physicians were the moderators of all care-related activities whether or not they knew the role or value of those activities. This led to a series of problems.

> *Physicians have been living outside the cycle of shared accountability for decades. A health care system simply cannot become effective until physicians are equal partners with the other providers on the health care team.*

- Judgments of clinical efficacy have been based on the value of treatments and practices to physicians, not necessarily on their value to patients.

- The clinical model of relationship subordinated all players to the will of the physicians, thus excluding the possibility of using partnership, dialogue, or consensus strategies to arrive at best treatment for the patient.
- Physicians have evolved into practitioners who independently provide services and receive payment for them, which allows them to avoid building sustaining and direct relationships with others at the point of care and to establish only a cursory relationship with the hospital organization.
- Physicians have only limited accountability for unnecessary costs. Systems, however, are beginning to hold physicians more accountable as closer examination of physician practices is uncovering the fact that some are needlessly expensive.

Health systems now increasingly realize that the relationship between physicians and other clinical partners in the continuum of care must become more functional and interactive (see Table 5-2).

It is clear that physicians must be incorporated into empowering and accountability-based structures. But exactly where? The answer is straightforward: at every place where the decisions impact the physicians and the other providers as well as those who set direction and establish policy for the clinical services of the organization. In other words, physicians must establish relationships at a whole range of locations along the continuum of care and the organizational system that supports it.

However, if this is to occur, physicians must want partnership and the health system must value it. First, in the transformation of health care, one must be present to win. As the script gets written by a whole range of providers along the continuum and they become more comfortable with their relationships, they will define the content of their relationships with physicians whether the physicians are present or not. This will occur in spite of the physicians' argument that they must captain the process. If the physicians do not enter the dialogue regarding the emerging clinical relationships, the other players may undertake a range of concerted strategies that may diminish the physicians' role.

**Table 5-2** Comparison of Current and Emerging Physician Relationships

| Current Physician Relationships | Emerging Physician Relationships |
|---|---|
| Hierarchical | Horizontal |
| Individualistic | Partnership based |
| Unilateral responsibility | Shared accountability |
| Directing clinical activity | Facilitating clinical activity |

Second, there is a dynamic unfolding as the continuum of care becomes the basis for the health care delivery process. More dialogue, more interaction, and more negotiation of roles and relationships are all essential for determining the functions and activities that must be combined to create best practices in service delivery. Comparing standards against actual performance and outcomes requires time spent in communication and collective activity (see Figure 5-1).

Third, there will continue to be a focus on cost and payment issues. With the price of care increasingly fixed, the cost impact of the various approaches to care delivery must be analyzed, and treatment practices must be compared as regards their contribution to the bottom line. The relationship between cost factors and quality indicators becomes very important to the viability of the health system. Continual cross-referencing and performance comparison activities will require much stronger, more accountable clinical relationships between providers, including physicians (see Figure 5-2).

## BUILDING VIABLE CLINICAL RELATIONSHIPS

A seamless organizational structure cannot be built without all stakeholders operating within a collective framework. The days of the nonpresent, noninvolved physician is long past. It is necessary to create mechanisms and structures that remove the physicians' option not to partner and participate with the other disciplines in reviewing, deciding, delivering, and evaluating clinical services. The organization must be designed to require physician involvement.

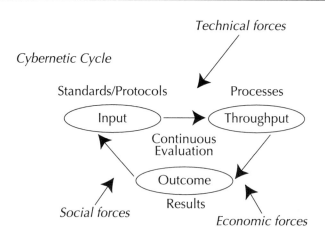

**Figure 5-1** Integration of Standards, Process, and Outcomes

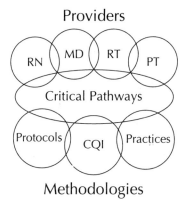

**Figure 5-2** Integration around the Patient

The following is needed to foster physician involvement:

- A direct relationship between physicians and decisional bodies at the point of care.
- Physician representation on system councils that affect the activities of the medical staff.
- Point-of-care involvement of physicians in protocol and critical pathway development, including associated evaluation activities.
- A change in the medical staff bylaws to make it possible for decisions about medical practice to be made in different ways and at a number of intersections in the delivery system.
- An approved mechanism that permits physicians to resolve medical issues in a broader context through dialogue between the accountable individuals at the point of care and also to resolve issues related to roles, practices, relationships, and expectations as a means of defining the real character of integration.
- A conflict resolution process that deals with the real issues and allows the people in relationships to settle differences without having to involve those "upstairs."

The medical staff can no longer remain isolated from relationships at the point of care. It is becoming impossible for anyone to maintain an identity that does not tie into the collection of relationships necessary to make the care system accountable. The old notion of "captaining" decision making and isolating oneself from the consequences and the interaction necessary to deal effectively with the intricacies of caregiving relationships is neither service efficient nor cost effective.

> *Physicians cannot remain isolated from the other patient care providers through use of artificial structures and boundaries that allow them to deal only with each other. Problem solving and patient-based decision making require collateral relationships.*

The greatest challenge presented by integration will be not the definition of the character of the relationships, but dealing with the power struggles for control of the system and the clinical relationships necessary to make it work. The old power equations and relationships negotiated in back rooms between a small group of stakeholders will not result in a sustainable distribution of power in a continuum-of-care system. Dialogue and negotiation of roles and relationships along the care pathway demand investment by the full range of stakeholders. Too many of the resources are tied up in the activities of those working at the point of care to make it acceptable for a few powerful persons to control the decisions that give direction to the health system.

A fact that is constantly forgotten in today's resource-intensive environment is that no matter where resources are budgeted, they are not used there. They are always expended by those who work at or close to the point of service. Unless a concern for cost-effectiveness is inculcated at every point along the service continuum, there is simply no chance that costs and quality will ever be integrated into a real value stream operating at the point of care (see Figure 5-3). Without such integration, health care will remain troubled and effectiveness will be a distant illusion.

Integrative care models and multidisciplinary team approaches to care facilitate the creation of a more supportive organizational structure than that characteristic of traditional hospital hierarchies. Collateral structures that reflect the relationship of the players to each other are more suitable for interdisciplinary work than more traditional structures.[16]

It is inappropriate, however, to create a service structure that parrots those already in place in nursing organizations. Those structures and their relational characteristics are specific to nursing. A broader cross-departmental and cross-service configuration is needed for organizing and structuring whole systems clinical decision making related to patient care. In addition, an operating structure more reflective of partnership roles and relationships between staff and management is required if a collateral point-of-care organizational design is to emerge. Finally, integration of the board, administration, providers, and community leadership

⟹ Cost drives much of the initial change activities. Change often begins as a response to cost.

⟹ Quality becomes an issue when a cost-based contract is in place. It is not possible to maintain quality services if cost savings is the only consideration.

⟹ Value is the relationship between cost and quality as expressed in what is done for the customer. It is value that the health system must achieve for the consumer.

⟹ Configuring all the players around the same purposes and integrating their activities is essential for the achievement of positive outcomes.

⟹ The contribution of each partner enhances the value of the contribution of all the partners in rendering services.

⟹ Ownership of all the processes related to patient services must be expressed at all levels of the health system by every player that influences them.

**Figure 5-3** Quality-Cost Relationship

must occur if the purposes of the health system and its mission are to be reflected in every act and function of all the players. Impact on outcomes and the determination and emphasis on value cannot be sustained without a structure that supports the effort of all providers to give service value to the consumers of health care.

**BUILDING ALONG THE CONTINUUM OF CARE**

Because of the move away from sickness care, service delivery will require an entirely new approach. The change to a process that manages lives instead of patients means a different script must be written.

The problem with changing the focus of service delivery to life management in a cost-controlled system is that none of the players are ready for what the move implies. It can never be business as usual, and the current configurations of health services will no longer be appropriate. Too many services are currently sickness based and institutionally located. In a life management system, hospitalization is viewed as a last resort and is avoided unless all other options fail. Because care is subscriber based

> *In a truly health-based system, the goal is to manage lives effectively rather than simply treat illness events.*

and capitated, the goals of the health service sector must include *not* admitting patients to hospitals when other more cost-effective and service efficient mechanisms are available. The idea is to keep subscribers in the continuum and out of the hospital, where high-intensity interventions and the extensive resource use quickly contract the financial margin.

This point-of-care orientation requires a decentralized structure that permits much of the decision making and clinical activity to occur at the point of care. Increasingly, the organization must be structured in a way that ensures the freedom of the provider to make decisions that have a direct effect on the resources of the health setting. It is clear that providers must have the kind and quality of information that allows such decision making to be effective and appropriate.

A decentralized organization needs far fewer managers (see Exhibit 5-1). Further, the supervisory role of the manager of yesterday is basically ineffective in such a setting, and the model of the manager as servant represents a more accurate conception of the manager role needed in a decentralized organization. This means that the content of and expectations for the role also change. Purveying information, integrating services, coordinating resources, and facilitating functions and activities become the major tasks.

## THE BASICS OF DECENTRALIZATION

The old "line and box" set of organizational relationships do not make sense in point-of-care systems. Leadership is not based on the status of roles but on the relationships between roles. Horizontal relationships challenge old notions of organizational power, influence, relationship, and control. They also demand different kinds of managers with different skills. Parental organizational designs, which support hierarchical and paternalistic approaches, must be replaced by newer models of partnership and adult exchange.

**Exhibit 5-1** Features of Decentralized Organizations

| |
|---|
| • Fewer managers in the system<br>• Better skilled managers at all levels<br>• More self-directed staff problem solving<br>• Fluid organizational parameters<br>• Reduced department structures<br>• Increased disciplinary interaction<br>• Designing around the point of care |

What kinds of structures need to be created to support the new partnership-based organizational systems? They must be effective, responsive to service demand, able to integrate the wide variety of players, and sustainable in times of great adaptation to environmental and service shifts. The new organizational configurations must not have characteristics that make them as rigid and impenetrable as the industrial structures now being abandoned. They must operate well within lateral or horizontal relationships along the service continuum. They must be loose enough to be adaptive yet firm enough to ensure the accomplishment of goals and the creation of real accountability.

> **Redesign must be based on the point of service. Structure must be built around the provider-patient relationship if patient care is to be facilitated.**

Further, they must engender flexibility so the system can respond appropriately to outside forces. Developing new relationships with players along the continuum of care and possessing the ability to take advantage of opportunities for subscriber services and new service relationships are essential for organizations. Indeed, the ability of providers to create new service relationships and meet the attendant obligations is an important foundation of the new models of health service.

## PRINCIPLE-DRIVEN TEAM CHARACTERISTICS

Further, team-based approaches involve the use of group processes in deliberation and decision making (see Exhibit 5-2). Good relationships between the providers at the point of care are essential to good decision making. Processes and methodologies that develop group activities and decision skills will turn the health system into a learning organization. The principles and techniques of continuous quality improvement can be used to formalize and discipline the dialogue and deliberation process in team-based designs. The structure of the organization must foster an integrated methodology for effective decision making.

Power will be an important issue. The organization must take into account the reality of power initiatives and the possibility of unilateral power moves by players in the system. The challenge is to limit the ability of players with a single-item agenda from being successful in manipulating the system for their own purposes. The structure must support integrating initiatives and force the system to include invested and involved players in decisions that will affect their lives and work.

**Exhibit 5-2** Team-based Approaches

- Staff involvement in all care decisions
- Accountability of all roles clearly defined
- Continuous development of team members
- Behavioral adjustments to high-intensity interaction
- Focus on group rather than individual performance
- Changed orientation from processes to outcomes
- Continuous evaluation of effectiveness and relationships

Indeed, the structure must make it possible for decision making to be quick and effective by supporting accountability and making it difficult for accountability to migrate away from its appropriate places.

The structure should also enhance the organization's ability to respond to critical events that do not allow for extensive deliberation and interaction between the parties. During a time of great change, opportunity never waits for readiness. There must be a set of parameters that allow the organization to adapt quickly to service changes and to ensure that opportunities will not be missed because the group process is too ponderous and inflexible to respond appropriately.

No organization can succeed on the basis of group structures alone. This is precisely why individual role accountability is essential for point-of-care organizations. Decision making requires a defined locus of control and all the attendant competencies necessary to the role. Historically, there were many players positioned for leadership and decision making. The main problem was that they were not allowed to make independent decisions upon which the organization could depend. This is why so many organizations have anywhere from 3 to 13 levels of approval for decisions. Approval mechanisms are always an accommodation to poor decision making. The implication is that the decision makers do not have what is necessary to make good decisions and therefore their decisions need approval by any number of levels of management. If decisions are to be right the first time, the necessary resources should be available to those making the decisions *before or at the time of deliberation.* Decision-approving processes operate too late in the cycle to ensure

> *Exercising power must focus on results. Power should never be a tool for manipulation or advancing personal agendas.*

effectiveness. The main impact of many levels of approval is to cause the original decision makers to lose confidence and interest in making decisions in the first place. Over time, workers' interest and ownership in decision processes will decline and, if approval mechanisms are left unaddressed, will disappear altogether.

> *Approval mechanisms in organizations are always a sign of inadequate decision processes. In truly empowered systems, approval mechanisms are no longer necessary.*

Whatever structures are created, they must possess a true point-of-care design. The vast majority of decisions (upwards of 90 percent) should be made at the point of care by those who work there (see Exhibit 5-3). Further, there must be a connection between what gets decided at the board level and what gets lived out at the point of care.

## POINT-OF-CARE DECISION MAKING

One of the greatest myths is that workers can live in accordance with an organizational mission constructed for them by the board. Every attempt to get the staff to live by beliefs and values defined for them by others is doomed to failure. Living by beliefs or values depends on the extent of one's ownership of them. Simply telling individuals what the beliefs and values are does not create a commitment to them. What is needed is for the workers to play a meaningful role in the delineation of the organizational mission and values so that they express the relationships of those at the point of care. If point-of-service workers are not committed to the mission, it will not matter who else is committed to it.

**Exhibit 5-3** Decision Making at the Point of Care

- Skill building for staff to make good decisions
- Clear delineation of what decisions should be made
- Clear understanding of personal accountability
- Team-based problem solving at all times
- Flexibility in all process activities and absence of permanent structures
- Continuous evaluation and adjustment

## STAFF INVESTMENT IN THE MISSION

The set of principles listed in Exhibit 5-4 have varying implications for point-of-care organizations. Questions as to who owns the work, how quality is obtained, and who is accountable for the competence of any provider in the system rise high on the agenda.

In a work system where the competence of workers is so important and success depends on their fulfilling the obligations of their roles, the relationship between workers and workplace radically changes. Increasingly, roles are becoming more flexible and demand the application of skills in a number of different venues. Workers must apply their skills in many situations that call for fast, fluid, and flexible responses to changing conditions and opportunities.

*Hierarchy is not the foundation for organizational authority. Having the locus of control at the point of service entails that authority resides where the work of the system is done.*

This journey toward becoming relatively self-directed is a challenging one for workers. Most front-line workers are not prepared for the demands of the more adult set of relationships and interactions entailed by the new model of behavior. The role of the leader is to provide developmental and transitional activities, including role-playing, that will help workers learn the skills to meet new role expectations.

**Exhibit 5-4** Principles for Creating an Organizational Mission

- The staff must be involved in mission development.
- Ownership demands multilevel investment in the mission.
- All workers must converge around an agreed mission.
- The mission must be translated to have meaning for the staff.
- The organizational structure must facilitate staff involvement in the mission.
- All goals at every level in the organization should be directed toward fulfilling the mission.
- Mission-related activities must be broad based so that all stakeholders can actively participate.
- The mission must relate to the work of the organization and be based on community needs.

Still, the design of the organization must change concomitantly with the needed behavioral shifts. The structure must virtually guarantee ownership and accountability and ensure that there is no place in the system where individuals can hide from their obligations. As the content of accountability becomes clearer in the organization, performance becomes easier to define and to measure. The next step is the creation of an empowered council framework.

**IMPLEMENTING SHARED GOVERNANCE**

Mechanisms and strategies for integrating an organization are numerous and varied. They include empowerment, point-of-service decision making, worker investment, self-managed activities, cross-training, and multidisciplinary work groups. The real task is creating a structure that sustains the accountable behaviors necessary at the point of care to make integration work.

> *Shared governance provides the framework for sustaining a point of service-based organizational system. An organization cannot change behavior without altering the structure that supports it.*

It is to this task that the concepts and models of shared governance can be applied. If point-of-care organizations are to be effective, old designs that keep the locus of control away from the point of care must be revised or totally abandoned. Following the guidelines listed below will help restrict the locus of control to the point of service:

- There should be no more than two levels of management.
- Roles not essential to the work of the organization should be abolished.
- Uncommitted workers (even members of the loyal opposition) should be turned into committed workers or let go.
- There should be no more point-of-care managers than absolutely necessary.
- No decisions should be made away from the point of care without the active involvement of stakeholders.
- Accountability must not be turfed away from where it belongs.
- Structures must not encourage parenting management in the workplace.

The organizational structure needs to support decision making at the point of care and prevent most decisions from being made elsewhere. It is frequently necessary to eliminate positions in the organization that have a tendency to attract accountability inappropriately. In the old model, there are too many places where accountability can and does escape to. The organizational leaders must define areas of accountability and ensure that the system is designed so that those who actually do the work are the ones held accountable for it. They must look at the organization critically and determine if and why accountability has moved away from the places where it belongs. Below are some foundations and rules for implementing shared governance in point-of-service organizational systems:

• All structures in the organization must be designed to support the point of care, not the other way around.
• Any people in an organization who do not provide a service must serve those who do.
• Critical leadership occurs at the point of service; any other roles in the system should be directed to supporting point-of service roles.
• All service providers should seek solutions to their problems and answers to their concerns at the point of service. Seeking answers from any other place in the organization always impedes implementing the correct answer.
• These should be no management approval mechanisms in a point-of-service organization. Requiring approval of decisions suggest that decisions are often incorrectly made. Effective decisions are only made once and are correct the first time.
• Competence at the point of service, where the majority of key decisions have to be made, is essential. Competence elsewhere will be of no consequence if point-of-service workers lack the skills to do their work well and make good decisions.
• Whatever global, consultation, expert, or systems structures and roles exist in the organization, they should not assume accountability for operationalizing decisions affecting the work of the organization. Any operational locus of control that functions independent of the point of service impedes legitimate ownership and the successful achievement of the desired outcomes.

## DETERMINING ACCOUNTABILITY

Defining the accountability associated with particular roles is an important step in the process of identifying role obligations in shared governance (see Exhibit 5-5). As indicated earlier, management can no longer assume summary accountability for all of the activities of the organization and still expect accountability to remain with those who provide the services. A distinction must be made between manager accountability and service provider accountability so that the obligations of managers and staff can be differentiated. Further, the circumscribing of ac-

**Exhibit 5-5**  Manager and Staff Accountability

| Manager accountability | Staff accountability |
|---|---|
| Human resources | Practice and work issues |
| Fiscal resources | Quality of work |
| Material resources | Outcomes and results |
| Support structures | Competence of workers |
| Environment | Decisions of teams |
| Skills | |
| Teams | |
| Systems resources | |

countability unique to each role clarifies expectations for the role and establishes the basis upon which outcomes can be measured.

Organizational formats must be designed in a manner that supports the distinction between areas of accountability. The accountability of the staff should not be confused with the accountability of the managers. The structures that address the whole and the relationships between the service entities of the organization must honor the distinction. The coordination and integration of the activities and processes of the system should reflect the character of accountability established in the service configurations. Therefore, accountability for services should belong to the service providers, and the organizational configuration that focuses on related issues should comprise the service providers and those who offer essential support. Likewise, those whose job it is to meet the structural and resource needs of the system should act collectively to deal with support and resource issues.

Finally, there should be a forum for dealing with issues that involve all the stakeholders at the governance, policy, resource, and services loci of control in the system (see Figure 5-4).

### THE SERVICE OR PATIENT CARE COUNCIL

Health care services are increasingly becoming both multifocal and multidisciplinary. As new noninstitutional and nonindustrial models of health care emerge, new configurations that ad-

*Accountability is the foundation of the new organization. It is based on the clarity of outcomes, not on the certainty of processes. This is a major change in the focus of work and in the system.*

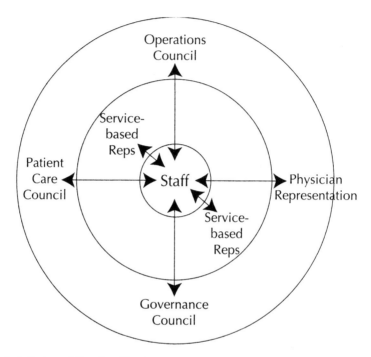

**Figure 5-4** Point-of-Service Design

dress the relationships of the players are essential.[17] In addition, the structures must support the seamless integration of the roles in the organization that facilitate the work. The reason is that the new models are designed around the relationships of the players rather than their status (hierarchy) in the organizational system.[18]

Service-based decisions, as much as possible, must be facilitated by a supporting organizational structure. In a shared governance health system, accountability for clinical decisions always rests with the staff. In a nursing component that employs shared governance, the practice council is the center of clinical accountability. In a clinically driven multidisciplinary setting, a broader frame of reference for decision making is necessary. Regardless of the service design (service lines, centers of excellence, product lines, case management, patient-focused care, continuum of care, etc.), a framework for clinical accountability is essential if a hierarchical structure is to be avoided and staff accountability for clinical services is to be maintained.

Although the staff must be accountable for their clinical work, their account-ability must be linked with the accountability of those in the organization who support the clinical work. Therefore, it is critical that both decision makers and processes must integrate services and structures.[19] It is in this context that the patient care council (or service council) takes form (see Figure 5-5). Designed to focus specifically on issues related to the services, the council comprises primarily patient-based service professionals and technical specialists. Like the nursing practice council, the patient care council focuses on service-based decision making. However, instead of having a unidisciplinary focus, the patient care council is accountable for decisions that affect all aspects of patient care delivery.

Councils are very different from committees. The purpose of committees historically has been to advise decision makers about specific elements related to a decision. A committee is empowered, generally by a manager, to undertake a narrow assignment of tasks or functions. Once having fulfilled its assignment, the committee ceases to have any value. Committees are generally not given broad

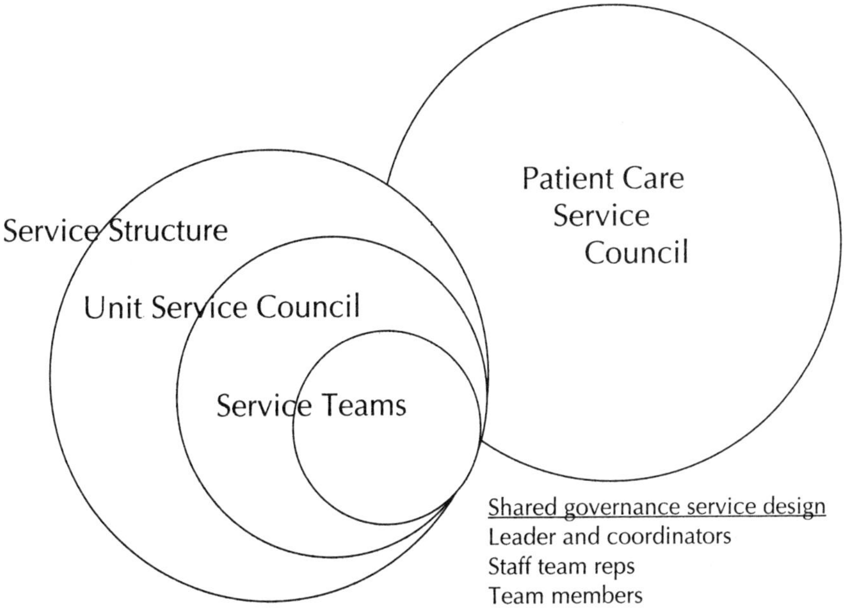

Service Structure

Unit Service Council

Service Teams

Patient Care Service Council

Shared governance service design
Leader and coordinators
Staff team reps
Team members

**Figure 5-5** Shared Governance Service Structure

authority related to a defined accountability. Further, committees tend to be focused on processes and tasks. They are assigned their work and are required to
fulfill specific functional obligations. Often their work is reported to the proper
authority (management) for review and approval.

A council, on the other hand, is an authority. The accountability of a council in
shared governance is clear and precisely defined. The expectation is that the council will see to it that the work related to the exercise of its authority will be carried
out and will result in the desired outcomes. The council membership includes all
the stakeholders that relate to the council's specific accountability. The members'
roles are based on their contribution to the council's meeting of its accountability
obligations. The council has control over its accountability and is not subject to the
approval of another individual or body. A requirement for approval would eliminate the functional and decisional value of the council. If the final authority resides
elsewhere in the organization, that should be the place where accountability also
resides. Levels of approval are eliminated in shared governance, with the result
that decisions are made more quickly and are more effective. Decision making is
enhanced if there is a close relationship between the places decisions are made and
the places they are implemented. In a council format, the fewer the places a decision goes before it is implemented, the more effective the decision process.

A council provides a single locus of control for a defined accountability and has
the full authority to do the essential work. There will only be a few councils in an
organization and each will have a defined context within which its accountability
is defined. Councils are centered at the point of care and radiate outward to those
arenas that support point-of-care decision-making efforts. Their chief mandate is
to ensure that the decisions made facilitate the fulfillment of the mission and priorities of the organization. Since health care is the reason health-based organizations exist, it is appropriate that all decision-making structures have a service- or
care-based core. This explains why the patient care council is at center of the
shared governance approach.

Since the patient care council is an interdisciplinary decision-making group,
there are specific tasks it is accountable for:

- Defining the approach to patient care and the delivery system issues that are
  addressed as a part of integrating patient care services.
- Resolving service conflicts between the participants and disciplines that impede the effective delivery of patient care services.
- Outlining the service structures necessary to meet the needs of patients, including the approaches that best respond to the community demand for patient services.

- Identifying the best clinical models for patient care delivery and their specific value and applicability to the kind of services offered by the organization.
- Making decisions about the most appropriate use of available resources in providing patient care services and meeting community needs.
- Defining the relationship between the organization and its community of service and linking community needs to the strategic objectives of the organization and responding accordingly.
- Facilitating creation of point-of-care processes and service structures that are suitable for the culture of service within which the organization finds itself.
- Integrating point-of-care processes and issues into the strategic and financial concerns of the organization, facilitating planning, and maintaining an organizational focus on service.
- Linking service providers, through a representational or network process, to both operational and policy decisions affecting service delivery.
- Integrating otherwise disparate clinical service configurations in an effort to ensure the principles and priorities affecting service provision are unfolded in concert with and applied consistently in all arenas of service in the organization.
- Directing the use of continuous quality strategies and evaluation methodologies to ensure the commitment of staff to the successful achievement of desired outcomes.
- Using critical pathway processes and integrating the disciplines along the continuum of care within an effective clinical data and information system.

As in all accountability-based structures, there must be an understanding that decisions are made and that authority exists in the group at the places where clinical action occurs. So many empowerment approaches fail because organizations do not understand that, for such approaches to work, power must be accompanied by involvement and ownership.[20] As soon as staff find out that their decisions have no weight, they soon stop making them and their involvement disappears.

The patient care council reflects a point-of-service decision-making approach. The units or services have their specific council format directed to integrating their team's work and dealing with service- or unit-specific issues. These concerns do not become the concerns of the patient care council. The specific unit or service councils make decisions reflecting their own work and relationships. It is from these unit or service councils that the membership on the organization's patient care council is drawn.

In a hierarchical organization, the manager is the locus of control. The manager is responsible for all the activities that fall under his or her auspices, and it is

> **The patient care council is the proper forum for the staff to deliberate those issues that reflect the staff accountability. It is the final locus of control for point-of-service decisions.**

through the management process that work gets done and results are achieved. In point-of-service models, accountability is distributed in a different way than responsibility is distributed in hierarchical models (see Figure 5-6). As a result, it is critical that organizational structures not impede the exercise of staff-driven authority and decision making. In shared governance, the councils are the loci of control and the distribution sites for the roles and expectations of individual players.

The patient care council is accountable for ensuring that expectations are fulfilled. The stakeholders and decision makers on the council define areas of ac-

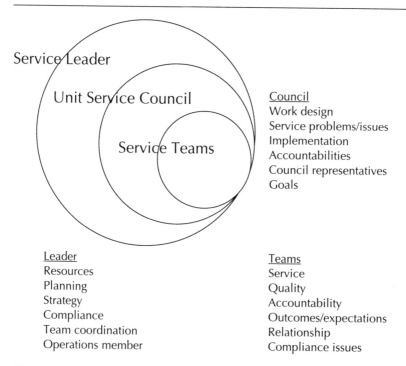

Service Leader

Unit Service Council

Service Teams

Council
Work design
Service problems/issues
Implementation
Accountabilities
Council representatives
Goals

Leader
Resources
Planning
Strategy
Compliance
Team coordination
Operations member

Teams
Service
Quality
Accountability
Outcomes/expectations
Relationship
Compliance issues

**Figure 5-6** Service Accountability

countability and make certain that the related obligations are met within the context of the organization's mission and purposes. The checks and balances in the council structure ensure that work is always consistent with expectations and always leads to desired outcomes.

> *The council design forces the system to keep decisions at the point closest to where work is done. It prevents the "turfing" of decisions up the hierarchical ladder.*

The patient care council is also the first place where service is linked to policy and governance. In order for the linkage to have organizational integrity, the key players must be invested in and facilitate the effectiveness of the process. Although most of the representatives on the council come from the service arena, the leadership of the organization must be represented as well. The medical staff service chiefs, the administration, and the board should also be represented. In fact, it is imperative that leaders from all the forums of authority be involved in the clinical or service-based decision making that occurs in the council. There are important reasons for this:

- The focus of the council is on patient care. Those who will be affected by decisions regarding care should be included in the dialogue about the pertinent issues.
- Constructing a format that makes it difficult not to participate and own one's work is essential for changing both the culture and context for service partnership.
- Medical staff leaders have often been prevented by practice and organizational barriers from fully participating in ongoing health care decisions and processes. It is no longer a viable strategy to keep medical staff at a distance from operational and clinical decision making.
- There has always been a format for ensuring that important decisions receive administrative approval. Most decisions must now be made in the service setting, often quickly, and by those upon whom they have the most direct impact. Organizational structure must now support this type of decision making.
- It is no longer possible for managers and administrators to know enough to manage critical decision making in all the arenas of health care. Increasingly the relationships of service providers with each other are more important than the providers' connection to the organization. Providers must be empowered to make their own decisions.

- Management is now obligated to create an environment that is fast, fluid, and flexible in its support of clinical and service activities. The market, payer formats, service configurations, and information systems are changing rapidly. This requires leaders to create a system of responses that makes it possible to act quickly and effectively.
- Unilateral models of decision making are no longer effective. Outcome orientations and point-of-care work structures make it impossible to make satisfactory service-related decisions outside the service setting. Those who are accountable for the excellence of their work must be invested in decisions that affect service and quality.

The organization has good reason to configure itself in a way that facilitates the work of the council. The focus of the council reflects staff accountability for the provision of high-quality services.

The role of management in shared governance structures is to construct and maintain a system of operational support that ensures that work defined by the staff gets done and patient care needs get met. Reconfiguring the administrative reporting relationships and redesigning roles in the organization can provide a more integrated and supportive administrative structure.[21] The various service- and ancillary-related vice-president roles, for example, may be condensed into one (e.g., service leader for patient services and/or quality). This would tend to make administrative support multifocal and interdisciplinary. All other administrative roles not focused on unit of service facilitation, integration, and coordination could be diminished, leaving essentially two levels of management—unit or service managers and service-quality administrators.

> **Management is precluded from controlling decisions made by staff on the patient care council. The staff must have ownership of decisions for which they are accountable.**

There are several reasons for reducing the administrative structure so that it is no larger than necessary for integrating the organization:

- Accountability has a greater tendency to migrate from where it belongs if there is a large number of management positions to which it can go.

- The councils set direction for the managers in the system. This is a radical departure from the hierarchical industrial model. The authority for setting policy and direction now resides with the stakeholders. The managers become agents of the councils in that their main task is to facilitate implementation of and compliance with the council's decisions.
- Point-of-service decision making and self-directed staff processes require that the staff be able to make decisions essential to their roles without the prior or subsequent approval of managers. Approval mechanisms qualify or interfere with staff accountability. The role of managers is to support the staff's skills and ability to act in a self-directed manner.
- The twenty-first century manager will relinquish planning, organizing, leading, and controlling activities to self-directed work teams in the shared governance structure. The more expansive systems role of the manager takes priority. This role requires broad leadership competencies in facilitating, coordinating, and integrating.

The patient care council represents a major departure from the traditional industrial model of organization. In a shared governance organization, the leaders commit to a different type of relationship between the players, who now act as stakeholders and investors and who therefore must develop a greater understanding of the business and work of the health care system. Superior-subordinate relationships and ego-driven unilateral behavior are no longer viable. The new approach requires a great commitment to the principles of equality, ownership, partnership, and accountability. It also requires the full involvement of all who contribute to the achievement of the level of quality consumers expect.

## THE OPERATIONS COUNCIL

In a shared governance organization, the accountability of and expectations for each role must be clearly defined.[22] So must the management and service functions. The shared governance literature defines management accountability as encompassing the human, fiscal, material, support, and systems functions in the organization.[23] Since the manager role is resource based and fundamentally links resources to the work of the organization, it is, as Drucker points out, primarily a contextual role.[24] The manager provides a supportive and adequate context within which the work of caregiving and service provision can unfold as unhindered by constraints as possible.

A forum for addressing the issues of stewardship, strategy, and resource provision is necessary for the effective integration of work and structure in the organization. This forum should be where the accountability of managers is defined and the structures and processes necessary for its exercise are constructed. The operations council is the organizational forum that meets these qualifications.

With a format similar to that of the nursing management council, the operations council also has similar, although broader, accountability (see Figure 5-7). The accountability of the operations council encompasses the following:

- Management of the human, fiscal, material, support, and systems resources of the organization.
- Creation of an environment that empowers service providers and is supportive of their independence and interdependence in clinical decision making.
- Application of the strategic and mission framework for services within a specific service arena or partnership.
- Assessment and evaluation of the environment and the support given to the service providers to determine the presence of variance or factors not contributing to the work.
- Identification of linkage problems interfering with the seamless integration of the service structures and identification and implementation of solutions.
- Planning and implementation of parallel and collateral responses to service issues or barriers between services or providers, with a focus on team-based approaches to solution seeking and opportunity finding.

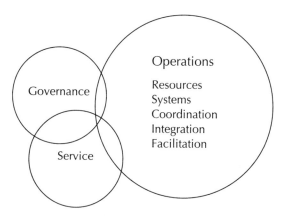

**Figure 5-7** Operations Council Accountability

- Development of the self-directive skills of staff so they can achieve owner-ship of work and issues and become nondependent on management for caretaking and dependency-related activities.
- Predicting and anticipating future issues and circumstances impacting the specific service area, with attention to identification of strategies and staff responses to the changes and variables affecting service provision.
- Fully participating in collective goal-seeking, visioning, and planning efforts in order to take advantage of opportunities for higher levels of service provision and enhancement of the quality of service activity.
- Full investment in the process of developing leadership skills in staff and others through modeling, mentoring, and participation in developmental activities.

Note the absence of clinical and service-related accountability. In fact, such service-related activities are purposely excluded from the definition of managers' roles in order to ensure that they are performed by the staff. In older industrial models of organization, the assumption that the manager was a "superworker" created a set of expectations that simply could not be fulfilled. In an accountability-based system, the manager's role is more clearly defined and the expectations for the role are specified in detail so that performance can be better measured.[25]

*Operational accountability is grounded in resources. The role of the manager is to ensure that the necessary resources are available to the staff in a way that they can use.*

The operations council provides a forum for the organization's management to focus on those issues that are within its area of accountability. The council, by design, breaks down the system's barriers to access, focus, accountability, and relationship between managers. It is not a place where communication and administrative reporting and control is exercised; rather it becomes a center of vision building, problem solving, outcome evaluating, and systems designing (see Exhibit 5-6).

All management roles and positions in the organization are represented on the council. Each service center or center of excellence representing a major service area sends a manager to participate in council decision making. Included is the elected chair of the service council, ensuring linkage to the council and its decision making related to the delivery of care and the provision of services. Also suggested for inclusion would be the senior officer for medical affairs, the chief oper-

**Exhibit 5-6** Operations Accountability in Shared Governance

| | |
|---|---|
| Membership: Board, Services, Executive, Management, Consumers | |
| Resources | Work:    Set operational policy |
| Systems | Build support context |
| Coordination | Implement council decisions |
| Implementation | Develop leadership |
| Operations | Evaluate processes |
| | Generate information |

ating officer, and a representative from the board of trustees. The size of the council and method of representation used are partially determined by the structure and culture of the organization.

The operations council is where the organization links its functions and activities (the obligation of the patient care council) to its structural and mission-related obligations. The checks and balances of the structure and the processes of shared governance are incorporated here. The integrity of the organization is provided for by the deliberation and decisions of this group. It is also the place where opportunity is provided for conflict to be played out.

The concept of shared governance, although idealistic, is not unrealistic. Power struggles and political intrigue do not disappear simply because the organization is configured in a more equitable and functional manner. Rather than assume that the conflict is dealt with, the organization should provide a forum to air differences and mitigate the consequences of political infighting so that they do not reduce the effectiveness of the essential relationships and decisions. Unilateral and isolated processes, which are favored by some "seat of the pants" leaders, must be abandoned. The shared governance approach does not assume that all styles of leadership are acceptable. Those that negatively impact the operational integrity of the organization, the delineation of accountability, and the efficient and appropriate delivery of services across the continuum of care are unsuitable and should not be allowed.

> *The operations council provides linkage within the organization, ensuring that all levels of the system support point-of-service activities.*

Giving the responsibility for all major resource approvals to the operations council ensures that everyone's agenda will be discussed and deliberated upon. It prevents the "end runs" that so many people attempt in order to get their personal agendas implemented regardless of their impact on the rest of the organization. It also allows responses to market shifts, service changes, and new opportunities to be worked out with the knowledge and investment of the leadership.

The primary role of the operations council is to ensure that the functions of the system are consistent with its mission, purpose, and direction. Since those who make decisions about policy (the board) and about service and care (the patient care council) are present at the deliberations of the operations council, decision making remains integrated. The elements of the organization's work, direction, structure, and work processes must come together to serve the purposes of the system and sustain the operational integrity of the relationships that move the organization toward desired results.

> *The operations council ensures that the usual "end runs" around the system that often occur are short-circuited. If a program or allocation is appropriate, it should stand the test of the council's review.*

## THE GOVERNANCE COUNCIL

In a whole systems design, there must be a mechanism for linking the decision making that occurs in all the arenas of the organization.[26] In the past, the disconnection between the board and the service providers meant that the service outcomes and the organizational strategy would rarely cohere. The commitment of the board to the staff or of the staff to the board was virtually nonexistent. Indeed, rarely did one group know anything about the other except for information carried by various stakeholders between the groups.[27] As a result, organizational decision making was fragmented and rarely fully successful in achieving ownership from the players at any level.

Hierarchical notions of governance lead to command and control relationships. There is overwhelming evidence that these types of relationships work poorly. Governance should be based on a partnership between the players in the organization, system, continuum, and professions as well as the members of the community. No one can function effectively minus good relationships with the others upon whom the service continuum depends.

It is in the governance council (or policy council) that integration and collaboration are most visible. This group, which includes representatives from the board leadership, the administration, the leadership of the patient care and operations councils, and the medical staff, has the responsibility of ensuring that the mission, goals, systems, and work of the organization are linked in a common framework in order to facilitate the achievement of service outcomes and maintain organizational viability (see Figure 5-8). Although its focus is on the organizational mission, strategies, and goals, one of its main roles is to tie the board, operations, and service structures together seamlessly. The accountability of the council is broader than the accountability of either the operations or patient care council. Since its primary concern is the fit between the community and the service environment, it concentrates its attention on direction and integration rather than support, functioning, and service. Specific roles of the council include these:

- It translates and interprets the board's mission, purpose, goals, and strategy for the health care organization.
- It defines major service centers of excellence for the organization.
- It provides a place in the system where the providers, administrators, and community link for the purpose of providing services to the community.
- It deals with conflicts between systems, services, and providers that could impede the achievement of the mission of the organization.
- It acts as an agent of the board in implementing the organization's mission and direction in ways that are appropriate and meaningful for providers and consumers of health care services.

The council's membership should include the board chair, the chief executive officer, the leaders for service/quality and for operations, the chief of the medical

**Figure 5-8** Seamless Organizational Design

staff, the chair of the patient care council, and the chair of the operations council. Community members, consumers, and other customers could also be on the council (see Figure 5-9).

Integration is the main purpose of the council. The problems of limited vision, inapplicability of the board's perspective, administrative shortsightedness, and clinical myopia could be severely reduced if all of the key players dialogue directly with each other. The council provides a supportive context for linking the components of the organizational system in a manner that encourages seamless and point-of-care decision making. Through the actions of the governance council, people come to realize that the organization is truly designed to support their work, and the leadership can be confident that all players are invested in its mission and will act as partners in the provision of health care services.[28]

Some might suggest that the governance council performs in much the same way as the board itself. This is not true, although the council could stimulate a change in the configuration of the board and its relationship to the organization. The council's primary role is to act as a functional agent of the board, linking the governance functions to the operations and service functions of the system (see Figure 5-10). It provides a forum in which the early steps in the implementation of board decisions can be deliberated and interpreted for the members of the organization. It serves as the quality interface relating the board mandates for service to the organization's performance-related activities. It is here where possible changes motivated by developments in the market and by new opportunities take form and are communicated to the board and where board decisions begin to be

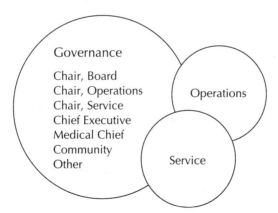

**Figure 5-9** Governance Council Membership

implemented. The members are key leaders from every accountable arena, and the council thus provides a means for them to deliberate fully and make decisions regarding issues that affect every central component of the organization's work.

The objectives of the operations and patient care councils are driven by the mandates that emerge from the governance activities of both the board and the governance council. The work of all the organization's loci of accountability is connected through the shared governance structure (see Figure 5-11).

> *The governance council's primary role is to ensure that there is a seamless connection between all the parts of the organization. Integration of the system with the community it serves is the focal point of this council's work.*

The structure itself is further supported at the point of service by the unit councils (also known as self-managed work groups or teams). Their role is to pursue the goals of the organization within the cultural framework of each service in the ser-

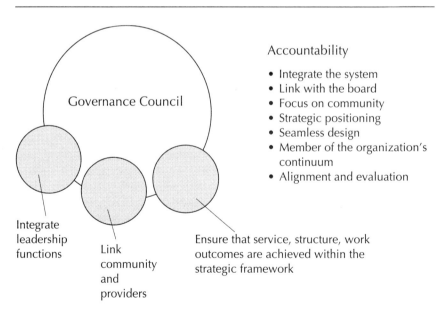

**Figure 5-10** Governance Council Accountability

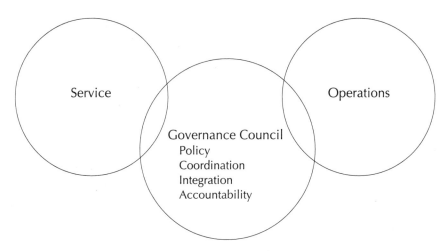

**Figure 5-11** Governance Council Linkage

vice continuum. Since care must increasingly be organized around patient popula-tions or the service continuum, the needs of the service relationships and the orga-nizational community get integrated and addressed at the point of care. It is the job of point-of-care providers to work out the fit between patient and service needs and the design, purposes, and direction of the organization.

## THE INTEGRATED ORGANIZATION

Clearly, specific roles in the organization would have to shift to support a more integrated networked organizational model. Administrative positions and vice-presidential roles would be reduced, possibly even eliminated. The key ad-ministrators in the streamlined organi-zation would be the leader for service/ quality and the leader for operations. All other administrators would support the service managers and the service providers.

New systems approaches to structur-ing organizations will not be accepted without challenge. The changes in rela-tionships, roles, and players will cause uncertainty and pain.[29] In the transfor-

*A truly seamless health system has a link to the community it serves. There are too many health systems that have no roots in the community within which they reside.*

mation to a service-based structure, every role will be questioned and subject to revision. In fact, the whole system of health service provision and the structures that support it will be open to revision.[30] The age-old adage "Form should follow function" is especially apt. No new or existing structure is permanent.[31] Each system must have design that facilitates achievement of its purpose and expedites its work.[32] It is to this end that whole systems shared governance is directed. It creates a transitional model for ownership at all levels of the organization. It reflects accountability at every level and creates a seamless structural and relational integration of the system (see Figure 5-12). Finally, it provides the basis for a whole community model of shared governance. Seamlessness within a health system is of little value if there is no link between the system and the community it serves.

More important than suggesting a model, as has been done in this chapter, is the promulgation of the principles underpinning horizontal and integrated approaches. Clearly, it is increasingly valuable to organizations to have a structure that is flexible and fluid in design. A system's structure should not interfere with its ability to do its work and to meet its social mandate. Therefore, it should pro-

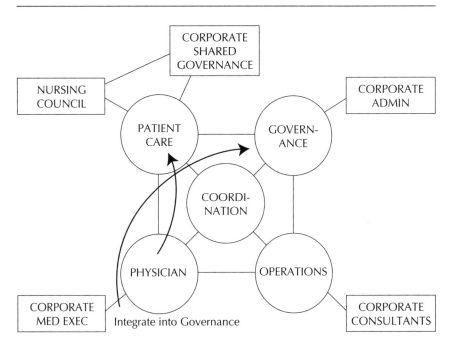

**Figure 5-12** Corporate Integration Relationship Structure

> **No structure should be permanent and inflexible. Each organizational structure must be able to transmute fluidly into new forms as demand requires.**

vide the system with the flexibility and responsiveness to reconfigure based on the need for a different context for service provision. As health care organizations become more decentralized and community based, there will be an increased dependence on the architecture of the information system. Structuring for a more "virtual" set of relationships in health care will require connections just now being conceived.

The shared governance structure is a transitional model that provides a foundation for the more service-driven, horizontal health care organization currently under construction (Figure 5-13). Through this provisional structure, self-managed

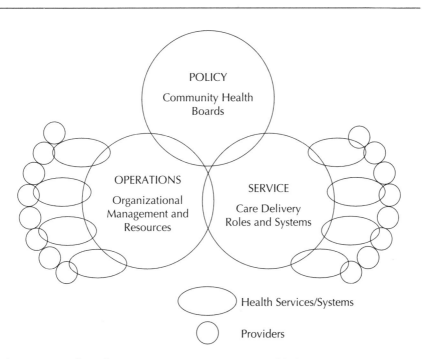

**Figure 5-13** Shared Governance Community Health System

and -directed activities and the linkage of those to the organized system can take form. The organization can respond to demands for service and adjust components in response to changes in service needs and payer relationships. Components of the organization can be redesigned and can offer their unique brand of service in the marketplace without having to wait for the whole organization to make the same shift. The role of the councils is to increase the independence of the services by struggling with the tension between local service identity and organizational integrity and systems fit.

Leadership in an integrated organization will have to link across the system from board to service. The seamless connections across the continuum are facilitated by the leaders' roles within councils, service pathways, and on work teams. In this way leaders now link with the organization, its members, and the community it serves (Figure 5-14).

No structure should be permanent and inflexible. Although a stable structure furnishes a sense of security, it eventually reduces an organization's ability to change. The best type of structure provides format and context but also facilitates adaptation and accommodation. Whole systems approaches to shared governance strongly support the journey to an integrated and seamless decision-making structure in health service organizations.

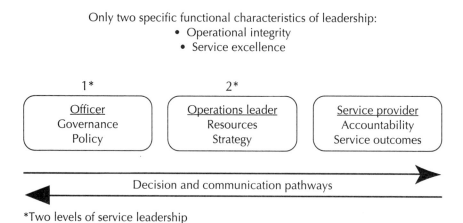

**Figure 5-14** Leadership Structure

## REFERENCES

1. T. Porter-O'Grady, "Whole Systems Shared Governance: Creating the Seamless Organization," *Nursing Economics* 12 (1994):187–195.
2. T. Porter-O'Grady, *Implementing Shared Governance* (Baltimore: Mosby, 1992).
3. V. DeBaca, K. Jones, and J. Tornibini, "A Cost-Benefit Analysis of Shared Governance," *Journal of Nursing Administration* 23, no.7–8(1993):50–57.
4. J. Jenkins, "Professional Governance: The Missing Link," *Nursing Management* 22, no. 8(1991):26–30.
5. K. Brodbeck, "Professional Practice Actualized through an Integrated Shared Governance and Quality Assurance Model," *Journal of Nursing Care Quality* 6, no. 2(1992):20–31.
6. C. Jones et al., "Shared Governance and the Nursing Practice Environment," *Nursing Economics* 11 (1993):209–213.
7. G. Edwards et al., "Unit-based Shared Governance Can Work," *Nursing Management* 25, no. 4(1994):74–77.
8. K. McDonagh, *Nursing Shared Governance* (Atlanta, Ga.: K.J. McDonagh Associates, 1991).
9. E. Lawler III, S. Mohrman, and G. Ledford, *Employees Involvement and Total Quality Management* (San Francisco: Jossey-Bass, 1992).
10. T. Porter-O'Grady, "Work Redesign: Fact, Fiction, and Foible," *Seminars for Nurse Managers* 1, no. 1(1993):8–15.
11. P. Drucker, *Managing for the Future: The 1990's and Beyond* (New York: Truman Tally Books/Dutton, 1992).
12. P. Drucker, *Post-Capitalist Society* (New York: Harper Collins, 1993).
13. A. Rheaume et al., "Case Management and Nursing Practice," *Journal of Nursing Administration* 24, no. 3(1994):30–35.
14. J. Katzenbach and D. Smith, *The Wisdom of Teams* (Boston: McKinsey & Co., 1993).
15. J. Goldsmith, "Driving the Nitroglycerin Truck: The Relationship between the Hospital and Physician," *The Healthcare Forum Journal* 36, no. 2(1993):36–40.
16. T. Peters, *Liberation Management* (New York: Harper & Row, 1992).
17. H. Maynard and S. Mehrtens, *The Fourth Wave: Business in the 21st Century* (San Francisco: Berrett-Koehler, 1993).
18. D. Nielson, *Partnering with Employees* (San Francisco: Jossey-Bass, 1993).
19. L. Schlesinger and J. Heskett, "The Service-driven Service Company," *Harvard Business Review* 69, no. 5(1991):71–91.
20. C. Handy, "Balancing Corporate Power: A New Federalist Paper," *Harvard Business Review* 70, no. 6(1992):59–72.
21. W. Kiechel, "The Leader as Servant," *Fortune*, September 1992, pp. 121–122.
22. T. Porter-O'Grady, "Shared Governance for Nursing: Part 1: Creating the New Organization," *AORN Journal* 53, no. 2(1991):458–466.
23. H. Mintzberg, *Mintzburg on Management* (New York: The Free Press, 1990).

24. P. Drucker, *The New Realities* (New York: Harper & Row, 1989).

25. A. Relman, "Assessment and Accountability: The Third Revolution in Medical Care," *New England Journal of Medicine* 319 (1988):1220–1222.

26. R. Coile, *The New Medicine: Reshaping Medical Practice and Health Care Management* (Gaithersburg, Md.: Aspen Publishers, 1989).

27. R. Stayer, "How I Learned to Let My Workers Lead," *Harvard Business Review* 48, no. 6(1990):66–83.

28. M. Wheatley, *Leadership and the New Science* (San Francisco: Berrett-Koehler, 1992).

29. C. Handy, *The Age of Unreason* (Boston: Harvard Business School Press, 1989).

30. T. Morganthau and M. Hager, "The Clinton Cure: Reinventing Health Care," *Newsweek* October 4, 1993, 36–43.

31. Wheatley, *Leadership and the New Science.*

32. W. Bergquist, *The Postmodern Organization: Mastering the Art of Irreversible Change* (San Francisco: Jossey-Bass, 1993).

# Chapter 6

## The Journey from Self-Management to Self-Design

The pursuit of a quest is a pilgrim's progress in which it is essential
to resist the transitory contentment of attractive way stations and
side roads, in which obstacles are overcome because the goal is
visible on the horizon, onward and upward.

Mary Catherine Bateson
*Composing a Life*

In today's environment, managers are seeing their long-standing beliefs and
practices disintegrating before their very eyes. Although they recognize that
the world is different than when they began their careers in management,
many continue to act as though the future will be an extension of the past. In the
stable world of the past, successful careers in management followed a conventional pattern. The necessary academic preparation and skills were known, the
steps along the career path were defined, and the fit of the managerial role into the
whole of organizational life was well understood. Some individualization of role
did occur—to make a fit between the role and the unique skills of the person. Yet
standardization of role performance was typically expected. Once established as a
leader in the organization, the individual was rarely confronted with the challenge
of solving multiple and new problems for the first time. Substantial changes have
occurred, however, and continuing to embrace this model of performance will
doom current health care leaders to certain failure.

### LEADING WITH A FUNDAMENTAL APPRECIATION OF REALITY

Today, the materials and the skills from which the leader role is designed and
sustained are no longer clear. Predictability has vanished, leaving health care managers feeling like Christmas turkeys who barely made it through Thanksgiving! A

closer examination of the health care environment reveals incredible disruptions. Downsizing, restructuring, work redesign, mergers, and acquisitions make health care organizations high-risk places for those seeking stability and security. Professional managers find their careers taking on not only new directions but subject to dramatic shifts in authority, span of control, reporting relationships, referent group, and place of employment. Even the most basic concepts used to construct the professional identity of managers have changed, including definitions of what constitutes quality care, what it means to manage, what is necessary health care, and who is the customer.

> *What works for someone in one period of time and in one set of circumstances may not work for anyone else in any other situation.*

It is a common illusion that stability will return after a period of dramatic change. In reality, change is continuous. Sudden and unpredictable periods of rough whitewater are indeed followed by brief periods of relative calm in which people can regain their focus and strength, but further substantial changes are inevitable and must be anticipated.

Dramatic change is an ordeal. No one likes it, and it generates significant discomfort. Even small changes can give rise to foreboding. People are never totally prepared for the new because it means adjustments in the self and in relationships. Even moving from one neighborhood to another a few miles away can create anxiety as old habits and patterns are disturbed by the unfamiliar.

Change produces a crisis in self-identity, and people constantly undergo self-tests to see if there is a fit with the emerging reality. In essence, contemporary health care organizations have populations of "misfits" moving through change with passion and intensity. No one can ever truly be fit because circumstances are continually

> *A sense of humor, faith in a higher power, and trust in the unknown are the hallmarks of wholeness in the face of fragmenting change.*

changing. In any case, the process of change is a challenge to self-esteem.[1] As the noted developmental psychologist Eric Erickson has observed, a person's identity should not be thought of as a fixed entity that, once acquired, endures for the rest of the person's life. Instead, certain crises, moments of opportunity or threat, bring the identity to the forefront to be addressed again and again.[2]

## THE EXPERIENCE OF CHANGE: A CREATIVE REWORKING

The view being presented here is not that managers are on a long and tortuous road headed for eventual extinction. There is and always will be a need for effective leadership. However, the leadership role must change with the times. Before individuals can move to outcome-based, resource-oriented, and service-driven leadership, they must abandon out-of-date mental maps and create new alternatives to getting the job done. The successful practice of leadership in the twenty-first century will be anchored in the purposeful cultivation of the ability to shift from one process to another, to improvise in new circumstances, and to cope with discontinuity.

> *Those searching for the quick fix, the "right degree," or instant solutions search with the wrong mindset for the twenty-first century.*

The challenge is to combine the familiar and the unfamiliar in response to the new context for leadership. Creative leaders approach new role demands with an attitude of self-design or improvisation. They see this time of transformation in health care as a period to play with career possibilities—to revisit their reason for choosing management as a field of endeavor and their vision for their lives. The creative reworking of leadership roles requires of the individual a certain learning resourcefulness, a preponderance of free-style actions and outcome-driven actions, and a tendency to reject stereotypical answers.[3] By applying these skills and strategies in the process of improvisation, managers will find it less burdensome to make sense out of their experience and achieve a fit with new role definitions. The real question for each individual is whether or not improvisation is a last resort or a purposeful way of working into the future.[4] Can the individual, in other words, switch from the discipline of a self-managed career to the art of self-design?

This chapter focuses on a detailed process for leaders to use in their own work of improvisation and self-design in preparation in order to develop a personal action plan for acquiring or strengthening the behaviors that will be needed by twenty-first century leaders. Embarking on the journey to self-design challenges individuals to ask the following questions:

- What are the creative opportunities that this crisis has brought me?
- What learning will I carry with me when my work changes? What will I discard?

- How can I make creativity flourish in the midst of distraction in my workplace?
- What are multiple demands and ambiguity teaching me right now?
- At what point will I know that self-design has become a significant strategy for me?

## PERSONAL MASTERY

The Chinese have a saying, "He whose virtues exceed his talents is a superior man; he whose talents exceed his virtues is a dangerous man." So it is with leaders. In order to effectively integrate the new demands for leadership in the twenty-first century, a personal reworking of the management role is paramount. Only in this way can leaders truly understand what is happening around them and make informed choices about their future. This means aligning their core principles, beliefs, and ethics with the new role demands of the manager.

> *An improvised leadership role will be different from a carefully planned and executed one; it is certainly more hazardous but is also rich with discovery.*

Learning does not occur if it is not related in some way to a person's mission and reason for working. When they are connected, managers and their staff do whatever it takes to get the job done. It is easy to recognize when there is a disconnect between individual and organizational goals. The effects of management training linger awhile and then fade away. Staff may be involved in restructuring, work redesign, or some other major change project, but they exhibit virtually no spark or curiosity.[5] They simply show up and park their brain at the door.

The covenant between organizations and individuals has changed. Organizations now offer, instead of lifetime employment, maximized employability.[6] Instead of demanding total dedication to the organization, managers must create conditions in which people can develop the skills they need to succeed in the blustery health care marketplace. They can do this by modeling personal mastery, recognizing the obstacles to their own and others' growth, and engaging in self-design. The steps leading to personal mastery are summarized in Figure 6-1. In the sections to follow, each step is described and examples and thought-provoking questions are provided.

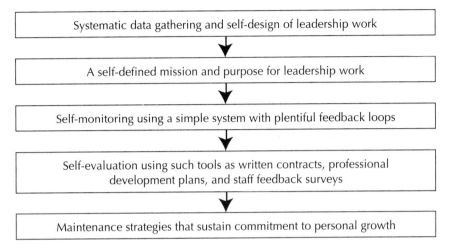

**Figure 6-1** Steps Leading to Personal Mastery

## NEEDED YESTERDAY: SELF-DESIGNING LEADERS

Individuals in positions of leadership have always been self-managing, that is, they have been able to manage their performance according to prescribed role standards. Self-management strategies used by managers typically addressed short-term deviations from role standards and were highly dependent on the accountability system in place in the organization.

What is needed today is an expanded definition of self-management that encompasses not only behavior but cognition. When thinking is added to the equation, leaders adjust their practices only after active involvement in the definition of performance standards and evaluation of the appropriateness of the standards. Concentrating on performance moves the focus from what needs to be done to why it needs to be done and how it needs to be done.[7]

*Self-design* is an expanded form of self-management for the twenty-first century. Included in a leader's self-design activities is a commitment to the continuous design and operationalization of a constantly unfolding management role.[8] The nature of the work itself, the degree of discretion that people have, the technology employed, the particular work climate, and the work systems in place are all part of the context in which management occurs and are subject to new delineation.

> *Organizational changes as well as personal changes are ideally implemented with a "no blueprints" mindset.*

In order to meet their awesome accountability to those who are providing health care services, leaders must engage in a persistent assessment of their management competencies and skill applications in order to deepen their knowledge and better understand the principles that govern their actions. As their knowledge expands, leaders become more skilled in seeing opportunities for reinvention and in identifying how the environment may be hindering growth. The confidence that comes with increased understanding provides the courage to remove obstacles to professional development. Clearly, self-design requires a professional development plan aimed at revising the way management work is performed. It must be regularly evaluated and refined or changed when circumstances require it to be.

## ASSESSING SELF-DESIGNING SKILLS AND BEHAVIORS

What is the level of your self-design skills? Are you putting your energies in the right place? Exhibit 6-1 contains questions that can aid you in determining the level of your self-design skills and in figuring out ways of improving them.

Successful leaders share many traits, including clusters of skills that form the basis for the self-designing response to change.

## THE PROCESS OF SELF-RECOGNITION

The first prescription is to gain self-knowledge and achieve an accurate assessment of one's unique competencies, skills, and set of experiences. Do you understand exactly where you are at every point in your career? Do you strive to understand your reactions to stress, failure, and success? Are you a practiced observer and student of your interactions with and impact on others? How comfortable are you in acknowledging your goals, competencies, and skills? The self-designing leader uses self-knowledge to accommodate personal realities while adeptly operating in ways that meet organizational goals. Professional and personal experiences can provide the insight upon which to build a successful professional future. Are you willing to put forth the energy to discover this type of special wisdom through a rigorous self-assessment process? Willingness is a key to self-design. Do you see your work as one long process of getting tired? Or do you work hard to get up every morning with confidence and say if this is not nice, what is?

**Exhibit 6-1** Questions for Determining Self-Design Skill Levels

- Are you able to acknowledge unpredictable situations as opportunities for learning and personal growth?
- Would you describe yourself as an effective problem solver or solution finder?
- Do you see obstacles as hurdles to overcome or opportunities for achieving mastery?
- During periods of personal or organizational crisis, do you know how to get the help you need to find your way?
- Do you work hard at letting go of old mindsets even when they are your favorites and give you comfort?
- Can you move toward achievement of your professional vision and your purpose in working without blueprints or guarantees of success?
- Can you bear up for a lengthy period of time with the discomfort of not knowing how things will turn out?

*Source:* From *Developing a 21st Century Mind* by Marsha Sinetar. Copyright © 1991 by Marsha Sinetar. Adapted by permission of Random House, Inc.

A creative reworking of the leadership role requires liberating oneself from excess baggage—those positive and negative aspects of personality that have ceased to be functional. The process of letting go is never easy but is essential to moving forward. For example, consider the case of a manager who has been rewarded for setting the highest of standards for himself. He will be unsuccessful as a coach because he lacks the patience to support people's growth (he is very disappointed when anyone fails to measure up to his standards). Or imagine a manager who believes that it is critical to stay well-informed. On the surface, this appears to be a real strength. She reads every memo and every new policy or procedure, and then spends significant time correcting people who seem misinformed. This seeming strength becomes a weakness because it precludes her from recognizing the degree of effectiveness of the information and communication systems in her department. In fact, she may become the information system, creating a situation in which her staff are dependent on her and thus reinforcing a child-parent type of relationship!

How do you begin to get a handle on the excess baggage you have brought to the performance of your leadership role? Remember the old adage that we are destined to repeat only those failures from which we have not learned? (See Exhibit 6-2 for some thought-provoking questions regarding excess baggage.)

It is important to continually examine your beliefs about your competencies and skills as a leader. Some of these beliefs come from the experience of past failure.

**Exhibit 6-2** Recognizing Excess Baggage

1. Do you finish everything you start—a boring book, a project, or a program—even if it is not work continuing?
2. Do you live by the adage, "If something is worth doing, it is worth doing well"? Some things are okay to do less than perfectly, particularly in unpredictable situations when using untried strategies. (Have the courage not to get that A!)
3. Do you describe yourself as a "peacemaker," often saying yes to preserve relationships rather than risking the consequences of saying no?
4. Do you feel an overwhelming need to be correct and thus agonize over decisions? Do you find yourself postponing decisions sometimes, even though it lessens their impact, because you are afraid of making a mistake?

*Source:* Adapted from *Excess Baggage: Getting Out of Your Own Way* by J. Sills, p. 50, with permission of Viking Penguin, © 1993.

For example, we sometimes make a decision to not engage in a certain behavior ever again because of the negative consequences that it engendered. When we do this, we fail to forgive ourselves for a mistake made and lose the opportunity to apply a tactic that might work in different circumstances. Being able to forgive oneself for past mistakes is an essential element of self-assessment.[9] Unfortunately, it is the rare workplace that has built-in rituals for forgiveness. Stories about big mistakes and failures are a part of the oral history of most organizations; they reinforce the norms for what is acceptable and what is not. No one wants to be the protagonist in a story of failure, but the fear of failure can cause people to lose confidence and behave in an inflexible manner.

If we value ourselves and learn to appreciate our own virtues, we are able to lead with a much more positive attitude. The point is not to deny the facts in a particular situation but to look at situations in a new and positive light. For example, we might think of fear about work redesign as really excitement that has not yet been discovered! Leading with a positive attitude is not blind optimism but is being adept at seeing the hidden opportunities in a situation.

> **Baggage is a self-imposed burden for leaders. How can you recognize your own baggage and jettison it?**

Working with a willingness to confront the realities that surround us means being able to hear the truth about ourselves and what other people are truly thinking. When we attain this mindset, we take responsibility for how we think and act and thereby create a climate in which fear and denial are not tolerated.

> *The test of a first-class mind is the ability to hold two opposing ideas in the head at one time . . . and still retain the ability to function.*
> *F. Scott Fitzgerald*

Undoubtedly, if you are in a position of leadership, you will make mistakes that have the effect of stifling people, demotivating them, or even intimidating them. For example, a manager in one organization had the habit of gesturing emphatically whenever she was passionate about a certain point. Only after years of this behavior, when a courageous staff person gave her feedback, did she recognize that staff were intimidated when she started to "point the finger at them."

If you value yourself, you will constantly look at your thoughts and actions to understand their impact on your goals and on other people. Consequently, you will be able to change before too much damage is done. By looking at Figure 6-2, you can quickly determine whether or not you are applying effective sets of self-design skills to your leadership role.

## CURRENT PARADOXES

Our professional socialization has taught us to plan for patient care without allowing room for mistakes. A rallying call of the CQI movement is "zero defects for one and all." Yet Handy has observed that there are no simple answers to anything, nor is perfection a possibility. This may come as a shock to many of us searching for the "right" solution. Does this mean that we abandon our quest for excellence? No! It means we recognize that the philosophy of zero defects, along with engendering a drive toward improvement, can simultaneously stifle innovation by creating an overwhelming fear of defects! The solution is to make sure that the zero de-

> *Leaders cannot even begin to address the crippling effects of inconsistencies and contradictions in their organizations until they understand and address the paradoxes inherent in management work.*

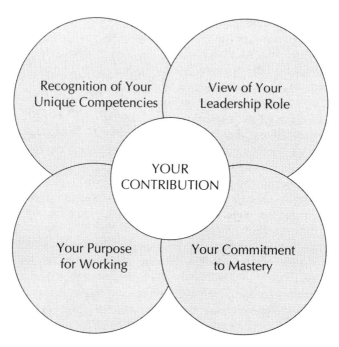

**Figure 6-2** The Processes of Self-Design

fects policy does not result in punishment for occasional failures and does not lead to inflexibility.

Leaders must understand what is happening in our times and how opposites can operate simultaneously in our lives.[10] In the disorderly world of health care, people are being buffeted by the contradictions and inconsistencies that accompany dramatic change. The more change there is, the more paradoxes there are to accept, cope with, and make sense of. Although leaders cannot make paradoxes disappear or achieve total resolution, they can understand them and then act to minimize their impact.[11] However, managers cannot even begin to deal with the paradoxes confronting their organizations until they have addressed the paradoxes inherent in their own work.

One paradox is that managers report they increasingly are putting in longer hours and have less time to perform their work despite having many time-saving technologies at their disposal, such as E-mail, desktop computers, and on-line information services. In some organizations, time has become a competitive weapon, as more work is gotten from fewer people.[12]

Is your use of time out of balance and do you choose to ignore that fact? If the answer is yes, then you need to reflect on what you have defined as your fundamental or core leadership tasks and obligations. Are you holding on to so much that you cannot balance your expenditure of effort and also lack the flexibility demanded for improvisation? Because of downsized management structures and reduced support roles, the range of essential management tasks tends to become too broad. Consequently, some of the productivity that downsizing and the attendant revisions sought to enhance is threatened. Some managers may find their time filled with doing things that are no longer necessary. Others may have too much to do because they are doing work that should be done by the caregivers. The main danger of over-extending the core of management tasks is that it restricts our room to grow, to experiment, or to be flexible in how we respond to current realities. We will have no alternative but to look to prescribed rules for action rather than look to our own wisdom.

> *When the core accountability of the management role is overdefined, the manager's productivity is not enhanced but jeopardized.*

Another paradox of organizations is that organizations currently need to be both global and local, both large and small, both centralized and decentralized.[13] Leadership groups are now struggling with the resulting perplexities. As the movement toward integrated health care systems continues, one challenge for leaders is to know how to stay connected to self-directed or self-managed units. What connections do they need to build and where should the connections be? How can they create fluid connections? The important work of building connections will not be accomplished if leaders lack discretionary space in which to place network activities. Figure 6-3 indicates the consequences of having an overly broad definition of core leadership accountability.

Self-designing leaders spend time distinguishing core and discretionary activities. Leaders can no longer wait for someone else to define their work. The most effective leadership groups consist of managers who have constructed their own individual roles and have connected and configured their roles to enhance their teamworking abilities.

Exhausted managers have defined their core accountability too broadly and have held on to or accepted responsibilities that are not their own. They appear incapable of letting go outdated paradigms and practices. They find work is a

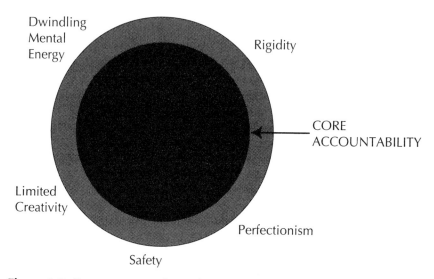

**Figure 6-3** Consequences of Overly Broad Core Leadership Accountability

grind because they have too much to do and never enough time to do it. They generally wind up burned out, haunted, and cynical.

Their dwindling mental energy is accompanied by an inability to sustain a focus on long-term targets. Because reactive solutions do not require the same kind of mental energy that long-term solutions do, exhausted managers tend to favor quick fixes and band-aids. They do not have enough time for creative thought or action. Their problem-solving is rigid and "by the book" rather than "outside of the lines." Perfectionism is a common defense because it precludes spending time and energy learning from mistakes. Risk taking is abandoned in favor of safe harbors because safe harbors do not require time and energy devoted to synthesizing thought and action creatively. Gradually work becomes a set of activities that daily negate one's professional vision and purposes.

> **Good moods have been replaced with a sardonic weariness in many of today's health care workplaces.**

On the other hand, when managers purposefully examine what they see as their fundamental accountability and seek a balance between core and discretionary work, the results are very different. Suddenly there is extra mental energy for devising creative

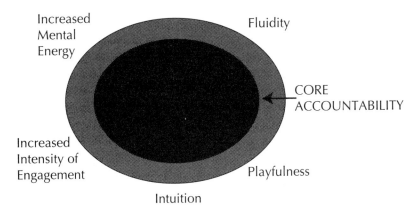

**Figure 6-4** Consequences of a Balance between Core Leadership Accountability and Discretionary Activities

responses to problems. Figure 6-4 shows what results from a balance between core and discretionary activities. Long-term targets receive sustained attention. Behaviors are altered as personal paradigms are challenged and polarities resolved. Intuitive actions occur regularly because individuals are attuned to their hunches and emotions. There is room for experimentation, imagination, playfulness, and learning from mistakes.[14] There is a certain vivacity and an air of enjoying work. It is no secret that creative juices begin to flow when people are in a good mood.[15]

Self-designing a leadership role means reviving the imaginative, inventive spark possessed by children. Effective leaders work hard to regain the spark within. Innovation is an everyday experience for them. They may regularly try taking a new route to work, use the stairs instead of the elevator, walk outside instead of through the tunnel, or often rearrange the furniture in their office. They constantly search for ideas that stimulate their own and others' thinking. New ideas are shared and explored aloud. They encourage others to participate in critical thinking.

The process of evaluating the balance between the "musts" and the "maybes" of leadership work is essential. Lack of balance has a wide-ranging impact upon self-concept, worldview, productivity, and relationships.

> *Designing one's own work allows a balancing of what must always be done and what can possibly be done.*

Pessimism makes people skeptical about their potential to change and grow. Some questions to begin your assessment of the balance in your work are contained in Exhibit 6-3.

## CREATING A NEW MISSION

Can you see yourself working in a way that you never have before? What will you be doing that you are not doing now? What will you never do? Whom will you be working with? What will be your work environment? To have a mission for your work means seeing something that does not quite exist.[16] Creating a new mission helps you to center on what you want and to pursue it. It is a highway into the future.

Have you ever written a mission statement before? Not one of those wordy documents produced at the end of a grueling retreat but one that is to the point and easy to remember. A personal mission statement should describe the major out-

**Exhibit 6-3** Assessing the Balance of Work

1. Do you define yourself solely in terms of your work?
2. Have you created a support system of trusted colleagues?
3. How much do you read to improve professional effectiveness? (Not only does reading expand knowledge but readers learn how to uncover links between seemingly unrelated events.)
4. Do you engage in exercises that heighten powers of observation?
5. Do you have a repertoire of tools to prevent you from being a victim of your environment?
6. Do you have a high endurance level in times of uncertainty and ambiguity? Are you able to be flexible? While not acting blindly, are you willing to act without knowing every consequence in advance?
7. Have you developed a keen sense of timing from thinking about your experiences of being engaged and disengaged?
8. Do you know when to act and when to pull back and do nothing?
9. Has your work provided you with the opportunity to develop skill in the use of words that give meaning and motivation?
10. Do you have the freedom to demonstrate "robust action" or a management style that combines expeditious decision making and flexibility?

*Source:* Adapted from H. Levinson, *Career Mastery* (San Francisco: Berrett-Koehler Publications, 1992); R.G. Eccles, N. Nohria, and J.D. Berkeley, *Beyond the Hype* (Boston: Harvard Business School Press, 1992).

> *Do you have a clear view of what you want your work to become? Do you set daily priorities that serve to move you forward toward your dreams?*

comes of your work; focus on a condition that does not currently exist; and be compelling, inspirational, and easy to relate to.[17]

## DEFINING A PURPOSE FOR WORKING

Your particular leadership position exists for some reason. Why were you hired? Why does your position continue to exist? Have expectations changed since you were hired? Unfortunately, the organizational structures of many health care organizations contain "leadership" roles that have no purpose but remain in place because no one wanted to deal with the politics necessary to eliminate them. For example, one organization had a person ensconced in the corporate offices, fondly referred to as "the marble palace." She was called Vice-President of the St. Elsewhere Way ("The St. Elsewhere Way" was the title of the organization's vision statement). This person had little idea about how her work activities affected the organization's customers or how they felt about their care experience. In fact, she may not even have known who exactly those customers were.

Taking the time to craft an aim for your work has several benefits. It should bring meaning and value to what you do, particularly in those times of "intangible" success. It will also remind you that your work is not a destination but a journey. Questions to begin the exploration of your mission and purpose are found in Exhibit 6-4.

Defining a purpose for your work helps you to maintain, in these times of transformation, a central focus on your activities and to resist fragmenting pulls in different directions. To use Handy's metaphor again, it enables you to distinguish the *core* of your leadership accountability from the activities that should remain

**Exhibit 6-4** Questions for Exploring Mission and Purpose

1. Why was I hired?
2. What value does my position add to the delivery of patient care?
3. Why does my role continue to be supported?
4. Why do I continue working in this position?
5. Why do I come to work every day?
6. What are my core leadership tasks and obligations?

peripheral. Sample leadership vision and work purpose statements are provided in Exhibit 6-5.

## COMMITMENT

Making a commitment to act in accordance with your mission and purpose statements is the third step in the process of self-design. It means "walking the talk" and moving beyond rhetoric to action. A commitment is a promise that you make to yourself and from which you will not vacillate.[18] Sustaining a commitment is never easy. There will be obstacles all along the way, and sometimes they will engender hopelessness or even cause defeat. Genuine sacrifice is required if your mission and purpose statements are not to remain mere words on a piece of paper.

> *By taking the time to create a vision and a purpose for your life, you will approach your work with a broader, more critical, and more strategic outlook.*

Every person who works must try to perform in a manner consistent with core beliefs and principles. It is the nature of organizational life that situations will arise that challenge us to act in ways other than our stated mission and purpose entail we should act. Commitment requires a clear understanding of ourselves and where we want to go. Without commitment there will be little change and no accountability for work.

Covey has described three threats to commitment: (1) passions, (2) pride and pretension, and (3) aspirations and ambitions. In order to moderate the impact of passions upon work performance, he urges self-discipline and warns against over-

**Exhibit 6-5** Sample Leadership Vision and Work Purpose Statements

### Leadership Vision Statement
My vision as a leader is to become artful in seeing hidden connections, making them visible, and applying my current understanding in order to connect people and resources in the delivery of care.

### Work Purpose Statement
The purpose of my work is to create the necessary conditions for people to identify, acquire, and apply the knowledge and skills that will enable them to thrive in turbulent times, thereby improving their lives and contributing to the success of my organization.

> *If you are committed to creating the conditions for honesty, then, besides asking for feedback, you will listen no matter how painful the feedback is and will never punish the messenger.*

eating, overimbibing, failing to exercise, and not getting enough rest. Unless we pay attention to the ways in which we need to temper our behavior, we will be victims, not the masters, of our own indulgences. When self-discipline is a part of a leader's repertoire, it is easier to stick to a commitment, particularly in difficult circumstances. Pretension and false roles come from disharmony between core values and principles. Such disharmony can be overcome by crafting mission and purpose statements, which are basically honest and direct expressions of what a leader believes. Aspirations can get in the way if they dominate decision making or if they are not linked in some way to service. If personal agendas are disconnected from patient care needs, then every situation has winners and losers instead of just winners.[19]

## CONTRIBUTION

When leaders act in a committed way, their contribution to organizational success is multiplied, because they understand just what it takes to be and to stay committed regardless of how difficult this can be. Systems and processes are continually examined as to their impact on commitment. Leaders engage in coaching activities designed to integrate individuals' goals with those of the organization.

> *We make a living by what we get; we make a life by what we give.*
> *Winston Churchill*

To make a substantial contribution, leaders must view themselves as stewards who have chosen service over self-interest. Only when managers have defined their leadership mission and purpose and begin to pursue these in a committed way will they be fully accountable for the outcomes of their enterprises. This means that the delivery system has to function well and produce the correct balance of quality, cost, and customer satisfaction. In the new paradigm for leadership, managers must combine humility with a commitment to partnership, choice, and service.[20] Questions regarding commitment and contribution are contained in Exhibit 6-6.

**Exhibit 6-6** Questions Regarding Commitment and Contribution

1. Do I let personal gratification limit my effectiveness?
2. Are my professional mission and work purpose in harmony with my organization's goals?
3. Do I balance my personal goals against the demands of service?
4. Do I keep my commitments even when obstacles tempt me to disengage?
5. What will be my legacy?
6. Do I coach those who will follow me in the art and discipline of self-design?
7. How have I made a difference in the delivery of care?

## SELF-EVALUATION

Self-designing leaders engage in the deliberate evaluation of their leadership practices using tools such as written contracts, professional development plans, and staff feedback surveys. This section describes a leadership evaluation tool developed by the authors: *The Shared Leadership Practices Survey.*

This two-part survey is relatively new. (An exhaustive search of the literature revealed there was no tool that assessed the degree to which managers possessed the new leadership skills necessary for success.) The first part is a 45-item inventory that assists leaders in the self-assessment of their competence in areas such as facilitation, collaboration, coaching, systems thinking, conflict management, and empowerment as well as the degree to which they apply the shared leadership skills necessary for success. An accompanying staff assessment provides another source of information. Each of the items can be used to distinguish those practicing shared leadership from those who are not. Staff members are asked to evaluate their managers' actual practices and the desirability of each practice.

The tools can be used to evaluate the success of leadership training programs, leadership development, and guide the implementation of new partnership structures.

We recommend no less than five randomly selected staff assessments per leader. This gives the leader a snapshot of his or her leadership practices and should stimulate the collection of more feedback and self-exploration. In responding to the 45 items that make up the tool, the person is asked to indicate how characteristic each item was of his or her leadership practices. Staff selected to provide feedback use a second instrument. They are asked not only to evaluate actual leadership practices but also to indicate what they desire from the leader.

The instruments generate three scores for each leader: (1) a self-assessment score, (2) a score representing the staff assessment of actual practices, and (3) a score representing the staff's degree of desire for shared leadership practices. Scores can range from a high of 315 to a low of 45 (the higher the score, the more traditional the leadership practices; the lower the score, the more the leader is demonstrating shared leadership practices). Work is presently being done to identify shared leadership practices along a continuum from novice to expert.

Group and individual scores can be calculated for each of the following: the self-assessment, the staff assessment, and the degree of desire for shared leadership practices. The self-assessment score reflects the beliefs and values of leaders as well as their perception of how well they are practicing shared leadership. The first staff score reflects the staff's actual *experience* of their managers. When survey results are communicated using terms like *feelings* or *perceptions,* managers have a tendency to distance themselves from the feedback. *Experience* is an objective word and suggests that something is working, regardless of the actions being taken. The second staff score is an indicator of staff values and beliefs about leadership practices and therefore can be considered a measure of the workplace culture.

A review of the gaps between each set of scores can be used to help leaders to better understand how they work. The information collected highlights for managers how their perceptions of their practices compare with staff members' actual experience of their leadership and with what staff members desire from leaders. An action planning worksheet is included in the instrument packet to guide interpretation and discussion. Three gaps are important to consider:

1. The difference between the leader's self-assessment and what the staff desire.
2. The difference between the staff's actual experience and what they desire.
3. The difference between the leader's self-assessment and what the staff actually experience.

For example, consider the following set of scores:

Self-assessment: <u>90</u>    Staff Actual: <u>168</u>    Staff Desired: <u>210</u>

Gap 1 suggests there is a great difference between the manager's and the staff's beliefs and values regarding leadership practices. Gathering information about new leadership expectations and dialoguing about what this means for the alignment of staff and manager accountability are in order. Gap 2 imparts both good news and bad news. The bad news is that there are probably experiences, rules, and norms that are impeding the full expression of shared leadership practices.

The good news is that in spite of the obstacles some shared leadership is being experienced by the staff. The tasks called for would include gathering more information about barriers to shared leadership practices and to developing plans for their removal. Gap 3 suggests that the manager needs to develop more competency in the application of shared leadership practices. However, if the staff are asking for more command and control approaches, as reflected in a high desirability score, then workplace interventions must also occur.

Sample items from each instrument are located in the Appendix. For further information about the instrument, please contact the authors: Cathleen Krueger Wilson, 4651 East Palomino Road, Phoenix, AZ 85018 or Tim Porter O'Grady, 1710 Barnesdale Way, NE, Atlanta, GA 30309-2602.

## MAINTENANCE STRATEGIES

By engaging in the dual processes of self-design and personal mastery, leaders can acquire the capacity to not only produce results but also master the knowledge that underpins the strategies used to produce them. Working hard to master something is accompanied by a predominant willingness to understand one's own performance. This understanding is an important maintenance strategy. The predominant maintenance question facing today's manager is "Are my leadership practices balanced with my core principles and a realistic vision of the present reality in my organization?"

The goal of personal mastery is to create a state of "creative tension" between principles, practices, and reality.[21] In order to keep up that creative tension, managers must be constantly searching for barriers to the truth. For example, in one organization a hospital CEO who thought he was creating a learning organization asked his leadership team to bring case examples of mistakes made so that everyone could learn from them. The request was an abysmal failure because managers left the meeting feeling insulted. The CEO did not recognize that his brand of humor was experienced by others as a type of put-down. Another deterrent to honesty occurs when an individual risks expressing an honest feeling and the group or the person listening goes on as if the statement had never been made. The feeling of devaluation experienced in that kind of interaction, particularly if it is normative, has long-term negative consequences for any organization.

When a health care organization is led by managers who pursue personal mastery as a part of their leadership work, the results are astonishing and contagious. There are hospital departments undergoing work redesign where multidisciplinary groups confront challenges that arise with grace, open dialogue, and genuine equality of authority. Emotions are acknowledged and treated with respect. Everyone is afforded real opportunities to work through the disturbing aspects of any changes, and as a result sustained commitment to the new system is achieved.

Dollars are allocated to the growth and development of every group. This means replacing the practice of spending priority dollars on education to meet Joint Commission on Accreditation of Healthcare Organizations' guidelines with expanded support for training that enhances job performance. The organizational philosophy behind this commitment is that people are indeed the key to the successful delivery of quality care.

The more traditional forms of motivation are not in evidence when personal mastery is pursued by leaders. There is a recognition that extrinsic rewards or fear of job loss, for example, are not enough to sustain quality contributions. People will contribute because they want to learn and because the work is connected to personal goals. Finally, there is rarely a time when leaders meet and shake their heads, bemoaning still another failed communication attempt. People are kept informed of their organization's performance in terms of both cost and quality as well as the implications of that performance.[22]

## MORE FEATURES, MORE OPTIONS, AND MORE FLEXIBILITY

Today's organizations need to change fundamentally to succeed in the health care marketplace. The challenge of leaders is to stop focusing their change efforts on what is and engage in the creation of what does not yet exist. True transformation alters the underlying principles, assumptions, and beliefs on which decisions are made. To create structures that support point-of-care decision making and operational independence, leaders must take on the hidden context of their organizations. The past has to be confronted, along with the interpretations for action that are the result of past experiences. This is the only way to see what is possible for the future.[23]

The continuum of care will drive the relationship between providers and patients. Consequently, the critical work of leaders is to engineer a new context for the delivery of patient care. Assumptions about how work should be organized, authority relationships, the degree of control that people have over their work, the flexibility of roles, and the interdependence of stakeholders are key elements of the context in which care is delivered. Creating a new context is exceedingly difficult work, requiring a move away from traditional beliefs about the delivery of care into the unknown. The journey has to begin with the leaders' self-exploration and assessment of their readiness for real transformation.

## REFERENCES

1. E. Hoffer, *The Ordeal of Change* (New York: Doubleday, 1959).
2. M.C. Bateson, *Composing a Life* (New York: Atlantic Monthly Press, 1989), 17.
3. M. Sinetar, *Developing a 21st Century Mind* (New York: Villard Books, 1991), 15.
4. Bateson, *Composing a Life,* 4.
5. P.M. Senge et al., *The Fifth Discipline Fieldbook* (New York: Doubleday-Current Books, 1994), 193–194.
6. R.H. Waterman, J.H. Waterman, B.A. Collard, "Creating a Career Resilient Workforce," *Harvard Business Review* 72, no. 4(1994):87–91.
7. C. Manz, "Self-Leading Work Teams: Moving beyond Self-Management Myths," *Human Relations* 45, no. 11(1992):1119–1140.
8. Ibid., 1125.
9. D. McNally, *Even Eagles Need a Push* (New York: Delacorte Press, 1990), 54.
10. C. Handy, *The Age of Paradox* (Boston: Harvard University Press, 1994), 12.
11. Ibid., 12.
12. Ibid., 27–32.
13. Ibid., 69–74.
14. Sinetar, *Developing a 21st Century Mind,* 31.
15. D. Hall and D. Wecker, *Jump Start Your Brain* (New York: Warner Books, 1995).
16. McNally, *Even Eagles Need a Push,* 73.
17. Ibid., 73–111.
18. Ibid., 149–165.
19. S.R. Covey, *Principle-centered Leadership* (New York: Summit Books, 1991), 48–57.
20. P. Block, *Stewardship* (San Francisco: Berrett-Kohler, 1993), 3–19.
21. Senge et al, *The Fifth Discipline Fieldbook,* 194.
22. Ibid., 219–232.
23. T. Gross, R. Pascale, and A. Athos, "The Reinvention Roller Coaster: Risking the Past for a Powerful Future," *Harvard Business Review* 71 (November–December 1993):97–109.

# Chapter 7

# Building toward Outcomes: From Responsibility to Accountability

On the street of By and By, one arrives at the house of Never.

Cervantes

E
veryone in health care is affected by the transformation currently underway. The challenge is to convert that transformation into real action that leads to desired results.

Results have been included as part of work responsibility for some time.[1] However, the layers of process, including rituals and routines, have often made it difficult to identify the desired results. Now as the workplace and the influences from the environment that affect it act in concert to challenge all processes, every activity is subject to deep analysis.[2] Issues related to what is or is not appropriate in doing work rise to the surface and throw the value of all functions and activities into question.

Every component of the organization is being scrutinized. No job or role is exempt. Functions, activities, content, and expectations are all open to review. What was once safe in the old model might now be unnecessary in the new, and the whole world can begin to look turned upside down.

## NEW NOTIONS FOR A NEW PARADIGM

The whole framework of work has been fundamentally altered. The notion that each job has specific functions and activities that belong to it and have some permanence or stability is no longer true. Actually jobs are disappearing from the workplace. The notion of job is an industrial creation reflecting an age that is quickly passing. The loss is significant.

In the previous age, roles and functions were clear and relatively stable. The content of a job could be fairly precisely defined before a person even accepted it,

> *Outcomes drive all processes. A focus on outcomes is essential to the effective delivery of services. Value is found in the outcomes, not the processes.*

and the functions could be clearly identified. If the person learned to function well and perform the tasks with competence, continued employment was virtually ensured. The job would remain essentially unchanged, except for revisions due to mechanization, the variable most likely to affect the character of the job.

In this new age of technology, jobs as we know them are disappearing. The need for the old type of job no longer exists. The whole nature and function of work and the relationship of the worker to the work are being altered forever. There are several ways in which technology is changing the workplace:

- Computers can do what people used to do. It doesn't make sense to continue to employ people to do what machines can do as well or better.
- Knowledge of concepts is more important than knowledge of tasks. Workers gain knowledge about the character and content of the work in academic settings instead of on-the-job training.
- The location of work is shifting. Increasingly, computer technology is making it possible for workers to do work in a number of different places and yet remain connected through communication technology.
- Computer literacy is essential to success to any role. There are no roles that will not require some level of computer skill.
- The content of work will need to be adjusted continually. There will be no fixed or permanent functions in any role. Adaptability and fluidity will be vital talents for future workers.
- Mobility will become an important part of service provision. As technology makes it easier to provide services outside of traditional service settings, bringing services to consumers will occur more often than bringing the consumers to services.
- The relationships between roles will be more closely assessed. It is the interaction between the parts of the system and the various players that determines how effectively the work is done. An increasing focus on interaction and relationship building will be required of persons and organizations in the future.

Organizations may appear to expect more of their workers over the next two decades. The truth is that they will not expect more but will expect a different set of skills.[3] The new set of skills is based on the refocusing of work from the center of the workplace outward.

- There is increasing dependence on the effectiveness of the decisions of workers.
- More interdependence between the various providers is now required, increasing the need for strong relationships.
- Less direction is provided outside the work site.
- Managers will be more focused on context issues than content issues at work and less willing to parent workers in their decision making.
- There will be continuous learning processes in place to ensure workers adapt to changes and maintain competency.
- More group decision making and interaction will occur in the workplace than previously. Unilateral decision making will decrease dramatically.
- Expectations regarding results are more important than the tasks and functions associated with a job. What happens as a result of the work is vital to the work itself.
- Clearer delineations of expectations for each team member will result from the focus on the point of service.
- The outcomes that each member of a team is held accountable for will be closely tied to the outcomes of the entire team.[4]

## RESPONSIBILITY VERSUS ACCOUNTABILITY

The words *responsibility* and *accountability* are often used interchangeably. Also, definitions are devised that do not get to the core of the difference between the two concepts. The main difference has to do with locus of control rather than content.

### Responsibility

Responsibility, as currently understood, is an industrial age concept. It is typically explicated using the established relationship between employee and employer. Employees have historically been held responsible for performing expected functions within the context of the duties and parameters that defined their work. The content of their responsibility and the expectations regarding the quality of their work have been the prerogative of the employer.[5] It was the obligation of the workers to deliver the quality of work within the parameters provided by the employer.

Workers in the past were also held responsible for complying with the additional requisites of the work defined by the employer. Either direct

> *It is the end of the age of the job. There are no more jobs.*

definition or sanctions imposed by the employer have been used to communicate the appropriateness of specific actions by the workers. The worker's level of compliance as seen through the eyes of the employer determined rewards and advancements.[6]

The problem with this responsibility-based approach is that it fosters a high level of paternalism. The employee-employer relationship is built on the assumption that the employees lack knowledge, investment, and ownership and as a result have to be carefully oriented, observed, managed, and supervised if the employer-defined outcomes are to be achieved. In this framework, the workers are held to perform at the level of excellence through satisfying the manager or owner rather than necessarily achieving excellent outcomes. The *value* of the work is linked to the satisfaction of the manager or owner, whose approval is needed for continued employment, rather than based on the inherent quality of the work.[7]

An additional aspect of responsibility is its historic focus on tasks and functions.[8] Individual workers are responsible for something, almost always something they do, in which case the actions themselves are the focus. The actions are judged appropriate based on the script written for them, and the workers are held to have met their responsibility if their performance of the actions is evaluated as satisfactory.

> *Responsibility concerns the processes of work. Accountability concerns the outcomes of work.*

Responsibility-based job descriptions emphasize tasks and functions. Indeed, a job description is usually a laundry list of functions expected to be performed by the person who holds the job.[9] In linear, assembly-line approaches to work, the processes and their interactions are the focus of the organization. Increasing process efficiency and effectiveness has historically been the chief goal of the management. The tasks imbedded in a process essentially serve as a checklist for compliance, and rewards are tied to the efficacy with which the sum of the tasks are performed as well as the attitudes and attention the employee brings to them. It is no surprise, then, that many employees see their job as a checklist of actions. This perception spawns remarks such as "It's not my job," "That's not in my job description," and "That's extra, so it'll cost you." The rituals and routines of the work process encompass the attention of the employee. They become the framework for work in responsibility-based approaches.

As noted, an employee's work responsibility is employer defined and task based. In addition, the employee, by virtue of having work responsibility, is responsible *to* someone. The superior-subordinate relationship places control for the

> *The relationship between the worker and the manager is often parental. The worker is oriented more toward satisfying the manager than achieving clear outcomes.*

actions in the hands of the superior—the manager. It is the role of the manager to define the activities of and expectations for the work and to assess how well the work is being done and the degree of congruity between the performance of the worker and the expectations for the work. The worker is responsible to the manager for the satisfactory completion of the work, since the responsibility for ensuring that work is complete and satisfactory is, in the final analysis, the manager's. The manager is given this responsibility by the organization. In short, in a traditional industrial-model organization, responsibility is delegated from the top of the hierarchy down to the bottom.

**The Problem with Responsibility**

It is important to recognize when a change is so significant that our current understanding of concepts and processes is no longer adequate. Older notions of work and work relationships prevalent during the industrial age are becoming subject to challenge and closer scrutiny. The emerging new constructs for work identified in Chapters 1 and 3 are having a significant impact on our understanding of work and work relationships. As a result, several concepts related to the workplace are being called into question and new views are beginning to achieve ascendancy:

- Partnership must define the foundations of work relationships both inside and outside the work setting.
- Investment is required of all the players in an organization if it is to thrive in the new world order.
- Competition should be internal rather than external. One competes with one's own standards for customer satisfaction rather than with another organization's behaviors.

> *Workers are now so focused on the content of work as the only measure of its worth that they can no longer define the meaning of the work in light of what it does or does not achieve. They have a process fixation.*

> *The job orientation in the workplace immobilizes the workers by creating fear of loss. Refocusing on roles and relationships is essential to break the impasse.*

- An organization cannot afford to have on board any players who are less than fully committed to its goals.
- Decision making should be shared with those upon whom the decisions depend for their successful implementation.
- The point of service is where resources are preserved or expended and thus where the effectiveness of the organization is determined.
- The organization depends more on the skill of its workers than the workers depend on the organization. Desirable knowledge creates demand and mobility.
- The focus must be on outcomes. That is where the value of all processes is most evident.
- Vertical integration is a temporary precondition for horizontal integration.
- The needs at the point of service drive all the structural requirements of the organization.
- The fewer the levels of management, the more effective the organization. Four or more levels signal the existence of organizational and structural flaws.
- The larger the executive team, the less effective the organization.

**Job and Role Expectations**

Three decades of research on effective structuring along with the emergence of the global paradigm and the information age are changing our views about workers, relationships, and the workplace. These factors have converged to force leadership to rethink the configuration of work, the character of relationships, and the processes intended to achieve organizational effectiveness. They also challenge the delineation of responsibility and our dependence on it as a legitimate construct for work expectations. The new paradigm calls for a more legitimate and effective mechanism for delineating roles and expectations for the players in the workplace (See Table 7-1). It is out of this reality that the concept of accountability emerges to replace the processes associated with responsibility in the workplace.

**Accountability**

Accountability, which differs from responsibility in several important ways, forms a new foundation for performance expectations and the achievement of outcomes (see also Chapter 3). It also forms a foundation for the new type of relation-

**Table 7-1** Jobs versus Roles

| Jobs | Roles |
|------|-------|
| Functional | Expectation oriented |
| Process driven | Outcome driven |
| Delegated | Inherent in role |
| Defined parameters | Fluid and flexible |
| Event based | Continuum focused |
| Content defined | Expectation defined |

ship between workers at all levels in the organization and challenges many of the older notions once associated with responsibility in the workplace.

First, accountability has more to do with results or outcomes than processes. The measure of the processes or the performance of activities is the results achieved.[10] The worker and the other partners first agree on the desired outcomes and then on the processes intended to achieve them. It is this fundamental focus on outcomes that distinguishes accountability from responsibility. And it is this focus that changes everything.[11]

To begin with, it no longer matters what the processes are by themselves independent of their results. Any processes that do not achieve the desired or required outcomes are simply changed or dropped. No worker can define him- or herself simply by the content of the work processes. Indeed, an attachment to processes is actually deleterious to the work and impedes the achievement of its purpose.

> *The tighter the relationship between process and outcome, the more value created by the work.*

In addition, the structure and function of work are altered. Workers can no longer be concerned merely with quality of their performance of tasks or functions. Instead, the outcomes of the work constitute a better measure of its value. It is within this framework that accountability is imbedded. The workers' performance is validated by the intensity of the relationship between processes and results. The tighter the relationship, the more valuable the work. Evaluating the relationship depends on the clarity of the outcomes and the functions and actions that achieved them. It is here where the challenge is greatest for the workers and the workplace. If value is in the outcomes, it is essential for the workers to know the expected outcomes and to judge their work in terms of these expectations. That creates some significant functional alterations in the organization's expectations for the work:

- Work descriptions must not be laundry lists of tasks and functions unrelated to the results.
- Performance evaluation must not focus on compliance with functional requirements as a basis for financial or professional advancement.
- The definition of expectations must not be done unilaterally. Outcomes cannot be achieved unilaterally, and team-based approaches require a different format for outlining expectations and performance.
- Relationships are more important than functions and form the basis for outlining role expectations.
- Job categories should not be defined by their functional content. Indeed, jobs as we know them will disappear and be replaced by more flexible definers such as "role."
- The traditional role of managers is no longer viable. Leadership now has a different meaning and must be exercised in different ways.

A second important difference between accountability and responsibility is that one is accountable *for* rather than responsible *to*. Accountability is generated from within the role rather than transferred from the organization to the role.[12] This arrangement results from the fact that there is an inherent relationship or partnership between those who occupy roles and the organization of which they are a part. They share in the dialogue that defines expectations and outcomes and negotiate with each other in determining what resources are necessary and how the processes should be designed and implemented as they move mutually to achieve the goals to which they have all committed.

> *Where partnership exists, the parties are clear about what they expect of each other. All elements of their roles are negotiated between them; there are no assumptions.*

This interaction demands a different configuration of roles and relationships and a different understanding of the work. Leaders also come to a different understanding of the role they play, which is basically to create a milieu that will result in the dynamic necessary to get to mutually agreed outcomes. Creating this milieu is largely a matter of facilitating interactions and relationships between the workers. The workers must play an essential role in defining the expectations and then give evidence of the part they played in achieving the desired results. The burden of obligation is always on those who are accountable. Creating the proper configuration will be challenging, since it requires a more adult notion of relationships. The checks and balances necessary to make it work consistently must be built into the culture.[13]

Finally, accountability can never be delegated. Each role and the accountability associated with it are essentially connected. In a sense, the role defines the accountability, and the accountability also defines the role. This is reflected in the fact that the person who fills a role plays the major part in determining the content of the accountability. Further, accountability is never defined in isolation. Since outcomes are usually influenced or achieved through the activities of many people, their interaction is as much a part of the content of the accountability of a role as the activities of the particular role. Therefore, the functional components of an accountability-based role are never defined in isolation from its relationship to other roles, are never permanent, and demand the investment of the individual in defining them.

Accountability is dynamic, not stable. Since it is always outcome related, it will be adjusted as the requisites for the desired outcomes change or the evidence indicates a need for adjustment. Since it is dynamic, accountability will accommodate the shifts in the context that influence the activities undertaken within the specified role.[14] More importantly, it will always be adjusted with the full participation of the person who fills the role.

Defining a role based on desired results is not only different from defining a job function but more challenging. It requires that several considerations be taken into account:

- No roles should exist in the organization whose expectations and outcomes are not clearly enumerated.
- Success in a role is defined by what happens as a result of the work rather than the work alone.
- Performance evaluation is an assessment of achievement rather than an assessment of function.

> *Roles must always be adjusted to reflect the variability in expectations and outcomes. There are no permanent functions.*

- The functional content of a role must not be assumed to be permanent. It must change when results demand change.
- Success in a role is measured by the fluidity and flexibility of the individual as well as his or her proficiency.

- Role content is negotiable and is never under the absolute control of any specific member of the work team.
- Accountability entails an obligation to match processes with outcomes, not an obligation to eliminate a focus on means in order to emphasize ends or vice versa.

> *Partnership requires dialogue. The ability to interact continuously is essential for sustaining relationships.*

- Role-specific accountability can be defined by social mandate, law, professional obligations, or other factors. The duty of those with mandated accountability is to ensure that the expected outcomes are clear and that they are achieved.
- The organization should not unilaterally define accountability. If it attempts unilateral definition, it prevents the ownership necessary to obtain the desired results. Outcomes can never be sustained without individual ownership of them.

The application of accountability, with its orientation toward outcomes, requires a whole new way of thinking about work and relationships. The interaction of the players and their relationships are of increasing importance and become the center of leadership activity.

As the continuum of care begins to take center stage in delivery of services, the relationships of the team members and their commitment to the outcomes toward which they are directed determine the success of the organization. It is at the point of service where the health care organization lives its life. Continuous dialogue is essential.[15] Dialogue regarding revenue, costs, integration, and systems can occur in the executive offices of the health care organizations of America. If the health care outcomes that can only be achieved at the point of service are not obtained, all the structuring and financial strategizing in the world will not sustain the system.

Ownership and accountability are essential to the future configuration of roles and activities. Further, they should support the seamless integration of roles throughout the organization. All members of the organization should bend their efforts toward achieving the same outcomes and sharing the same rewards to the extent of their contribution and accountability. As indicated in previous chapters, every role is defined by how it supports the point of service. Therefore, in accountability-based systems, all roles are defined with regard to their potential contribution to the activities along the continuum of care.

In whole systems thinking, the accountability of a role is determined by the role's contribution to the mission and purposes of the organization. The defining of the content of the role should also take into account this contribution. In partnership models, roles are not differentiated by their position on a hierarchical ladder. Rather, they are distinguished by the content of their contribution to achieving the desired outcomes. There should be no secret or arbitrary function or control, and therefore bossism, paternalism, and arbitrary behavior have no place in an accountability-based system. Valid are only those decisions and relationships that facilitate the members' performance of activities and tasks necessary for success. Several components must be in place to make accountability work effectively:

- Team-based approaches to decision making and strategy or activity determination should be in use throughout the organization.
- Continuous quality improvement techniques should be applied by groups or teams as they make and implement decisions.
- The preponderance of decision making must occur at the points of service.
- Each role should be defined within the context of its accountability for achieving desired results.
- Team-based evaluation of performance should replace individual job-based evaluation.
- Rewards should be tied to performance outcomes, not to an individual's level of manual dexterity and functional proficiency.
- The management team should develop an outcomes orientation to leadership and relationships and create the context for effective team-based relationships and performance.
- Acknowledgment should be given to what people do with their skills, not simply to their credentials. Having an ability is no guarantee that it will ever be evidenced.

The transition to accountability-based thinking and structuring will be challenging because there is so much process orientation and functionalism in health care. This is not to suggest that process competence is not important. Skill in performing complex clinical activities is essential to the delivery of the effective treatments and interventions. The providers of services, from professionals to aides, should be as competent as the services require. Competence is a fundamental requisite of work; it is, however, not the purpose of work. It is a foundation, a beginning point. Increasingly, health care work demands a high level of proficiency from individuals prior to their assuming the obligations of their roles. This is because of the greater sophistication of new technologies, which requires individuals to be well trained before using them in the provision of clinical services or the application of interventions.

All processes must be directed toward achieving outcomes. Value is in the results of work, not the activity of work. However, no single activity accomplishes results by itself. Just as it is the concert that produces the music, it is the interaction of the activities that leads to achievement. The attention of the players must be on the relationship between what they do and where it leads.

This means that managers must develop a different orientation if they are to be effective in an accountability-based organizational system. They must focus on role accountability and how their activities facilitate the achievement of outcomes. As mentioned in earlier chapters, the role of managers is significantly different in a point-of-service system, and their accountability requires a different orientation to skill. Since the managers create the context that makes it possible for others to own their work and the decisions that relate to it,[16] they must give up parental roles and process functions and focus on the accountability that belongs specifically to their role.

> **Work relationships are not an end unto themselves; they serve a purpose. They must be founded on a mutual commitment to the outcomes to which they are directed.**

There is a much stronger relationship between managers and teams. A true partnership replaces the older parental and dependent relationship. Everyone is familiar with the role of everyone else. The functional obligations are clear in advance of performance, and there is universal understanding of the activities of each player. Absent are ambiguities of role and function. Management caprice (not common but recurrent) and staff somnolence in decision making are no longer acceptable. The team-based approach to decision rendering, the delineation of areas of accountability and their consequences in advance of performance, and the use of continuous quality techniques for team processing discipline the relationships and interactions. This ensures behaviors that support the outcomes that will be the measure of the efficacy of those behaviors.[17]

Further, there are no secrets. There is no need for them and they serve no one's interests. All elements necessary for the work must be available to those who do the work. Failure to achieve desired outcomes is evidence of an inadequate distribution or use of resources. What is not working must be changed. Results are the measures of process. Every member of the team has an obligation to be frank and open about what is or is not contributing to the achievement of outcomes. The team becomes clear about the issues and is pushed by leaders to dialogue and deal with challenges wherever they may arise.[18] Skills that are necessary for dealing with challenges but are lacking among team members must be made available to them. The organization must become the center of learning. Everyone must pursue learning as a condition of membership and employment. Learning becomes the foundation upon which the organization continues to develop and grow within the context of its service framework.

In accountability-based organizational structures, managers must model the learning experience, including the struggle involved in changing. They must be willing to disclose, experiment, alter past behaviors, address unfinished business, and push the team partners toward circumstances and behaviors that will change their interaction and work processes. They must make it safe to experiment and to risk

> *Real wisdom comes with the recognition that outcomes are achieved through collective enterprise, not through the efforts of any one person.*

so that there are no unilateral work processes that operate at cross-purposes with the team.[19]

The real challenge for everyone is to recognize that nothing is the same as it was. There is a need to mourn the losses and begin to sort through what the forces of change are bringing and how they can be effectively harnessed to create energy for change in every place where work is done. Some will become disadvantaged. They must continue to trust the process and harness the resources that will make learning easier. No one can be granted permission to forget, decline, or sidestep the obligation to deal with the issues and the changes that he or she must confront in his or her own work and relationships.[20]

## LEADERSHIP ACCOUNTABILITY

Building an accountability-based organizational system requires a clear differentiation of the roles in the system. The manager's focus is different from the focus of those who directly provide services to the patients. The manager has a defined obligation to make essential resources available to those who need them. The manager is also responsible for defining the decision framework for the organization and supporting those who make the decisions. The manager should not, however, make decisions for the staff. Supervising the work of the staff is also a waste of energy and resources if the staff are not held accountable for achieving expected outcomes (Exhibit 7-1). If the staff are not held accountable, the manager will continually be doing his or her own work as well as tasks that belong to the staff. This is parenting in its purest form and there is simply no room for it in an accountability-based organizational system.

The manager must be aware of his or her specific accountability if the manager's role is valued. Further, the value of the role must be explicated in terms of the role's relationship to and impact on outcomes. *In an accountability-based organization, no role can be justified that does not have a positive impact on outcomes.* This applies as much to the manager's role as to any other role in the system:

- Providers' roles relate to the work they do and the delivery of services to the patient. Providers are accountable for the *content* of that work.
- The manager's role relates to the resources of the system and their use. The manager is accountable for the *context* of work.
- Contextual accountability encompasses human, fiscal, material, support, and systems processes. These processes form the foundation of the manager's accountability.
- The manager's role includes ensuring that the staff have what they need to provide services to patients.
- The manager does not make unilateral decisions about the content of the providers' work. Providers do not make unilateral decisions about the context or resources for their work.
- All decisions concerning the application of resources and the content of the work are rendered through a team process. Once consensus has been achieved, compliance is required.

**Exhibit 7-1** Individual Accountability

1. Every person owns his or her own efforts.
2. The relationship between people is vital to obtaining outcomes.
3. There is no laying blame for what did not happen.
4. No person engages in unilateral hero behavior.
5. The expectations for each person are clearly enumerated.
6. Individual actions contribute to meeting collective expectations.
7. Performance evaluation focuses on outcomes, not processes.

- The manager's role includes ensuring that the decisions of the team, group, and organization are implemented as decided and that the outcomes agreed to are evaluated systematically to determine whether and to what extent they have been achieved.
- A manager on a work team focuses on the issues that relate to the team's role and helps the team meet its obligation to achieve its objectives. Development of the team and enhancement of its effectiveness are prime areas of concern for the manager.
- The manager sees to it that the team has the resources and the skills to surmount any obstacles, resolve any conflicts, and achieve the desired outcomes.
- The clinical work of the team focuses on patient care. The work of the manager focuses on the milieu within which the work is done. The set of interactions between system and provider, system and community, and system and resources frame the functional accountability of the manager at any place in the system.
- The resources that maintain the linkages between provider systems and support the interactions fall within the accountability of the manager. Horizontal linkage and the negotiation of resources and relationships are fundamental obligations of the leadership role. This does not preclude involvement in or consultation with the team whose role it will be to provide services along the continuum.
- In self-managed work environments, the capability of the work teams to delineate and negotiate relationships, resources, and roles is supported by the leadership. The skill building, support systems, and information necessary for the interactions along the continuum of care form the functional framework for the manager's role.

The significance of this change for the manager is considerable. The move from director and controller to facilitator, coordinator, and integrator is a considerable journey. Managers who are skilled in the industrial style of management (i.e., most managers) will have a challenging time switching to a new set of behaviors. A partnership is different from a parental relationship. When parenting skills have been developed to a high degree, it is difficult to surrender them for behaviors more appropriate for an adult relationship.

Views about workers will also be challenged, including the belief that work will not get done appropriately unless it is supervised and controlled. In addition, building toward collective decision making will challenge many who have become successful unilateral or "hero" decision makers. The claim that group deci-

> *The role of the manager is to create the context for the staff's work. The manager should not be concerned with the content of the staff's work.*

sion making is not fast or effective is a nonvalidated excuse for not doing the work necessary for competent team-based decision making. Favoring unilateral decisions simply because they are quick to make, sacrifices long-term effectiveness for speed.

But what of the content of the manager's role? How can a manager's role be defined without enumerating the functional activities expected of the manager? As noted previously, functions and actions change as the conditions and circumstances demand. Defining them and building a role upon them would be like building a house on sand. A solid foundation upon which the role can be built is accountability for the outcomes. The role description, in this case, would consist of statements of expectations rather than lists of functions.

Unfortunately, leaders have extensive experience defining functions for a job description but substantially less experience defining expectations and accountabilities from the perspective of outcomes. However, that is what they must learn to do. (See also Appendix B.)

It is only through defining the accountability of the role that any relationship between the role and what it produces or impacts can be identified. The value of the role is directly related to its impact on the outcomes of work. The only real evidence of value is the effective and balanced correlation be-

> *Role descriptions, unlike job descriptions, enumerate expectations, not job tasks or functions. It is as important to know what work achieves as to know what the worker does.*

tween cost, quality, and time. It is only by tying the role to that set of variables and evaluating outcomes can its value ever be clearly calculated.

Every role must have an identifiable accountability. However, determining the accountability cannot be done without considering the role's relationship to other roles. Defining accountable roles is generally a team process. Different teams require specific sets of guidelines to identify the accountability essential to their functioning. The assumption that having few levels and layers of management is preferable, and the assumption that the focus of all roles should be on the point of service are the type of guidelines that are applied in determining an individual role's accountability content.

As suggested earlier, the role accountability of the manager should differ radically from the role accountability of staff. Indeed, obligations for the service or clinical work of the staff or team must be excluded from the definition of the accountability of the manager. Including such obligations would risk making the role parental in nature. The manager should be held accountable for work *context* rather than for work content. The definers of context become the framework for defining accountability for the manager's role. Although delineating these parameters for the role of manager may be challenging, it is necessary if the manager is to be a partner rather than a parent.

As indicated earlier, there are five basic areas of accountability—human, fiscal, material, support, and systems resources—that Mintzberg indicates fall squarely within the content of the accountability of the manager's role[21] (see Exhibit 7-2). They are resource driven and focus on context, not content. Each entails specific role obligations that provide the content of the manager's role in various functional levels of the organization.

## Human Resources

Managers have traditionally had the task of providing the right people for the right work in the right place at the right numbers and at the right time. They still have this task. They are accountable for ensuring that staff are available in a balance that is appropriate given the demands and the material resources. This does not mean that a manager unilaterally undertakes all human resource activities. Team-based approaches to operating the human resource system and self-scheduling and human-assigning by staff can be used to coordinate resources and service demands. The role of the manager is to see that such a system is in place and works effectively and that the human resources are appropriate given cost parameters and service demands.

## Fiscal Resources

The creation, management, and evaluation of the use of the fiscal resources of the organization is a central function of managers. The object is to match service operations and goals with the fiscal resources dedicated to achieving the organization's purposes. It is imperative that there be a close relationship between the fiscal resources and the work of the providers. Managers budget dollars but rarely spend them; that is the work of the providers. However, it is still important to make sure

**Exhibit 7-2**  Areas of Management Accountability

- Human resources
  - The right person in the right place
  - Consistent with the budget
  - Matched to clinical need
- Fiscal resources
  - Appropriate financial plan
  - Accurate operational budgets
  - Good monitoring system
  - Good variance analysis and correction
- Material resources
  - Renewable supply system
  - Right supply and equipment for needs
  - Viable capital plan
  - Good variance analysis and correction
- Support structures
  - Empowered environment
  - Problem-solving skills for teams
  - Connection to right resources
  - Form always follows function
- Systems structures
  - Effective information system
  - Good quality control indices
  - Solid linkages with the organization
  - Strong developmental program

fiscal resources are used effectively. The system that addresses this issue and applies and evaluates the use of fiscal resources falls within the accountability of the manager. Here again the manager may work with mechanisms that depend on staff involvement such as cost center budgeting, staff-driven financial plans, staff fiscal control mechanisms, point-of-service cost evaluation, and per subscriber cost parameters. The role of the manager is to ensure that whatever methods are used work well and facilitate the effective use and stewardship of the fiscal resources.

**Material Resources**

Many of the same principles apply to both material resource and fiscal resource management. Ensuring that the providers have what they need to perform their work is essential. Material resource allocation and use techniques can also be staff driven. Capital planning and acquisition processes can be team based and team evaluated. The role of the manager is to ensure that there are appropriate mechanisms to handle material resource issues effectively and without exceeding the parameters provided for the sources.

## Support Resources

Creating a milieu that makes it possible for the staff to be self-directed and deal with clinical and service issues and that empowers the teams to control their relationships and work is part of the support role of the manager. Primary tasks include resolving development issues, enhancing the learning context, providing the tools to problem solve, and providing access to the expert resources of the organization. The manager must be concerned with the competence of the staff in managing their work and the environment of empowerment that pervades the organization. Offering opportunities for empowerment and ensuring a proper and sustainable milieu are of critical importance.

## Systems Resources

Linking all the parts of the system together to facilitate the work is a fundamental task of the manager. Systems resources such as experts, service supports, organizational structure, quality measurement, data collection and generation, outcome measurement, and competence enhancement provide the kind of support necessary to sustain a team's efforts. If the manager is to ensure that the team will continue to function effectively and has the resources it needs, systems information is essential. The manager must make certain the systems data are presented in such a way that they can be understood and are useful. Indeed, the manager's role centers on the generation and interpretation of the information necessary to support the work of the providers. Information from budget data to clinical outcome data can have significant implications for service or care delivery. Accurate and meaningful systems data assist the providers in making the right decisions and validating their work.

Although these areas of accountability represent the main work of managers, they should not be defined in terms of processes (e.g., as lists of functional activities). If accountability is to be tied to outcomes, it must be stated in terms of *outcomes*. The outcomes should be the definers of the functions that lead to them and therefore the language of performance should be constructed in outcome terms.

(See also Appendix B.) Expected outcomes form the foundation of role expectations for every role in the organization. Performance in a role is ascertained by the level of achievement of the outcomes that define the role. Evaluating performance by achievement avoids the need to enumerate a list of the functions and activities that form the work of the role. Role-related functions are widely variable and are dependent on resources, skills, and service requirements. In contrast, the outcomes toward which all clinical activity is directed are relatively invariable.

For the manager, role outcomes relate to the five managerial areas of accountability. The manager has an obligation to abide by the mandates of that accountability as identified by the partners (including the manager). In other words, the manager, in assuming the managerial role, promises to perform in such a way as to meet the expectations for the role. What is to count as evidence of adequate performance is defined by the role, in particular, by the outcomes that are expected to result from the manager's performance.

> *There is no real accountability without consequences. They must be identified at the same time as the accountability. Without them, achievement of desired outcomes simply cannot be sustained.*

In accountability-based approaches, the manager is answerable to all those upon whom his or her role touches. Since the structure emphasizes horizontal relationships, vertical interactions or reporting mechanisms are not adequate. Hierarchical processes do not fit the accountability model, which emphasizes horizontal, adult-to-adult interchanges. For example, the manager typically receives feedback regarding the impact of his or her performance on other players. In general, those who work in the same capacity, those who are affected by the manager's work, and those in related roles should always contribute to the evaluation of the effectiveness of the manager's performance.

In an organization that has self-managed work teams, the work teams are obligated to reach an understanding of how the contextual issues are to be addressed. The accountability for resources must exist somewhere in the organization. The teams must negotiate resource issues and identify the desired outcomes of resource distribution so that performance can be measured against them.

## DEFINING ACCOUNTABILITY

Unlike process-oriented approaches to work definition, accountability approaches focus on expectations. Instead of listing a range of activities, an accountability-based role description lists the expectations for the role. The expectations give the role purpose and shape. In addition, listing the expectations ensures that evaluation of the outcomes will indicate the effectiveness of the means.

Within an area of accountability, those things that act as measures of the expectations or functional delineators of the accountability best define the role. For example, in the case of material resources, one expectation might be stated as follows:

> The unit capital purchase priorities are consistent with the corporate mission
> and purposes, and the amounts do not exceed the allocations available.

The expectation (or desired outcome) with regard to capital expenditures is clearly defined. How to achieve this outcome is left to the manager. (There is a wide variety of approaches to achieving outcomes in a highly decentralized workplace.) It would be expected that the corporate parameters have been negotiated and clarified by the corporate council accountable for setting the parameters. The process should have included the players accountable for achieving the outcome—the consistency of priorities and corporate mission. The manager undertakes whatever actions are necessary to achieve the outcome, and the measure of his or her performance would be the achievement of the outcome within the parameters negotiated. (See also Appendix A.)

Translation of the accountability into specific actions by the manager and the involved teams is part of the process that individualizes the accountability. For example, the dollar amounts, standards of measurement, and potential equipment purchases need to be determined through team dialogue so that point-of-service team members are clear about the constraints and possibilities for capital purchasing. The identification of the functions and activities, however, always belongs to the team members at the point of service. The measure of their performance is delineated in the accountability.

The accountability of a given role should be delineated in a process that includes those who depend on the performance of the role. Delineation of accountability replaces delineation of responsibility and functions. The changeover depends on the implementation of specific reforms in the organization designed to support an accountability framework.

- Shared decision making in the organization exists in all places where decisions are made about the work.
- Persons at all levels of decision making have access to each other and share the accountability for setting direction for the organization.
- Each member's role in the group or team to which he or she belongs is clear to all the other members.

> *Accountability can only be invested in individuals, not groups. The role of the team is to ensure that the accountability of its members is fulfilled and the desired outcomes are achieved.*

- Every role accountability has been integrated with the overall team accountability for outcomes that the team defined.
- Outcomes and organizational and clinical goals are integrated along a value stream that is service friendly and patient based.
- Ownership that emerges from the integrated organizational design operates at all levels and results in the type of excitement that keeps workers and leaders invested in their work and the organization.

Accountability insures the investment of the workers in the clinical processes and the goals of the organization. No longer is the work compartmentalized and farmed out to individuals who are only interested in their own component. Effective functioning results from a high degree of integration and the investment of each and every player in the desired results. It is results that indicate the effectiveness of every aspect of the work.

## BUILDING TOWARD ACCOUNTABILITY

Constructing an accountability approach to defining work is a new challenge. It requires managers to keep focused on the products of work and the outcomes of processes. At every level of the organization, accountability should be the tool that is used to switch the focus of the providers toward outcomes and sustain the organization's commitment to its goals.

As discussed previously, every role in the organization should have defined activities that are directed toward achieving desired results. It is thus essential to be clear about the specific outcomes related to the role and to evaluate team members' functions within the context of those outcomes and indicate their contribution (or lack of it) to the achievement of the outcomes. The role must be described in terms of the outcomes, and the design of the documentation that identifies the role's accountability is critical to enumerating them.

- An integrated system means an integrated approach to the roles of all the players. From mission to performance, all expectations should be defined in accountability or outcome statements.

- All roles are defined within the context of their contribution to the purposes and goals of the organization. Each role's expectations should be related to those purposes and goals.
- It is the role of leadership in accountability-based approaches to facilitate the enumeration and the delineation of functional activities that allow the workers to achieve the outcomes for which they are accountable.
- Routines and activities are defined by the workers in their teams as a response to the teams' accountability for defined outcomes. These functional processes should be kept to the minimum necessary to maintain safety or consistency. Those that have outlived their usefulness should be relinquished.
- There are no hard and fast functional delineations for roles. Workers should adapt processes as the demand for revision arises. The goal is to keep people from creating new and permanent rituals not directly related to the desired outcomes.
- Role descriptions are as brief as the relationship of the roles to outcomes allows. The accountability definers should be all that is contained in role descriptions. There should be no functional definers located in these descriptions, since outcomes are the only determinants of a role's value.
- Role functions reflect the partnership that is characteristic of the horizontal organization. There is no superior-subordinate content in accountability-based roles. A role's potential contribution to achieving mutually agreed outcomes is what determines the functioning of the role.
- Teams always define functional expectations for their members. The definitions reflect the team's accountability and outcomes are adjusted by the team when they do not appear to contribute toward the achievement of the intended outcomes.
- Shared governance strategies support accountability-based designs in that the continuum of accountability is couched in a seamless organizational structure that supports and sustains an accountability-based operational and clinical system.

In accountability-based systems, the consistency and predictability of tasks and functions is not a concern. In fact, since service demand and technology often change, workers need to be adaptable so they can respond appropriately. An organization need only worry about consistency in regard to its mission and

*Defining accountability disciplines work, forcing it to serve its purpose of achieving something measureable toward an outcome that matters.*

purposes. Partners and players may shift as the demand for service is affected by payment, technology, or service changes. The organization must be able to revise its activities quickly to respond to demand adjustments. The accountability of each role must be broad enough to encompass a number of shifts in functions and tasks and still meet the defined obligations.

Control is necessary to maintain discipline in processes. The locus of control, however, is different in accountability-based approaches. Instead of being defined within a hierarchical and superior role, control must be present in the process that measures the achievement of the desired outcomes. Accountability and the measurement of performance become the best control mechanisms. The advantage of using accountability as a control mechanism is that it is imbedded in the work itself.

> *Flexibility is required of teams as they confront the vagaries of health service. The ability to respond quickly to the market is essential to thriving in it.*

In order to avoid the parental temptation to take responsibility for others, it is appropriate to delineate the measures of a role and have the team assess the congruence between the activities of the role and the expectations for the role. This keeps attention focused on the role rather than the person. Team members can look closely at the relationship between the functions and the accountability by assessing the impact of work activities on the achievement of the desired outcomes. This process should occur at all levels of the system.

What this mean is that accountability will cross all roles and units in the organization. It also means that every role must have access to any other role in the organization that could influence its ability to achieve the outcomes for which it is accountable. Decisions made by an operations council will clearly have an impact on a clinical team somewhere along the continuum. This team should be able to access the operations council representative and obtain from the council what it needs to achieve its defined results. This applies to board, administrative, and medical staff roles as well. Further, flexibility in the relationships between teams and the cross-referencing of teams along the continuum will be necessary to ensure the integrity of the processes and the efforts at obtaining desired outcomes.

The rules of partnership apply to the exercise of accountability in a team-driven organization (see Exhibit 7-3). Since accountability is fundamentally individual, not collective, partnership demands that individuals identify for each other what they most need from each other. It is in that framework that partnership takes form. There is a value in the relationship, and it is that value that must be the basis of engagement between the parties. Each person in the partnership agrees to the purposes of the partnership and to work to achieve the outcomes to which the partners are committed.

Clarification of functions and activities is the mutual work of those who have already agreed to the partnership. The relationship has taken form and the

> *Accountability demands clarity and honesty. In the workplace, a new relationship between the partners that is frank and open is a requisite for sustaining commitment.*

activities that exemplify the accountability get enumerated at this point. There is ongoing dialogue because the functions are tenuous and their continuance depends on their contributing to the achievement of the desired outcomes. Dialogue is also the foundation for building and maintaining the relationship over time.

Clarity presumes honesty. If a relationship based on accountability is to work, communication must be unrestrained. Since accountability depends on agreement about roles related to outcomes, all dialogue and exchange of information must reflect the agreement and must be open and honest. Personality dysfunction must not be an impediment to interaction. Individual neediness and the desire for control are no longer acceptable in any relationship since they obstruct communication and damage the relationship. Any communication or personality difficulties must be worked on and resolved early in the process. Otherwise, they will cause serious problems at later, more critical junctures in the partnership. The team must continually evaluate the work and activities of the players and the impact they

**Exhibit 7-3** Team Accountability

- Each team defines for itself the content of its work.
- It has a formal process for conducting its business.
- It has a framework for problem solving.
- It uses total quality management techniques for undertaking work processes.
- It holds its members accountable for their contribution.
- It builds solid relations between members.
- Its members can hold each other accountable for performance.
- It responds flexibly to service or market changes.
- It undertakes continuous measurement of the quality of its work.
- It seeks to obtain value in all of its work.

have on the agreed outcomes. The outcomes become the moderators of the relationship, and all the players must engage in continuous dialogue about how best to achieve them.

Once accord between the partners is obtained, it must be maintained. There should be no backing off from the agreement. There is nothing more disconcerting and harmful than the vacillation of one or more of the partners. The purposes of partnership must be served. If any of the agreements is breached, sabotaged, or adhered to in a lukewarm fashion, there is no chance that intended results can be achieved. A continuing relationship requires a commitment to do whatever is necessary to maintain it (see Exhibit 7-4). Failure to perform requisite activities indicates that the foundations of the relationship are simply not firm enough to sustain it. Testing, monitoring, and validating the underpinnings of the relationship are tasks that belong to the leaders. While the teams are building their relationship and developing ways of working together, the context for their joint work becomes the central concern of the leaders—a concern around which they coalesce their efforts to ensure that the organizational and relationship supports are sufficient to strengthen the partnership.

There should be a clear understanding that once the relationship has been agreed upon, there can be no abdication of the commitment. In this time of quick partnerships and easy relationships, some of the character of partnership and accountability gets lost in the shuffle. If a horizontal agreement is to work, there must be some understanding of its tenure. The time frame for the relationship must be articulated as clearly as the content of the relationship. Of course, reasons can always arise to develop new relationships and terminate those that exist, especially in a business enterprise. Shifts in relationships, however, should be antici-

**Exhibit 7-4** Developing Team Accountability

---

- The teams forming a partnership must learn group process skills essential to deliberation.
- They must focus efforts on defining relationships between members.
- They must develop techniques for problem solving.
- They must foster a commitment among members to resolve interpersonal conflicts.
- They must use continuous quality improvement techniques for solution seeking.
- They must evaluate continuously and redesign or adjust as necessary.

> *Accountability is about building relationships in horizontally integrated systems. Partnership between those who are not related to the same employer is the emerging model of organization.*

pated. While a relationship exists, the parties should be fully committed to build on it and make it work in their mutual best interest.

Increasingly, no one party, hospital, doctor, or corporation can independently sustain the kinds of services that will be necessary to provide a comprehensive continuum of care. Unilateral control is simply not a tenable way to get in place the range of services necessary to create a fully comprehensive continuum of health services. Building partnerships carefully and equitably with people who have the same interest in providing good services along the continuum will be critical to the viability and integrity of the services. One thing often forgotten in this cost-driven phase of health care transformation is that the long-term success of health care systems and providers depends on service and continuity. Cost is only one item in the value chain; quality and service are what sustain health care systems.

> *The vertically integrated ownership model is no longer the sole model of whole systems integration. Horizontally integrated models demand the development of real accountability.*

The desire for dominance and control is strong in the work world. Fierce competition has dominated the consciousness of health care leaders for decades.[22] Now that newer models of work and health service are emerging, the behaviors that were once emulated are now disastrous. Building a partnership requires not only different behaviors but a significantly altered conceptual framework for the work of leadership. There are still gurus who declare the need for a strong boss with a good unilateral vision who can get the troops to do what "he" wants them to do.[23] The problem is that such behavior is not viable in a multifocal, multiservice, multidisciplinary continuum of care system. For one thing, no leader could possess the breadth of knowledge needed to address unilaterally all the issues that arise in a continuum of care system. In addition, a leader in this type of system needs a different set of skills to get disparate and sometimes desperate players "singing off the same sheet of music" and heading in the same direction.[24]

This is not to deny the need for leaders who facilitate, integrate, and coordinate processes and activities defined by those who will perform them. Making sure the system functions in the manner prescribed by its stakeholders through keeping the players on their tasks and providing the necessary support, tools, and follow through is the essence of the leader's role in an accountability-based system.

## OBSTACLES TO IMPLEMENTING

Simply because accountability is the route to effectiveness in a point-of-care delivery system does not mean that people are excited by the notion or willing to start on the journey. For generations in the work world, the parameters of work were measured by a different yardstick. Performance and job function were linked, and work content defined each role. Busyness in doing "things" became the measure of effectiveness, and the amount of things a person could do and the character the person brought to the work constituted the grounds for promotion. Staff are clear about how that world works and how to deal with it in a way that is comfortable and somewhat satisfying to them.[25]

> *The age of "bossism" is over. If we are to build community, we need to join in the effort to build real and sustainable partnerships.*

Now there emerges a new context for work and a new paradigm within which it is defined. Doing a good job, knowing one's functions well, being faithful, and being good at performing activities diminish as contributors to success in the workplace. Workers get upset and confused by the new focus on outcomes, value, accountability, and integration and by the changes in the way work gets done and who does the work. All the work-related expectations are being revised. In addition, the role of the leader and the number of people acting as leaders are changing, thus threatening the stability of the environment.[26] In short, the amount of

> *Just because accountability is now expected of every worker does not mean that every worker is pleased with the change.*

change inherent in the shift to an accountability-based approach can be overwhelming and can cause the following difficulties and challenges:

- Focusing on outcomes instead of processes creates the impression that content of the jobs of various players in the system are being devalued.
- There is fear that not all jobs are required when the content of the work is examined too closely. People are afraid that scrutiny of their work will uncover insufficient substance to justify its continuance.
- People know about their activities and functions. They do not necessarily know about the outcomes or value of their work. Moving from what appears to be the concrete (functions) to the unclear (outcomes) creates concern over the viability of their jobs.
- Job function builds security around the activities of the work; accountability builds role security on the value of the work. The first focuses on the activity, the latter on the results. This is a frightening shift since currently many jobs have no results.
- Workers know what they do very well and are comfortable with this knowledge. Surprisingly, health care workers are often uncertain whether what they do makes a significant contribution to discernible outcomes. Now they must find out, and the truth can be unsettling.
- The shift in focus to outcomes and accountability engenders a way of thinking about work that is 180° from the old perspective. Thinking in new ways about work is challenging and even scary for workers.
- Determining their own obligations and measures of performance is another new challenge for workers. For one thing, they usually lack the necessary skills.
- Movement from separate and individual work structures to a strong dependence on team processes intensifies the relationship between the players. Proximity does not necessarily mean relationship. Building interdependent relationships between team members necessitates confronting issues historically left unaddressed.
- Reaction to accountability is severe when people first understand what it entails. Valuing results means there must be some. When achieving results has not been a job requisite, many will object to the new focus. Investing people in the change will be difficult.
- People generally choose safety over risk. Redefining roles and accountability is a high-risk exercise. Workers will be reticent to take it on. Pushing the players into the process will require real leadership and facilitation skills.
- Leaders themselves are products of the same work history as the workers and they will face the same change challenges. It should not be assumed, for

example, that they have the skills to lead a self-directed work team in an accountability-based system.

Accountability cannot exist without empowerment of the team members.[27] Accountability is always invested in an individual role but is reflective of the expectations for the entire team. The team has an obligation to fulfill the expectations to which it agreed, and each member is accountable for achieving specific outcomes that contribute to their fulfillment.[28] The team assesses its compliance with the expectations and the contribution of each of the members. The interaction between the team and its members is critical to the delineation of accountability and the team's success in complying with the agreed expectations.[29]

- The team defines the role it plays in fulfilling the organization's mission and purposes.
- The team interprets goal expectations or outcome requirements within the context of its own role, focusing on those issues that make up the foundations of it own work expectations.
- The team determines and articulates the role and performance obligations of its members by considering the contribution each member makes toward the achievement of the goals or the performance expectations for each member's role.
- Individual accountability (outcomes) is elucidated in a process involving all team members in order to identify those functions and activities that are directed toward achieving the desired results.
- Team members maintain a dynamic dialogue concerning the team's work and activities as a way of ensuring that all members are moving in the same direction and are acting in a manner consonant with the agreed accountability for their roles.
- The continuous quality improvement focus of the system is manifest in its evaluation of the team's activities and the achievement of the outcomes to which the team is committed.
- The relationship between the accountability and the outcomes becomes the database for determining the efficacy and validity of the functions and activities (processes) of the team members.

In an accountability-based system, mature relationships are demanded if the system is to work. There can be no more approaches to work and organization that protect people from their obligations.[30] Performance must be an element of the relationships between the players. The intensity of the relationships challenges the teams and their members to meet the standards they have set for themselves. The work of the teams must be congruent with the goals of the system and the service or clinical outcomes the teams have accepted as their contribution to the fulfillment of the mission and purposes of the system.[31]

In a continuum of care, the relationships between the players reflect their dependence on each other. When teams converge around their accountability to support the continuum, they bring with them the expectation that each has performed as agreed. When evaluating outcomes and uncovering evidence of broken places in the system, team members are motivated to address their own activities in light of the whole.[32] Since the whole will be affected by performances along the continuum or within the components, all parties will be interested in the corrective adjustments made in the performance of any team or team member.

> *Workers should no longer be protected from the vagaries that affect what they do and how they do it. They must know what limits them and what makes them successful.*

There is an obligation, when focusing on outcomes, not to get stuck in processes. Accountability is always about outcomes, not processes. Processes are simply the means through which outcomes are achieved. The trick for the team is to keep its investment in the outcomes. Members must not become attached to functions or activities. Rather, the effort should be to identify the activities that support the achievement of desired results and to drop the activities that do not. The temptation is to get attached to what one does, and thus it can be threatening to be told to abandon activities even when they are ineffective.

In transitioning toward accountability, the leadership has to deal with the fact that the self-esteem of workers is tied to the expertise they bring to a function or activity. Clearly, expertise is important. Yet, attainment of an effective skill level is a normal expectation, not something to be treated as extraordinary. A normative level of skill in the performance of functions must be defined. This will preclude the use of categories such as "good," "some-

> *No one component of work can fulfill by itself the obligation to bring about sustainable outcomes. It is the aggregate of everyone's actions that achieves desired results.*

> *The goal of team processes is to keep members' eyes on the outcomes. Value is in the achievement of desired outcomes, not in the mere execution of processes.*

what good," "really good," and "excellent." The degree of goodness of a performance is not as important as its effectiveness in helping to achieve intended results.

The assumption that the expertise demonstrated in an individual act is as important as any other factor in rendering service is at best superficial. No expertly performed act by itself engenders a particular outcome. Outcomes are dependent on aggregates of acts.[33] It is the level of fit and the intensity of the relatedness of acts that determine the effectiveness of work. Producing an excellent carburetor for a car engine is wonderful if all the other parts are functioning properly. It will not make a modicum of difference to the driver, however, if all or some of the other parts are defective—the car still will not work. Fit of function and activity in relationship to the whole is more important than the excellence of any one portion of the system or the service. *The goal is global excellence in the entire system.* That can only be achieved through the interaction of the components or teams and their devotion to building the continuum of actions and functions that achieve sustainable outcomes.

The expectations, relationships, and interactions of the teams, members, and services along the continuum constitute the foundation for effectiveness and the framework for fulfilling the accountability imbedded in each role and the expectations of those who depend on the team for their care.

## DIALOGUE AND ACCOUNTABILITY

The effectiveness of the communication between the partners is critical to the ability of a system to change the way it operates.[34] The changes, including radical alteration of roles, are significant enough that they will demand continuous and critical dialogue between all members of the staff. Every person must undergo development. There are no exceptions. The essential task is to create a learning organization.

Mutuality and ownership demand an understanding of the dynamics necessary to obtain and maintain them. They do not happen by accident. Dialogue skills, just like any other skills, must be learned. It should never be assumed that people have them simply because they are disposed by personality and interest to favor interaction over autocracy. Building relationships and fostering continuous interaction takes skill and time. The transformation cannot be achieved without them.

Relationships in a horizontal system are based on equality, increasing the need for genuine dialogue. Conversation between partners becomes the cornerstone of maintaining accountability and facilitating the achievement of desired outcomes. The effectiveness of such conversation depends on the directness and openness of the partners,

> *Dialogue sustains the essential relationships between people and continuously clarifies their interactions to the benefit of those they serve.*

especially in regard to the issue of what can actually be done. There is nothing that impedes the achievement of the results as much as the commitment of one party to something that will not or cannot be accomplished.

Contracting for outcomes strengthens the bond between the parties in a relationship. This is especially true for relationships in the continuum between entities that are allied but not part of the same organization. Within the context of the contract, the accountability and the content of the relationship can be more clearly identified and structured so that all the parties are certain of what is expected of them.

> *The point of dialogue is to expand the frame of reference of the participants so that through their interaction they extend their mutual understanding.*

Just as it is necessary to be frank about the limitations of service, so is it necessary to disclose all influences that might affect the partnership and enhance or reduce the chances of success. In the old competitive market, it was sensible not to lay everything on the table or let the "competition" know what you were thinking or doing. In a partnership, that kind of behavior is suicidal. Complete disclosure means interchanges regarding all the challenges and compromises that must be dealt with as the relationship matures. The teams will have to face the circumstances and conditions of their relationship along the service continuum if barriers and constraints are ever to be addressed directly. Failing to build on the truth impedes the development of trust and impinges on the quality and character of the relationship and ultimately compromises the achievement of agreed outcomes.[35]

There will be substantial dependence on comparative data. If the organizational response to data is not mature and the parties resort to factionalism and blaming, no possible value can be obtained. The data are gathered to evaluate the character and effect of the work and the relationships. Uncovering worthwhile adjustments is itself a step toward enhancing the work of the players. The mature organization responds to the evidence by adjusting whatever needs adjusting so that the processes work better and are more effective in achieving the desired results.

Health care is predominantly relationship based.[36] The work of the providers, mostly professional, is essential to the success of any health care organization. Building in ways to support them in their efforts while critically evaluating the effectiveness of those efforts is absolutely necessary. The value equation suggests that the balance between time, cost, and quality is what sustains the achievement of desired outcomes. New rules, new relationships, and a new context for operating a health care system are demanded in accountability-based approaches. The implementation of accountability-based approaches is perhaps the single most significant shift players involved in the provision of health care services will undergo in the forseeable future.

---

## REFERENCES

1. M. Kerr, E. Rudy, and B. Daly, "Human Response Patterns to Outcomes in the Critically Ill Patient," *Journal of Nursing Quality Assurance* 5, no. 2 (1991): 32–40.
2. R. Kidder, *Shared Values for a Troubled World* (San Francisco: Jossey-Bass, 1994).
3. L. Paine, "Managing for Organizational Integrity," *Harvard Business Review* 72 (1994): 106–117.
4. F. Adams and G. Hansen, *Putting Democracy to Work* (San Francisco: Berrett-Koehler, 1993).
5. W. Bennis, *Beyond Bureaucracy* (San Francisco: Jossey-Bass, 1993).
6. G.E. Pinchot, *The End of Bureaucracy and the Rise of the Intelligent Organization* (San Francisco: Berrett-Koehler, 1994).
7. R. Hallstein, *Memoirs of a Recovering Autocrat* (San Francisco: Berrett-Koehler, 1993).
8. C. Hakim, *We Are All Self-Employed* (San Francisco: Berrett-Koehler, 1994).
9. L. Forsey, V. Cleland, and B. Miller, "Job Descriptions for Differentiated Nursing Practice and Differentiated Pay," *Journal of Nursing Administration* 23, no. 5 (1993): 33–39.
10. K. Nair, *A Higher Standard of Leadership* (San Francisco: Berrett-Koehler, 1994).
11. W. Schutz, *The Human Element: Workers and the Bottom Line* (San Francisco: Jossey-Bass, 1994).
12. T. Porter-O'Grady, *Implementing Shared Governance* (Baltimore: Mosby, 1992).
13. H. Coeling and J. Wilcox, "Steps to Collaboration," *Nursing Administration Quarterly* 18, no. 4 (1994): 44–55.
14. S. Stumpf and J. DeLuca, *Learning to Use What You Already Know* (San Francisco: Berrett-Koehler, 1994).

15. W. Isaacs, "Taking Flight: Dialogue, Collective Thinking, and Organizational Change," *Organizational Dynamics* 22, no. 2 (1993): 24–39.

16. A. Frohman and L. Johnson, *The Middle Management Challenge: Moving from Crisis to Empowerment* (New York: McGraw-Hill, 1992).

17. B. Dumaine, "The New Non-Manager Managers," *Fortune,* April 1993, pp. 80–84.

18. J. Katzenback and D. Smith, *The Wisdom of Teams* (Boston: McKinsey & Co., 1993).

19. M. Graham and M. Lebaron, *The Horizontal Revolution: Guiding the Teaming Takeover* (San Francisco: Jossey-Bass, 1994).

20. K. Myers, "Games Companies Play and How To Stop Them," *Training,* June 1992, pp. 68–70.

21. H. Mintzberg, *Mintzberg on Management* (New York: The Free Press, 1990).

22. G. Beneveniste, *The Twenty-First Century Organization* (San Francisco: Jossey-Bass, 1994).

23. S. Bing, *Crazy Bosses* (New York: Morrow, 1992).

24. C. Elliott, "Leadership without Bosses: Shared Leadership in the Creation of a Health Network," *Healthcare Management Forum* 7, no. 1 (1994): 38–43.

25. B. Posner and L. Rothstein, "Reinventing the Business of Government," *Harvard Business Review* 72 (1994): 133–143.

26. R. Ackoff, *Ackoff's Fables* (New York: Wiley, 1991).

27. P. Block, *The Empowered Manager* (San Francisco: Jossey-Bass, 1991).

28. W. Byham, *Zapp! The Lightening of Empowerment* (New York: Harmony Books, 1991).

29. C. Chowaniec, "Democracy and the Living Organization," *At Work* 3, no. 2 (1994): 17–19.

30. Dumaine, "The New Non-Manager Managers."

31. G. Parker, *Cross-Functional Teams* (San Francisco: Jossey-Bass, 1994).

32. R. Wellins, W. Byham, and J. Wilson, *Empowered Teams* (San Francisco: Jossey-Bass, 1993).

33. P. Kritek, *Negotiating at an Uneven Table* (San Francisco: Berrett-Koehler, 1994).

34. E. Schein, "On Dialogue, Culture, and Organizational Learning," *Organizational Dynamics* 22, no. 2 (1993): 40–51.

35. M. Magnet, "The Truth about the American Worker," *Fortune* 125 no. 9 (1992): 48–65.

36. S. Bunkers, "The Healing Web," part 1, *Nursing and Health Care* 13, no. 2 (1992): 68–73.

# Chapter 8

# The Manager as Learner: The Art and Science of Self-Management

The results are in: Reengineering works—up to a point. The obstacle is management. The only way we are going to deliver on the full promise of reengineering is to start reengineering management—by reengineering ourselves.

James Champy

O rganizations do not act, people do. It follows that organizations will truly change only when people change, especially the management group. It is the management group that sets the context in which *all* work unfolds. The way in which work is defined, the degree of judgment and control people have over their work, the technology employed, the work systems in place, and the organization's culture are shaped by the values, attitudes, and the behaviors of those who occupy leadership positions. It can no longer be ignored that success or failure in these formidable times is the direct result of the manner in which individuals operationalize the management role. Even the authors of a watershed work on re-engineering report that re-engineering efforts are seriously compromised or fail altogether when the management group does not change as well.[1]

The acquisition of new leadership competencies will occur only if a carefully designed and executed program for leadership development is instituted. All too often leadership development is at the bottom of the educational priority list. The Joint Commission on Accreditation of Healthcare Organizations, standards, other mandated educational activities, new clinical knowledge and skill acquisition, and identified corrective education seem to supersede the development of managers. Today's challenging environment demands that health care organizations invest in effective leadership development programs so that individuals are supported in the obtaining of the new competencies necessary for success.

This chapter describes the philosophy, the methodology, and some of the content of a leadership development program for practicing health care managers that has been successfully instituted in health care organizations across the country. The requirements for effective leadership development programs, the unique characteristics of managers as students, new training methodologies, and the key skills developed through participation in the program will be outlined in the pages to follow. Actual training exercises can be found in the Appendix.

## BEYOND SURVIVAL: SUCCESS IN THE TWENTY-FIRST CENTURY BUSINESS ENVIRONMENT

The leadership role in health care is being redefined in order to meet the demands of the future. The twenty-first century will see greater global competition and a purposeful flattening of organizations to enhance partnerships. Increasingly, health care leaders are recognizing that success will come from interrelated, interdependent activities. As health care organizations change from being stand-alone facilities into integrated delivery systems, the focus of operations will shift from departmental quarterly performance to systemwide long-term strategies.

More enlightened definitions of the stakeholders will require health care managers to develop greater intercultural understanding along with a certain political sophistication. Furthermore, managers must become proactively innovative. They must maintain current operations while at the same time implementing dramatically new approaches to the delivery of care. Maintaining the old and implementing the new at the same time takes a fine-tuned flexibility and an ability to think in a highly strategic manner.

A sensitive concern for the customer is resulting in more responsible, flexible, and ethical approaches to meeting stakeholders' needs. Management decision-making activities are shifting from a pure numbers approach to a continuous improvement approach that involves examining the content and the processes of care delivery. Suddenly, a qualitative approach to problem solving is gaining acceptance as a means of identifying opportunities for improvement.

Core competencies are being defined by organizations. This means that resources and energies must be realigned to support those things that are done well while discarding programs and activities that are not. Managers can no longer direct tasks but must lead in both the process and the content of care delivery. Discarding a fragmented ineffective policy is not enough. Instead, managers must address the fragmenting mindsets and behaviors that produced the policy in the first place. If these are not addressed and changed, they will produce a new policy or program that has similar flaws.

For example, in one multihospital system, there had been little sharing of resources for staffing beyond the occasional floating between hospitals. Each hospital had its own set of policies for staffing and a separate administrative structure. Contract labor expenditures were costing the system a fortune. Attempts by each institution to change staffing policies in order to reduce costs proved ineffective. It was not until managers recognized that the staffing offices were not thinking or acting as an integrated whole that a solution was reached. All of the staffing offices were merged under one manager, who traveled from site to site and trained the staffing office personnel in whole systems staffing.

## NEW ORGANIZATIONAL FORMS AND LEADERSHIP COMPETENCIES

The evolution of new organizational forms will require a certain entrepreneurial freedom, with self-directed units linked through information networks rather than corporate offices. Consequently, the managers will need to apply a toolbox of strong new leadership skills, such as alliance building, systems thinking, principled negotiation, team building, and group facilitation. The old win-lose model of problem solving and competition is no longer practical.

Yet competition is promoted over collaboration in the professional schools preparing today's health care managers. Teaching methods still center on individual learning and academic performance. It should come as no surprise that this tradition continues in the application of management techniques

> *If one is not compromising then one probably has no allies!*
> Charles Handy
> The Age of Paradox

such as management by objectives, individual performance appraisal, and one-on-one supervision. Traditional managers do not see groups, they only see the individuals within groups. Not only do traditional methods of managing run contrary to the team-based models of organization, but they are increasingly difficult to sustain as managers assume broader spans of control.

Health care organizations are being increasingly restructured around teams. This restructuring is based on the fact that most of the work in health care organizations is performed by groups of people. As members of work teams, individuals end up with far greater knowledge and a better understanding of patient care needs than if they worked independently. When organized and developed effectively, multidisciplinary teams of caregivers will optimize the quality of care, and the members will be more satisfied with their work. Unfortunately, the traditional command and control model of management is not effective with teams. A certain synergy or coming together in concert is needed for work groups to impact patient outcomes positively. If the managers try to meet the challenges of leading and motivating work groups in traditional ways, the workers will continue to solve interconnected problems in a disconnected manner.

In the integrated delivery systems of the twenty-first century, managers will need to become adept at stimulating the contribution of the whole person to the delivery of care. An interesting paradox is that working in a team also means that members must not limit their focus to just their own contributions but to the whole system and the impact of each member's work on the work of others. Creating conditions that release the group's and each individual's potential is essential when leading and developing a team. Whole systems thinking and strong facilitation skills have never before been in such demand.

The new business paradigm for health care organizations emphasizes the optimization of social and technical aspects into organization and work design; views people as scarce resources; requires the self-management of departments and teams; demands participation and involvement from everyone in the organization; integrates individual and social purposes, including dignity, meaning, and community; and recognizes that the bottom line is directly related to the workers' willingness to produce (commitment). The new requirements are quickly making the traditional skills of managers obsolete and are challenging staff leaders new to participation in organizational decision making. Both managers and staff leaders need the opportunity to develop, practice, and maintain new leadership competencies.

## ANTICIPATING THE FUTURE

There are several scenarios that could confront practitioners of health care management in the future. Managers may find themselves working in a strongly divided health care environment, beset with insular, reactive, and focused interests. This may happen if their organizations fail to develop the networks and alliances necessary for success. In this scenario, managers will need to apply strong interpersonal skills to maintain morale and to convince local, state, and national governments of the need for their services. They will also need to be flexible and innovative in order to achieve cost-effectiveness.

> *The new health care management paradigm demands a finely honed interpersonal adeptness.*

Another possibility is that there will be a continuation of today's volatile growth, with sharp swings in performance. The responsive creation of "lean and mean" organizational structures, purposeful risk-taking, and real innovation would be necessary in order to capture new opportunities for service delivery. In this scenario, managers will only be successful if they apply finely tuned people development skills, such as coaching and facilitation. Their staff, in order to remain productive, will need leaders who can support individuals and groups through radical change and also through the ethical dilemmas that come with increased competition.

In the best scenario, the health care environment would be characterized by solid growth and partial stability after a period of considerable delivery system restructuring. If this occurs, managers will be challenged to apply the full range of new leadership skills in developing and maintaining complex partnerships, inculcating mission and vision in a diverse workforce, creating and working with unusual contractual arrangements, and utilizing a higher level of strategic thinking.[2]

## NEW COMPETENCIES

Managers have a tremendous impact in any organization. Innovation will fail without good management. The most desired organizational outcomes will remain unattainable unless managers identify, acquire, and apply the necessary resources. No matter what the conditions of the business environment, the general task of management remains constant: to create the conditions for joint performance through promulgating common values, instituting the right structure, and developing staff. However, the way in which this task is accomplished must change because the workforce consists of highly educated knowledge workers instead of unskilled workers.[3] The challenge for an information-based organization delivering health care is to define just what the appropriate management structure needs to be. Who will be the managers? What will be their role and function? Where will these leaders come from and how will they be prepared? Exhibit 8-1 contains a set of managerial competencies for the twenty-first century that various management theorists have identified.

### Management and the Learning Organization

Senge suggests that contemporary managers will respond to the demands of the new business environment by developing competence in five specific domains, including systems thinking, personal mastery, mental models, shared visioning, and team learning. The skillful application of these competencies will produce organizations capable of continuous learning.[4]

**Exhibit 8-1**  New Competencies for Health Care Managers

*Senge*
- Systems thinking
- Personal mastery
- Mental modeling
- Shared visioning
- Team learning

*Champy*
- Association
- Collaboration
- Communication
- Mobilization

*Drucker*
- Coach
- Technologist
- Visionary
- Facilitator

*Systems thinking* allows managers to see the interconnectedness of everything and to work purposefully to eradicate those structures and processes that produce fragmentation in the delivery of care.

*Personal mastery* is addressed in greater detail in Chapter 6. For managers, it is a lifelong creative process of self-examination. Managers who pursue personal mastery (1) engage in continual values clarification in order to know what is truly important at the time and (2) attempt to see the current reality as it really is so that needed professional development can occur. New models of care delivery, along with uncertain outcomes, unanticipated constraints in the access to care, and complex ethical dilemmas, demand managers who can clarify their values and then guide action to ensure quality. The pursuit of personal mastery simply expands the opportunities for producing those results for which managers

> ### The most difficult problem ahead is defining the management structure and the preparation, the testing and the succession of top managers.
>
> **Peter Drucker**
> **The New Realities**

are held accountable because it confronts them with both the positive and the negative consequences of their actions.

*Mental modeling* accompanies the reflection and inquiry of systems thinking. It utilizes a set of tools that help individuals and groups to identify the unique way in which they have organized their knowledge, values, and perceptions as guides to action. Mental models explain why people who work in two organizations within the same system see a situation differently; they have simply paid attention to different cues. Since mental models are usually unconscious, managers help staff to make them explicit and then judge their soundness. This process allows for deeper understanding of the implications of different or flawed models, leading to the resolution of conflict or the reduction of resistance to change.

*Shared visioning* helps managers to bridge the vast networks of integrated systems by designing processes at every level and for every role. People can then articulate what really matters to them knowing they will be heard—and not only by their coworkers and colleagues but by top management as well. These processes will produce the shared meaning and commitment to action so necessary for effective action.

Finally, *team learning* is based on the recognition that an important management accountability is managing intelligence. Team learning is not the same as team building. It is creating the opportunities for people to learn collectively and to share knowledge and intellectual abilities. As the most complex of Senge's five domains, team learning involves looking outside oneself or one's reference group in order to develop new knowledge or to link with the intelligence of others.

### Management and Re-engineering

Champy echoes Senge's thesis, challenging managers to replace outdated practices with association, collaboration, communication, and mobilization.[5] In the complex process of redesigning quality care, no one should be conceived of as acting alone in doing his or her work.

*Association* is reflected in the mindset of managers who see every person as an associate and create a culture in which "they" have become "we." Re-engineering efforts that only change the name of employees to associates or partners are not enough.

*Collaboration* encompasses skills in recognizing and acting upon opportunities for partnership. It is based on the principle that partnerships are critical to the accomplishment of objectives and that effective processes for the choosing, judging, and rewarding partnerships must be developed and maintained.

*Communication* has always been the hallmark of competent managers. Managers must be able to translate the meaning of the specific values and behaviors that their enterprises need in order to move forward. The teaching, doing, and living of these values and behaviors is also an important part of communication competence.

*Mobilization* is more than spurring people to action. The turbulent health care marketplace requires rapid responses to suddenly changing circumstances. Quick responses will only occur if the managers are adept at making their organizations and the people who work in them understand what needs to be re-engineered. Understanding leads to accepting what needs to happen in order to respond to the environment in an effective way. Mobilization cannot occur without teaching people how to abandon a narrow specialty focus and instead think critically about their experiences, share observations, and then reach joint conclusions. This is the work of team learning.

## Management and the New Economic Realities

Drucker, in his discussions of the new realities of the workplace, describes management as a liberal art. The new manager must embrace innovation while providing the stability of structure. Management is not only a bag of techniques or analytical tools but also a technology and an art. As a *technologist*, the manager purposefully uses technical tools, including those of project management, consultation, information sciences, and fiscal administration.

The new manager must also be a *coach*, continually looking for opportunities for joint performance, tapping into culture, experience, and tradition in order to stimulate commitment and action.

As a *visionary* for his or her organization, the manager will create opportunities for the joint setting of patient care objectives. Not only will people help to set these objectives, but the processes used will ensure that organizational objectives are tied to individual goals and thus have real meaning.

As a *facilitator*, the manager must help his or her organization attain its goals. The manager must develop effective facilitation skills, providing the means for people to identify the true purpose of their work, communicate this effectively to others, and identify when they need to ask for help.[6] The knowledge and skills involved in adept facilitation enables individuals and groups to move through processes that allow them to accomplish their work.

*Merriam Websters' Collegiate Dictionary* defines *competent* as "having requisite or adequate ability or qualities. . . . having the capacity to function or develop in a particular way."[7] The competent manager will have gained not only new requisite knowledge, self-knowledge, and the wisdom of experience but the capacity to apply and act on that knowledge in the pursuit of organizational goals.

## KNOWLEDGE FOR ACTION

It is critical, when considering investment in a formalized leadership development program, to ascertain exactly what training can do and what it cannot do. Organizations suffer as much from ineffective training as they do from the absence of training. Expectations and outcomes must be clearly defined at the outset. One expectation is patently clear: the knowledge gained from participation in leadership development programs must be demonstrated in the actions of the managers.

> *Although managers are very skilled in identifying what the staff need to do to change, they are less capable in identifying their own needs.*

Leaders in a health care organization who are not provided with the opportunity to learn and practice new behaviors will not be able to contribute to the success of the organization. Without selected strategies for leadership development, the leaders will fail to build the necessary structures and processes that link the professional workers to the processes of care delivery. Instead, they will continue to use the command and control model of the past. Compliance may be achieved but not the commitment vital to surviving the stress of restructuring.

Without a formal timeout to develop or strengthen new leadership skills, managers will continue to struggle with unrealistic burdens. They may persist in trying to be in control of everything and to intervene compulsively at all levels of the organization. This will be increasingly difficult as their numbers are reduced and their workloads increased as a result of restructuring efforts.

There is not a health care leader anywhere who would not agree that new ways of managing are desirable. However, just ask a group of managers how these ideas will actually be translated in their own workplace—how they will "walk the talk." What will be different?

> *Leadership development programs that exist in isolation of the norms, expectations, and the assigned leadership accountability of a particular organization produce, at best, only short-term cosmetic effects.*

What will they do more of? What behaviors need to stop? How will it be verified that antiquated management practices have been truly abandoned? How will the managers get from the old way of working to the new way? Are there programs or policies or processes that need to be replaced? Although the managers may be aware of new leadership competencies, they will likely have little practical knowledge about how to actually perform in a new way.

> *The transfer of learning to real-time action may be embarrassing or threatening for managers because application requires substantive change.*

In addition, managers' application of new knowledge and skills in the health care workplace can be defeated by organizational defenses. Some managers may assume the theory espoused is inconsistent with the way things really work or even refuse to consider the possibility that it is accurate.[8] Some may hesitate to act in a different way because they suspect that the new behaviors are not really supported. If by chance new skills are tested, errors in their acquisition and the application may not be detected because of defensive routines. When organizational defenses are unyielding, leadership development will not produce the desired results.

Managers who are honestly interested in developing new skills often have to stumble on their way alone. Management development activities in their organization may be nonexistent or consist of annual or biannual programs on trendy topics provided by the latest business guru. All too often, managers have difficulty operationalizing new ideas into their own practices because their thoughts are a mishmash of personal and formal observations, half-recalled ideas from their readings, or flashes of insight gained during a particularly inspiring talk.

Sometimes training is provided as a means of looking for a "quick fix" for identified inadequacies, addressing remediation issues in targeted groups, or rewarding workers during a difficult period. These approaches do not produce sustained behavior change. To assist managers in the acquisition of practical knowledge, a corporate-wide program encompassing *specific cathartic experiences* must be carefully designed and implemented. For example, one organization incorporated sociodramas into their coaching workshops. Participants were given coaching scenarios to role-play on a stage in front of their peers. As each case was dramatized, the entire group critiqued the performance, including the actions of the manager, the response of the employee, the conditions in which the coaching occurred, and so on. Participation in the dramas and the critiques was a cornerstone learning experience for this particular management team.

The foundational work in planning a leadership program begins with a key set of questions that must be asked and answered by those charged with planning a leadership development program (see Exhibit 8-2).

*The combination of re-engineering efforts, downsizing, and corporate restructuring can leave an organization with a cadre of survivors who are reluctant to take risks or innovate.*

Real learning is intimately connected to action. The successful implementation of new leadership behaviors requires a systematic and planned approach. At the outset, three critical issues must be resolved: meaning, definition, and measurement. Without resolving these issues, any attempts at education for the purposes of behavior change will remain pure rhetoric.

## Meaning

The first issue is one of meaning. *Why should managers change how they operationalize their role?* The answer may be initiative driven or simply a response to the changing health care scene. Regardless of whether shared governance, patient-focused care, or systems integration is the type of initiative, clear definitions of the organization's goals must be articulated in such a way that they are easy for managers to act on.

It is evident that health care manager work is changing. Are the incumbents ready to embrace these changes? In the majority of cases, they are not. Without an

**Exhibit 8-2** Foundations of an Effective Leadership Development Program

- What is happening that demands that managers change their practices?
- How does the application of new leadership skills contribute to the organization's achievement of its goals?
- What specific actions are required from managers? Which practices should continue and which should stop?
- How will the rate of learning and progress in the application of new competencies be measured?
- What opportunities will there be for the development of new competencies?
- How will the application of new practices be rewarded?
- What will the consequences be of choosing not to develop new leadership competencies?

understanding of the revisions needed, they enter leadership development programs wary of broader accountability and unclear about just what their new role and skills should be. The rationale for change must be clearly and repeatedly articulated by the top leaders in the organization and by each manager's own supervisor.

## Management and Leadership Practices

The second issue concerns management and leadership. *Which management practices should continue and which should stop?* Leadership development programs will not produce the desired behavioral changes outside the context of actual organizational behavior. The transformation of knowledge into action will come only when top leadership demands that learning is applied in the continual examination and revision of management policies, procedures, and operations.

For example, in one organization a nurse executive espoused his support for leadership development but rarely attended the programs himself. He loved new ideas and perceived himself to be on the cutting edge of nursing administration. He prided himself as a people developer but failed to provide his team with the opportunities to practice what they were learning. Although participants in the leadership development program identified organizational practices that were outdated, there was rarely any attempt to change them. If there was an attempt to change, it was half-hearted and sometimes unknowingly squashed by the nurse executive. The development program ended on an unsatisfactory note, with everyone, including the trainer, unhappy with the lack of real behavior change.

## The Rate of Learning and the Level of Application

The third issue concerns measurement. *How will progress be evaluated? What tools or strategies will be applied to assess the rate of learning and level of its application to managerial work?* Measurement is critical to the success of development programs because managers, for many reasons, differ in their approach to such cornerstone activities as motivating people and acquiring and deploying resources. Sometimes the difference is simply a matter of different technical skills or experience. Other times managerial strategies are influenced by hidden agendas such as political gain or the desire to act in accord with perceived norms in the management group. In addition, the manner in which individuals fulfill their leadership accountability may be affected by how practices were modeled by a respected mentor. In the saddest instance, a person may simply not fit the management role and may suffer from a lack of honest feedback because no one has the courage to address the problem. Unless the accountability system is congruent with the competencies being promoted in the leadership development program, skill-based, political, and relationship-related issues will not be recognized and treated as the real barriers to actual behavior change that they are.

Clearly, any successful management development program must operate within the context of the managers' performance frame of reference. Accountability systems that support the acquisition and application of new leadership competencies have many elements. Job descriptions and performance reviews are examined and modified in order to emphasize the new skills. A timeline for holding individuals accountable for practicing new skills, via performance review, will be determined early on. The managers' supervisors will also participate in the development program so that opportunities for practice can be identified in supervisory meetings. The executive team models the new behaviors whenever there is an opportunity, including their own learning and practice attempts. The development and the implementation of a strong leadership development program must garner the same commitment as any other strategic initiative embraced by the organization.

Real learning entails action change. Without accountability and reward systems tied to the leadership development program, the intrinsic and extrinsic motivation needed for change will not be experienced by most of the participants. (The rare exceptions are the natural learners and innovators who exist in every organization.)

For example, one executive team implementing a dramatically different organizational structure could never manage to find the time to identify the behavioral changes it expected to see in managers. Actually, an insufficiency of dedicated time was a characteristic of the team's work in general, which eventually led to failure of the restructuring attempt. Participants were mandated to attend the leadership development program. However, the level of learning was superficial. It was apparent in the course of training sessions that the only place new competencies were being applied

> *Crisis management and shared leadership do not work together . . . ever.*

was the workshops. In fact, the executive team continued to operate in ways that prevented participants from applying new skills to their work. A predominant activity in the organization was crisis management. This prevented managers from fostering participation, engaging groups in dialogue about the meaning of the drastic change, and coaching key groups in self-management (not to mention examining their own management practices). It was apparent that the participants did not feel supported in even taking the time to attend the program. They viewed the members of the executive team as people who talked the new leadership language but repeatedly found excuses why command and control decisions had to continue. The leadership development program eventually was ended.

Contrast this experience to that of an organization where the leadership group conducted a baseline evaluation of each manager's skill set prior to the start of its leadership development program and did another evaluation at the end of the program. Individual feedback sessions were provided for each manager in order to develop a continuing development plan. Another organization arranged for "learning labs" to continue after the leadership development program had finished. These were the actual training groups from the leadership development workshops, which now met once a month for reinforcement of principles and problem solving. In a similar vein, companies like Boeing of Portland and ESCO Steel use "executive coaches" who function like personal trainers. Executives are assisted in doing more of what they need to do and doing less of what is ineffective. Interpersonal skills, rather than technical expertise, are the focus.[9]

The quality of personal management behavior is the result of a complex interaction between individual competencies, knowledge and experience, personal traits, and attitudes about work. Failure to recognize this complexity can result in the provision of management development programs that are irrelevant, poorly defined, and deficient in resources. The most common reasons why management development programs fail are indicated in Figure 8-1.

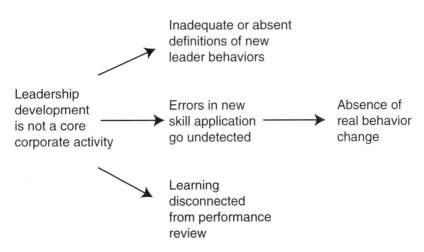

**Figure 8-1** Why Leadership Development Programs Fail

## CREATING A QUALITY LEARNING EXPERIENCE

### The Manager as Student

At least one year needs to be devoted to the development of new managerial knowledge and skills. This can be achieved through a leadership development program structured around monthly, full-day workshops, with homework and practice in between sessions. During the course of the program, some organizational practices may be identified as obstacles and changed in order to support new practices. However, these changes are most likely only the tip of the iceberg. In order for managerial practices to truly change, the leadership development program should be followed by the systematic and in-depth examination of all systems, practices, and procedures for their impact on manager attitudes and behavior.

> *Managers do not come to class with a clean slate. There is undoing and doing that must occur.*

The leadership development program must be tailored to managers' unique characteristics as learners. Most health care managers are experienced and generally successful people in their organizations. They therefore find it difficult to return to the role of learner. For one thing, they are not in the habit of formulating and expressing tentative judgments about what they are learning. In fact, managers have been expected always to have the answers. The design of learning experiences must take this fact into consideration and allow for practice in sharing incomplete or half-formed ideas.

Unfortunately, managers do not come to the learning experience with a clean slate. They will possess preconceived ideas and strong emotions about many of the issues raised in the development program. Every learning experience must challenge the manager to reorganize what is understood and what is felt. This can be accomplished in several ways. First, have each learning group keep a flip chart taped to the wall on which managers can record the key things they have learned. Have them do this after every significant exercise. Second, at the end of the day have each participant articulate aloud, in front of the group, what key ideas, concepts, or experiences will be taken back to the workplace for application. This not only assists with the reorganization and application of new knowledge but also develops comfort with team learning.

Assuming the role of learner is difficult for managers because participation entails changes in managerial practices. The prospect of making changes is at best anxiety producing and at worst immobilizing. Managers must be able to attend the learning sessions free from blocking, tension, and distractions in order to learn effectively. If beepers are going off, phone calls are being taken, or intense meetings are scheduled just prior to the workshop, real learning will doubtlessly be compromised. It is essential that every workshop begin with a warm-up exercise that helps the learners leave behind distractions and focus on the work ahead.

As adult learners, managers are self-directed. They are aware of their specific learning needs. As pragmatic problem solvers, they learn more effectively through experiences that allow them to apply what they have learned immediately. Training workshops thus need to be fast paced. The teaching needs to be a particular blend of brief lecturettes interspersed with experiential activities that afford the opportunity to practice concepts as they are introduced. Inner-group/outer-group exercises, videotaping, simulations, case analyses, and exercises in which outcomes are produced using the new skills are examples of effective learning methods. However, be cautious in using games and role-playing. Both approaches are experienced by managers as far removed from the real world and can lead to the rejection of the knowledge that the exercises are designed to reinforce.

## Trainer Expertise

Management development programs must not only be topic sensitive but also produce opportunities for team building and addressing cultural barriers to the adoption of new behaviors. For example, a program on empowerment raised real issues in one group of managers, who discovered they did not really know why the organization had selected a shared governance model. The trainer dropped the agenda for a time and explored several questions with the group. How was shared governance being supported in the organization? Was there a clear link between the mission and objectives of the organization and shared governance? When it was discovered that no link existed, the program participants used their learning groups to develop a link. The trainer then used the experience to teach how a sense of purpose and mission is empowering. In another organization, radical restructuring had left significant confusion about priorities. In the course of teaching systems thinking, this confusion was identified as a real-world issue and used by the trainer as a mindmapping problem. The process helped the leadership group to identify its priorities as well as a model with five key priorities that are always included in every project.

## Recognizing and Solving Learning Problems

There are some particular motivational problems that may surface in management groups. There may be anxiety about testing new ideas and skills because they

254 THE LEADERSHIP REVOLUTION IN HEALTH CARE

deviate from the accepted norms in the management group. This anxiety seems to dissipate with time and experience as trust builds within the learning group. If it does not, the trainer is obligated to point out managerial group norms that interfere with the application of new practices.

Some participants may not feel that the training was their idea but something forced on them by higher-level executives. If this is the case, the commitment of the necessary time is done grudgingly and with resentment. This obstacle to learning can be prevented as the development program is being planned by including the management group in the actual planning and emphasizing their accountability as continuous learners.

When managers are put in a position of sharing what they understand and demonstrating how to do something new, they experience a certain vulnerability. Depending on the degree of competition in the leadership group, this vulnerability can create learning problems. If not addressed in the course of the program, managers will retreat into forms of self-defense, such as expressing cynicism about what is being taught, telling themselves that the trainer is oversimplifying the reality of management work, or criticizing the exercise instead of focusing on their own behavior.

Several strategies can be applied by the trainer to overcome defensiveness. These include having each learning group develop guidelines that describe how they will treat each other during the course of the leadership development program. A sample can be found in the Appendix. Also, whenever defensiveness appears, the trainer needs to determine whether it is being expressed because of the needs of the individual or the behavior of the group. If defensiveness is occurring because of group behaviors, the training agenda must be temporarily dropped. Actions taken need to focus on providing support, dispelling fears, and identifying negative peer pressure.

> *In order for real learning to occur, the realities of job security must be confronted.*

Especially difficult to deal with are the hidden agendas unrelated to the educational agenda. Is the timing of the leadership development anticipatory of future needs, concurrent with a major change, or reactive because of an identified problem? The latter timing creates certain learning problems because managers may feel as though they are being sent to training for having failed. Another outcome from reactive timing is mere compliance, with no real intention to change.

Learning problems also occur when managers see their involvement in leadership development as a sure-fire indication that either their jobs are disappearing or really changing. For some people, this awareness is a real surprise. A few will look forward to the change, but the majority will struggle with job security issues during training. These individuals will be as excited at the workshops as they are at a funeral. Their participation will be focused on proving the trainer wrong or debating whether practice should change at all. Individual coaching and support outside of the formal workshops must be pursued with these individuals.

**Program Evaluation for Continuous Improvement**

Training for change demands a significant allocation of human, material, and financial resources. An evaluation model based on operational results must be implemented after review and input from key organization leaders and program participants. The evaluation model should include a customized combination of methodologies that may include subjective and objective evaluation, focus groups, ratings by others, and internal or external outcome evaluation.

A standardized assessment tool developed by the authors is described in Chapter 6. When this tool is used for program evaluation, an analysis of staff and manager perceptions about new managerial practices will determine if practical knowledge was indeed obtained.

Good evaluation information can be used to (1) provide qualitative and quantitative information to be used in assessing the outcomes of training, (2) give feedback to participants about their own development so they can use it in personal career planning, and (3) develop an organizational baseline for new leadership behaviors in order to guide their ongoing development and maintenance.

**An Action Perspective**

The difficulty in reaching a fundamental appreciation of the realities of new management practice is partially due to the fact that many of the new leadership concepts are too abstract to become a framework for real action. Managers are bombarded with buzzwords and nostrums guaranteed to produce innovative organizations or to ensure success. In order to meet the exploding accountability of management in everyday organizational life, individuals may be sorely tempted to resort to the plethora

> *The leadership imperative is to take action.*

of panaceas being sold by contemporary management experts. It is a major error to give in to such temptations by using a shot-gun approach to leadership development, such as a series of presentations on the most popular concepts of the day.

In order for new management competencies to be applied in the course of everyday management work, the philosophy and design of the leadership development program must be based on an action orientation. For example, recognition of the need for communication must be accompanied by the performance of actual communication that spurs the imagination, creates an image of a better future, encourages action, or feels good. A manager's true understanding of coaching is evidenced when individuals and groups are actually able after a coaching session to identify for themselves what is keeping them from their goals. Clearly, an action orientation in leadership development dictates a learning methodology quite different from traditional educational approaches.

Experience has shown that the majority of managers and professional staff leaders do not have all of the requisite skills to move from the traditional command and control model of the past into the facilitating, integrating, and coaching roles demanded for success in new organizational forms. Leaders sense that changes are needed but may not intellectually identify precisely what needs revision. In order to meet the demands of these turbulent times, there must be sufficient opportunities for leaders to examine and practice the new competencies for success from a cognitive, attitudinal, and behavioral perspective.

## Program Design

The leadership development program described here differs from traditional education in several ways. Throughout the program, activities consistently reinforce the core philosophies and values of management practices in high-involvement or empowered organizations. Learning activities differ from the common role-playing found in group training; they are lifelike simulations of real-world situations in which leaders under pressure must share their authority and expertise with others in order to resolve problems. This approach assists managers in developing a broader, more self-critical, and more strategic view of their managerial practices while at the same time providing opportunities for team learning.

> *The wicked leader is he who the people despise. The good leader is he who the people revere. The great leader is he who the people say "We did it ourselves."*
>
> *Lao Tsu*

Simulations are used to cause the emergence of certain behaviors in the training sessions. These behaviors are used as exemplars, for everyone's learning of effective and ineffective practices. Practice exercises, conducted in groups, also provide the opportunity to reinforce what is learned.

The trainers are not only trainers but successful consultants with significant management experience. They sprinkle the sessions with accounts based on their background as members of organizations undertaking major change.

Also, the leadership development program is designed to strengthen the overall management team by addressing team issues as they emerge in training, identifying the various strengths of individual members, surmounting obstacles to collaboration and leadership in the organization, and providing opportunities for managers from different departments to learn together. These high-level outcomes are pursued through the purposeful assignment of managers to "practice lab" groups, which will evolve new principles of management practice to be tested against the participants' experiences. The membership of each group consists of no more than eight people; they come from different departments and have different levels of experience in the managerial role. After the program has been completed, the practice labs commonly continue as support and continuous learning groups, extending the learning long past the end of the formal development program.

Instead of receiving a "canned program," each organization gets a customized package that takes into account where it is along the continuum of change. The core content recommended for a one-year leadership development program in new leadership competencies is summarized in the Appendix.

## DEVELOPING LEADERS WHO CAN DEVELOP ORGANIZATIONS

Clearly the uproar in the health care marketplace demands a new emphasis on leadership development. Most managers, including top executives, have few of the competencies needed to fashion a context in which new organizational forms can unfold successfully. New systems of care delivery are destined to remain only distant visions until the leadership group has clearly obtained the competencies needed for their creation.

> *Learning is as critical to a knowledge-based, postindustrial economy as steel was to a materials-based, industrial economy.*

A new form of leadership development must focus on leadership roles, skills, and techniques in the new business paradigm. The knowledge gained through the development program must be practical and not just theoretical. Leadership development will not succeed if it is not a major corporate initiative that encompasses not only training but the examination of organizational practices that support or impede the application of new managerial practices.

As Sashkin and Burke predicted, leadership development in the nineties is a unique blend of organizational development and managerial learning. The degree to which a health care organization is able to move effectively into the future will be highly dependent on the practices of its leaders. There is no other option for leaders but to transition and transform.

## Month 1: The Manager as Facilitator

*Overview*

Leaders/managers in shared leadership organizations are challenged to move from director and controller to facilitator and collaborator. How much is understood about the development and the maintenance of work groups? What are the facilitating roles that can be developed in a group? Do managers really capitalize upon the strengths of individuals? How do leaders move a group to commitment and action? What is the best way to moderate problem behaviors in work groups?

This workshop provides managers and staff leaders the opportunity to assess and expand their facilitation skills, emphasizing less telling and more asking. Lecturing, discussion, small group work, and videotaping are the primary instructional methodologies. For nursing groups, the unique characteristics of specialty practice, nursing management, and advanced practice roles are also addressed as group facilitation challenges.

*Objectives*

At the end of the first workshop, participants will be able to:

1. Critically analyze three key facilitation roles that can be assumed in a work group.
2. Contrast the helping and hindering behaviors that people exhibit in the TQM process in a multidisciplinary work group or a team.
3. Identify two alternatives for intervening in a problem behavior in empowered groups.
4. Describe the construction, development, and maintenance needs of effective work groups.

## Month 2: The Faultless Facilitation of Groups

*Overview*

This workshop builds upon the first facilitation workshop, expanding the repertoire of tools available to the leader/manager in the development and maintenance of effective self-directed work groups. The session focuses upon the key group communication and problem-solving techniques essential to effective facilitation. Lecturing is kept to a minimum. Instead, opportunity is provided for self-assessment and immediate feedback through two videotaped exercises. Questioning, listening, and observing skills are emphasized. Participants have the opportunity to practice using four different group problem-solving processes, including one for reaching consensus. The practice exercises are realistic and fast-paced, reflecting the real-world experience of empowered groups.

## *Objectives*

1. Apply one method of tackling problems and making decisions in an empowered work group.
2. Present a method for consensus decision making.
3. Evaluate their personal strengths and weaknesses in communications and problem-solving skills in a group setting.
4. Explain two methods for bringing forth a group's knowledge, candor, and trust.

## Month 3: The Leader Manager as Coach

### *Overview*

Leadership has been studied from a variety of perspectives, resulting in various styles being researched, refined, tested, and presented in training. However, leadership becomes operational only though the leader's interpersonal interactions. As organizations move to adopt more worker self-management, the nature of the manager communication with subordinates *must change* from directing and controlling to counseling, mentoring, tutoring, and challenging or confronting. It is these coaching skills that are introduced in this workshop, with opportunities for self-assessment and practice. The fact is that in most organizations people could work 15 percent more or less without anyone recognizing the difference. Coaching is a strategy that, when applied by managers to individuals and groups, will tap into that 15 percent discretionary energy.

The coaching process involves assisting the other person to identify what is preventing that person from working in a particular manner. The real skill in coaching is to always make sure that the persons being coached for managers are often teachers who reiterate the steps of the procedure or clarify the procedure itself. Through lectures, videotapes, and experiential learning, participants come to realize the real potential of coaching to engender commitment to excellence in the workplace.

*Objectives*

At the end of the workshop, participants will be able to:

1. Describe how coaching interactions contribute to employee commitment and sustained, superior performance.
2. Define a process model for coaching and the requisite skills involved in each stage of the process.
3. Practice the process model with feedback through videotape.
4. Analyze the facilitators and the obstacles to coaching interactions in their workplace.
5. Apply the coaching model to peer review, shared governance council work, CQI, and advanced nursing practice interventions (nursing groups only).

## Month 4: Learning from Conflict

*Overview*

Conflict is an inevitable outcome of the strength of our diversity in organizations and of the journey toward change. In the new business paradigm, the leader/manager must be comfortable with conflict, the "noise" that change generates, and the information it can provide about people and processes.

Participants are assisted in identifying personal and professional meanings of conflict situations. Through structured exercises, the dynamics of group reactions to change and strategies for intervening in those dynamics are emphasized. Participants are also taught how to recognize the conflict potential in the mismanagement of agreement in groups by applying Harvey's Abilene Paradox to their own organizational experiences (see J.B. Harvey, *The Abilene Paradox* [New York: Lexington Books, 1988], 13–37). The Abilene Paradox is a story about a family that is a metaphor for organizational life. It points out to managers that all too frequently events in organizations gather momentum and take on a life of their own. The paradox comes into play because at the same time no one really wants to take part in the issues gaining momentum. Understanding this organizational dynamic helps managers to understand how they may be setting groups up for failure, fostering alienation, intensifying the fear of risk taking, or putting dollars into projects that everyone knew would not work.

Concepts of principled negotiation are taught to participants, with opportunities to practice negotiation and to receive feedback about negotiation skills. For nurses, how to deal with the politics of nursing groups is also taught. Mini-lectures, experiences tailored to the particular work groups represented, and videotaped exercises are the primary learning methodologies.

## Objectives

At the end of the workshop participants will be able to:

1. Distinguish between a supportive versus a defensive climate in conflict resolution situations.
2. Anticipate potential areas of conflict in work groups of which they are currently members.
3. Apply two strategies for resolving conflicts in work groups.
4. Recognize when to create learning opportunities out of conflict situations.
5. Evaluate a conflict situation that originates in the mismanagement of agreement.

## Month 5: The Empowered Leader/Manager: The Personal Journey

### Overview

Before managers and professional staff leaders can foster empowerment, they must be empowered themselves. This workshop introduces five characteristics of empowered people and identifies how individuals can be challenged to be self-directed in the way they want to live out their lives—at home and at work. Empowerment is one of those buzzwords that is frequently tossed around in organizations but has little definition. Participants work with the five traits of empowered people by applying the concepts to their own managerial practices. A special section of forgiveness is included, addressing the need for more organizational grace when it comes to mistake making. Through lectures, discussion, and practice exercises, participants are challenged to understand the dynamics of empowerment at a personal and management/leadership team level.

### Objectives

At the end of this workshop, participants will be able to:

1. Recognize and define the five major characteristics of an empowered person.
2. Assess how well they personally think that they exemplify empowering qualities.
3. Identify how well the management/leadership team exemplifies empowering qualities.
4. Recognize how they act and feel when they have responded in a confident and empowering manner.
5. Identify how oppressed group behaviors interfere with the expression of empowering qualities (nursing groups only).

## Month 6: Developing Empowered Work Groups

### Overview

This workshop builds on the previous one, by applying concepts of empowerment to the leadership of work groups. Participants practice leading groups to the development of a work vision and coaching individuals to identify their purpose for working. In particular, establishing a vision and purpose for one's work is presented as a strategy for effectively managing change. Strategies for fostering empowerment in health care organizations are identified and applied to case scenarios. In some cases, leadership groups have actually used this session to craft their future vision for the organization and practice communicating that vision (see Appendix).

As leaders in complex, integrated delivery systems, managers are challenged to maximize commitment and contributions. The empowerment framework is used to develop this skill and as a tool to analyze and intervene in obstacles to effective group performance in empowered organizations. The requirements of unique organizational structures, such as team-based, high-involvement, or shared governance models, will also be discussed in relationship to the continuum of self-management and empowerment.

### Objectives

At the end of the workshop, participants will be able to:

1. Create and communicate an empowering vision for their organization.
2. Identify the actions needed to achieve that vision.
3. Relate the concepts of commitment and contribution to vision and purpose.
4. Analyze their own organizational structure for evidence of empowerment and determine an action plan for further development.

## Month 7: Negotiating the Messy Terrain of Change

### Overview

The demands of our turbulent environment are driving significant organizational transformations. As in all change, transformation is accompanied by multiple, smaller changes, incomplete transitions, and uncertainty. The leader/manager wears many hats at one time: strategist, implementor, and recipient of change. It is no easy task to embark upon a journey in which you must both lead a change and be a recipient of the outcomes.

This workshop is one of two focused upon the successful management of change. It is a full-day simulation of the process entailed in designing and implementing a change or an innovation in a health care or service organization. The simulation is designed to bring forward problematic behaviors commonly expressed during times of change by both managers and staff. Participants will be challenged to identify and apply their attitudes about change, their change management skills, and facilitation techniques. For professional work groups, the workshop will stimulate reflection about the relationship of professional socialization experiences to change. Professional socialization experiences can be real obstacles to collaboration and partnership, as each specialty believes that its model is the correct one, which can interfere with quality decision making.

Following a debriefing and a lecture on contemporary change management principles, participants then apply newly learned techniques to a second change process. Discussion is tailored to the particular change initiatives being planned or experienced by their organization. This workshop is an ideal experience for leadership groups planning major change or struggling with the implementation of major change.

## *Objectives*

At the end of the workshop, participants will be able to:

1. Describe the characteristics of effective and ineffective strategies for leading a planned change.
2. Identify the common roles assumed by individuals in professional groups during the implementation of change.
3. Apply, through practice, the key communication, coaching, empowerment, and facilitation skills necessary to produce lasting change.
4. Integrate and execute a planned change within a shared leadership group.

## Month 8: Making Change Happen and Making It Work

### *Overview*

This workshop builds on the previous one, emphasizing the personal, cultural, and project management demands for implementing change. Participants are introduced to scientific concepts of project management and the project manager role. From a cultural perspective, the dynamics of resistance are explored, with tips for effective intervention. Project management techniques for managing time, cost, and accountability are presented.

Participants are provided with the opportunity to assess and to modify a present change initiative using the techniques presented. This workshop is particularly useful for individuals who have had limited accountability for organizational projects.

## Objectives

At the end of the workshop, participants will be able to:

1. Describe how the human experience of change is expressed in health care organizations.
2. List the steps and accompanying leadership activities in the project management cycle.
3. Identify the characteristics of an effective project manager.
4. Apply project management techniques to a planned or progressing change in their own organization.
5. Describe the features of selected project management software (optional).

## Month 9: Organizing Professional Work Systems (The Flying Starship Factory Simulation)*

### Overview

The new health care paradigm emphasizes a new definition of work that relies upon cross-functioning and integration, along with meaning and dignity in work. All health care systems are examining their work design. This all-day simulation transports health care leaders from a traditional work setting through a redesign process and into a high-performance organization experience. Through experience, lectures, discussion, and assessment, the *why* and *how* of productive health care workplaces is driven home. This workshop is particularly appropriate for multidisciplinary work groups prior to a work redesign initiative or major restructuring.

Developed by Block, Petrella, and Weisbord, the simulation reproduces a factory that makes starships and is organized in a traditional manner. Extra fees must be incorporated into the budget for this workshop, as supplies, setup, and workbooks for each participant must be purchased in advance. The simulation is described in greater detail in the Appendix.

Participants are randomly assigned work roles and their work is organized in traditional fashion. For example, each worker is rewarded on the basis of individual performance; only supervisors are held accountable for solving interdepartmental problems; departmental boundaries are clear, and so on. At the end of the first run of producing starships, productivity and quality indicators are measured and presented to the groups. This feedback is then examined in the light of sociotechnical design principles.

---

*Extra fees are charged for workbooks and materials.

Participants are given the freedom to restructure their work in order to enhance productivity and quality using these principles. In a safe atmosphere, they experiment with no supervisors, self-directed work teams, supervisors as consultants, team-based pay, and myriad other new approaches to work. A second run in producing starships is then conducted, using the newly designed work structures and processes. Measurement of quality and productivity occurs once more. At the end of the second simulation, outcomes for each run are compared and analyzed using the principles of sociotechnical work redesign.

*Objectives*

At the end of the workshop, participants will be able to:

1. Apply concepts of empowerment, teamwork, TQM, and change leadership into a whole systems approach to work redesign.
2. Describe how structure, information flow, and reward systems impact output, quality, and job satisfaction.
3. Apply facilitation skills to use teamwork in order to align the characteristics of work for maximum quality and dramatically improved results.
4. Understand how employee knowledge of economic, social, and technical traits of the system is the basis for work redesign in the continuous improvement environment.
5. Recognize that there are many "right" ways to redesign work to improve results.

## Month 10: Mastering Systems Thinking

*Overview*

A major challenge for contemporary health care leaders is the management of knowledge. Individuals and what they know form the crucial resources of the information age. However, individuals and groups vary widely in the concepts, assumptions, connections, and knowledge that they carry in their heads, which color decision making and work performance. Leaders who can articulate systems explanations for organizational problems will avoid being pulled into an endless spiral of continual interventions for problems that never seem to go away.

We all know that leaders should help individuals and groups to see the big picture. Just how to do this is not well understood. This workshop provides participants with the key principles of systems thinking as a managerial tool. Participants have the chance to see interrelationships, not just tasks or snapshots of care delivery. Through a series of individual and group activities, systems principles are applied in real-world problem-solving situations in order to identify areas where well-focused interventions can produce results.

Specific mental modeling techniques—mindmapping and causal looping—are practiced as methods of avoiding symptomatic solutions. Participants have the opportunity to bring current problems from their own workplace to use as practice cases.

### Objectives

At the end of the workshop participants will be able to:

1. Describe the value of systems thinking to managerial work.
2. Apply systems thinking principles to problem situations.
3. Practice mindmapping techniques as a means of problem identification or resolution.
4. Use causul looping to see connections to a larger system.

## Month 11: Developing Accountability in Health Care Organizations

### Overview

Now more than ever organizations need effective accountability systems. Unfortunately, years of entitlement philosophies have created workforces who park their brains at the door and are comfortable with being rewarded for simply showing up. Based on the popular management text *The Oz Principle*, by Connors, Smith, and Hickman (1994), this workshop challenges participants to identify barriers to real accountability in their own home organization. Individual behaviors, organizational norms, and management practices are scrutinized through a series of highly interactional exercises for their contribution to either victim or accountability behaviors in organizations. The workshop closes with the management group identifying their own accountability as leaders in the new paradigm of managerial practice.

### Objectives

At the end of the workshop, participants will be able to:

1. Identify accountability behaviors as they are expressed in the health care workplace.
2. Recognize and modify at least two managements practices that contribute to a lack of accountability.
3. List characteristics of nonaccountable or "below the line" behaviors.

4. Describe the results of a personal self-assessment regarding their own accountability behaviors.
5. Lead a work group in the development of shared accountability.

## Month 12: A New Day Is Dawning: Planning Your Career in the New Health Care Paradigm

*Overview*

As health care organizations move toward new forms and structures that emphasize self-management, traditional managers are re-examining their roles, functions, and career futures. This workshop is designed to give the participants the opportunity to identify the perceived areas of competence, motives, and values that are nonnegotiable or core for them. Through individual work, work in dyads, and work in large groups, participants are challenged to identify how they and others see themselves operating in eight categories related to their career.

Participants are taught a set of concepts for thinking about how careers develop and how career concerns are integrated into their psychological makeup. For professional nursing groups, the unique career patterns of nurse managers will be incorporated into the discussion. This work is described as one of the elements of personal mastery. Information collected during the day is then made meaningful by the construction of a draft career plan.

This program is particularly useful prior to redesigning a management structure. Participants are encouraged to move from the paradigm of a lifelong employment to that of maximizing their employability in the health care marketplace.

*Objectives*

At the end of the workshop participants will be able to:

1. Develop insight into their career competencies in order to manage career choices and moves.
2. Apply a set of concepts and a framework for thinking about how careers develop and how people integrate careers into their personalities.
3. Examine the future career choices possible in their own organization within the new health care policy environment.
4. Apply concepts of career development in nursing in order to understand the Why and How of their present career path (nurses only).
5. Develop a draft of a personal career plan.

**REFERENCES**

1. J. Champy, *Reengineering Management* (New York: Harper Business Publishing, 1995), 1.
2. H.W. Moulton and A.A. Fickel, *Executive Development* (New York: Oxford University Press, 1993), 1–16.
3. P. Drucker, *The New Realities* (New York: Harper & Row, 1989), 222.
4. P.M. Senge, et al., *The Fifth Discipline Fieldbook* (New York: Doubleday/Currency, 1994).
5. Champy, *Reengineering Management*, 128–148.
6. Drucker, *The New Realities*, 224.
7. *Merriam-Webster's New Collegiate Dictionary*, 10th ed., s.v. "competent."
8. C. Argyris, *Overcoming Organizational Defenses* (Needham Heights, Mass.: Allyn and Bacon, 1990), 43.
9. D.C. Burkhardt, "Coaching over the Rough Edges," *Oregon Business*, August 1994, pp. 60–63.

# Chapter 9

# Uncovering the Bureaucracy Within: What Happens When Managers Stop Controlling Everything?

> The old leadership model that managers are the thinkers and the clinical staff are the doers must be replaced with thinking and acting in every corner of the health care enterprise.

The kinds of risks we take are directly related to the outcomes that we are able to achieve. It is a strategic imperative that leaders risk owning and enacting new shared leadership practices. The object is not just to make people feel better about their work but also to increase the chances of achieving desired outcomes and enhancing organizational performance. The frenetic activities surrounding the reconfiguration of health care services demand leaders who are able to fully engage the providers of care in the design and implementation of mostly untested and radically different systems of delivery. Ignoring the importance of the relationship between leaders and providers is a recipe for failure. Anyone who reads newspapers knows that some reconfigurations are experiencing fatal systems inadequacies. Patients have had the wrong limb amputated, received the wrong blood products, and had their respirators disconnected by mistake. Why are such mistakes happening? The response of the clinical staff might be something like this: "If only we had been asked, we would have said this was going to happen," "If only our leaders had truly listened when we tried to tell them what might cause a problem," or "If only people who disagreed were not labeled as resistive, we would have spoken up."

The system flaws that cause these dreadful outcomes are the direct result of leadership practices that failed to engage the clinical staff as partners. New ways of delivering care are largely untested and have many unknowns associated with their application. It takes the involvement of everyone who contributes to the provision of care to ensure that the unintended consequences of new ways of working

269

> *It is possible for people to be represented on committees without altering the worst aspects of their work.*

do not threaten the quality of care or the security and safety of patients. Just as important, the health care workplace must be an open system where honest dialogue and problem solving are applied to the ethical and human dilemmas that are sure to appear with change.

In order to initiate and develop leader-provider partnerships, leaders must create conditions in which every person strives to uncover the bureaucratic mindsets, unconscious habits, and actual behaviors that have been internalized and internally defined as definitions of good management. This will be an uncomfortable journey. It will mean acknowledgment of our darker side. Recognition must be followed by a process of trial and error until the new practices produce better outcomes than the old ones. The command and control model of the past must be left behind.

For years the bureaucratic tradition has rewarded managers for acting as though they could do anything and were always in control—even when confronted with events clearly beyond their grasp. This has led managers to struggle with the temptations of self-importance, reinforced by reward systems that confer bigger offices, covered parking spaces, or more secretaries than are really needed. They know that they can achieve stature by appearing to always know the right answer. Why give this up? Those managers motivated by an overdeveloped sense of self-importance tend to adopt familiar solutions rather than deal with the messiness of real understanding. In times of great change, however, there are no familiar solutions.

When the amount of power over other people is an indicator of managerial success, the result is a culture of entitlement. Team members park their brains at the door, expecting not to be asked their opinion or to have to accept responsibility for their behaviors but to be rewarded merely for showing up. Further, an addiction to action has led managers to adopt reactive solutions. In times of dramatic change, sometimes no action is the best strategy for the moment. Reactive solutions either fail in the long term or lead to a series of additional reactive solutions and a pattern of defeat.

Managers and clinical staff alike will have to confront the traditional attitudes and behaviors that characterize their relationships. During the change process, people will struggle with denial and yearn for the old days. The process will begin with the recognition and articulation of new values. For most managers, actual behavior change will take some time to develop.[1]

Once managers embrace the power of letting go and empowering others, the workplace will see a fusing of intelligence and imagination, and networks will be identified and encouraged. The needs of one group will not be more important than another, and by actively seeking to understand differing perspectives, managers will enable teams to move toward a collective vision. A shared purpose drives powerful action because everyone is committed to the goals. Individuals and groups are challenged to explore the visible and the hidden dimensions of problematic situations and thus attain better understanding. Processes for identification and the connection of individual viewpoints are purposefully applied. The manager acquires and allocates resources according to the principle of equality rather than status. Disputes over power are avoided because team members trust that they have equal access to resources. All team members are assisted in owning the outcomes of their own processes. Below are in-depth descriptions of the attitudes, concepts, and behaviors representative of the participative, interpersonal, and integration leadership competencies described in Chapter 2. Case examples are provided in order to amplify understanding.

## THE POWER OF THE INTERPERSONAL

Changing the context of the manager–clinical staff relationship requires the understanding and application of sophisticated interpersonal skills. There are so many aspects to attend to in the change process. Becoming a partner means giving up the fierce individualism and competitiveness that has characterized American society in favor of sharing ideas and collaborating. Once a partnership is formed, issues of dominance emerge and must be addressed by both parties. Organizations do not make it easy to be a leader. There is so little room at the top that those who attain the pinnacle can make it difficult for others. Most people in leadership roles find themselves caught between pressures to produce from the top and pressures for more freedom and authority from the bottom.[2]

Core competencies of the interpersonal domain include (1) the facilitation and development of teams, (2) performance coaching of individuals and teams in a way that fosters accountability, and (3) the creation of effective coalitions. It is facilitation, however, that is the foundation for every competency in the interpersonal domain.

### Facilitation of Work Teams

#### *The Manager as Facilitator*

The business literature is filled with exhortations for leaders to recognize the "wisdom of teams," to build "team-based organizations," and to become effective "team builders." All of this emphasis on teams is symbolic of the recognition that

> ## Today's health care environment has created an alarming number of things that managers do not know anything about.

the outcomes of service are no longer directly produced by individuals working alone but result from the collective efforts of teams of sometimes diverse individuals. It was Eric Trist and his colleagues, struggling to define new ways for organizations to enhance their performance, who really put teams at the center of the leader's work. In his descriptions of sociotechnical systems, Trist envisioned the creation of work systems in which people complemented technology. People were viewed as capable of self-organization and self-management. Sociotechnical design principles extended interpersonal values into the workplace, where those affected by the change were involved heart and soul in the change process, not merely represented in committee membership.[3]

The leader who has developed expertise in the interpersonal domain will be able to engage teams in the solving of those deep-rooted and sometimes hidden structure and process problems associated with the way care is delivered in a particular organization. Effective partnerships require more than buzzwords, bandwagons, solutions, or videotapes that make people feel good.[4] True partnerships will be developed through the leader's application of facilitation skills to help teams sweat out together the important work to be done.

In the health care workplace, leaders are increasingly challenged to lead temporary project teams as a flexible response to fluid changes in the environment. The critical nature of multi-

> ## Self-control is the only way to live and work in new delivery systems without making mistakes so bad that we cannot say sorry enough times.

disciplinary problem solving, whole systems integration activities, and pluralistic work roles requires leaders who can make sure that teams remain productive in spite of the demands of their environment. As organizations move toward the use of self-directed work teams, leaders will be challenged to balance the coordinating efforts of multiple teams. These teams will not be able to be productive without concerted efforts by leaders acting in the role of facilitators.

All we really have is accountability, not power. The myth of power in the command and control tradition was that managers could actually exert enough power to control people, business cycles, or the competition. The paradox inherent in the facilitator role is that the more powerless we become the more influence we have. Managers have typically been rewarded for being in control. Once they let go of the overwhelming need for control, they are less critical of themselves and others. Team members no longer look for the managers to tell them what to do. The competent application of facilitation skills engages people in joint attempts to do something about what can be influenced and to forget the rest.[5]

> *Great thinkers need to learn to talk and great talkers need to learn to listen.*

### The Power of the Team

Clearly, teamwork is central to a health care organization's effectiveness. For example, membership in a capable work team results in improved coping skills (members will always have different degrees of coping ability in response to the human suffering accompanying health care delivery). In a functional team, each person is respected fully as an individual with mutually valuable knowledge and skills of value to others. Members support and validate experiences and ideas for ways to solve problems or improve their work. The sense of isolation that can occur when difficulties are experienced as unique to a given person is reduced by this kind of team support. The advice-seeking and advice-giving behaviors of team members can strengthen altruism, self-esteem, and collegiality. On the other hand, dysfunctional teams can unify people around negative behaviors, limit the potential for growth, and fail to achieve their objectives.

> *I believe in honesty so much that I must be willing to be honest about myself.*

Interpersonal learning is an important outcome of participation in effective work teams. Each member's interpersonal style will eventually manifest itself. The team becomes a microlaboratory for members to gain insight into how they partner with others; how they teach; and how they resolve conflicts, problem-solve, or collaborate. When people are more accepting of one another, they are more supportive of each other, more inclined to help one another, and more likely to suspend judgment and listen.[6] As work teams become more cohesive, the quality of their relationships improves, and the interpersonal skills gained are applied in interactions between work team members and other health care providers, patients, and families.

> **When things do not go as planned, the facilitator is more curious than judgmental.**

What does it really mean to be a facilitator? A facilitator is a person who recognizes the power of the interpersonal and is committed to carefully analyzing intention and action. As the result of interactions, people acquire new ideas and act on them. The power of position is replaced by the power of process. How an interaction occurs is as important as its outcome. The context of a discussion is as important as its content. Consequently, the facilitator of a work team approaches the task of facilitation with the following:

1. Thoughtful reflection and thoughtful actions. Self-exploration, openness of emotional expression, acceptance, genuineness, empathy, self-disclosure, and risk-taking characterize the facilitator's work.

2. A personal sense of empowerment and self-actualization derived from the deliberate pursuit of self-awareness and personal mastery. The degree to which teams are able to move toward action or be stuck in processes is strongly influenced by their ability to let go of crippling mindsets and outdated habits. The facilitator helps team members to grow in new ways and to empower growth in others.[7]

3. An appreciation for the power of teams. Work teams can instill hope or despair, impart knowledge or misperceptions, provide functional or dysfunctional role models, and be a potent force for interpersonal learning.

4. A tool kit of strategies that can ease a team through a process and enable it to achieve its goals (see Exhibit 9-1).

5. A respect for the power of process. The tendency toward reactive decision making is reduced because the team learns to value the lessons that dialogue brings.[8]

A facilitator remains neutral in the discussion, keeps the team focused, and suggests and teaches methods that help the team accomplish its work. The goal of the facilitator is to develop the team in such a way that it can facilitate itself. In order for this to happen, members need to be educated not only about action methods but also about the roles various members play as well as the effectiveness of their interactions in performing the work. In order to develop the capacity of the team to manage itself, the facilitator must shift from being an evaluator to being a neutral observer.

The bureaucracy internalized by managers is reflected in traditional behaviors in which they act like a judge. If indeed the ideas that are suggested are judged,

**Exhibit 9-1**  Facilitator Tool Kit

---

- A set of *warm-up* activities that get team members involved in the task, clarify expectations about the work, and help members focus on the work.
- A set of *action methods* to help teams make decisions, such as brainstorming, nominal team techniques, mind-mapping, consensus building, win-win conflict resolution, and force field analysis.
- *Process observation tools.* Develop a standard set to assist the organization in identifying common process issues blocking goal achievement.
- *Norm-setting guidelines.* The guidelines might be based on a set of effective behaviors that the team members agree to apply in their work. Have the team members review a sample list and then add their own. These might include statements about tardiness, confidentiality, respect, and so on.
- *Supervision processes.* Facilitators bring their own humanness to their work, which sometimes colors observations. Sessions led by a behavioral health specialist can help facilitators avoid turning their personal issues into team issues.

---

then the team fails to learn. The most potent learning comes when team members recognize themselves that there is a better way of doing something. A competent facilitator will encourage members to explore their thinking and examine the intended as well as the potential unintended consequences of their ideas, rather than evaluating them. Sometimes managers mistakenly assume that to be neutral is to act as a devil's advocate or simply ask a lot of questions. Such behavior is experienced by work team members as manipulation or an expression of the leader's dissatisfaction with the direction of the team, and it will shut down the team's development toward self-direction as well as obstruct learning.

A facilitator can either act alone or act in support of a designated group leader or chairperson. A facilitator is accountable for developing the work processes within the team while the chairperson is responsible for the quality of the outcomes. If a manager acts as chairperson, he or she has a certain authority and accountability for the outcomes of the team and is therefore not a neutral party. In this situation, it will be important for the manager to explain when and why he or she is shifting roles. In moving into the facilitator role, the manager should state he or she would like to assist in the accomplishment of a goal and rather than lead the discussion would like to act as a neutral observer of the team. The manager should appoint someone else to lead the discussion at that time and then notify the group when he or she is returning to the more directive chairperson role. This helps members to discard their previous perceptions of the manager as always directing the work and helps them to understand better the facilitation role. If members do not shift their perceptions as the manager shifts roles, they may be extremely hesitant to embark on any difficult discussions for fear of being judged.[9]

The facilitator is supported by a recorder and a process observer. The recorder position is frequently a default position and is often rotated and commonly avoided by members. However, a competent, committed recorder can really function as an additional facilitator. Recorders are encouraged to use flip charts or whiteboards to visually display pertinent information. Use of such tools allows members to see and review the status of the discussion, the options being considered, or their recommendations. It also affords members the opportunity to edit for accuracy or to seek clarification. An exciting technology aid available on the market today is a whiteboard with a computer chip and a printer capability. When the board is filled, the information can be printed out before it is erased. The person acting as a recorder must have good handwriting, excellent active listening skills, and an ability to remain as neutral as possible. To ensure objectivity, if a recorder wants to contribute an idea, the team members are asked for permission.

*Are you spending your time looking for power or enjoying the privileges of partnership?*

Another supportive facilitator role is that of the process observer. In all human interactions, there are two ingredients: content and process. Perhaps surprisingly, most teams fail to achieve their outcomes because of process issues. Content encompasses the tasks the group must perform whereas process issues include morale, cohesiveness, feeling tone, atmosphere, and power issues. The role of the process observer is to identify out loud any process obstacles or issues that have arisen. This information is used by the facilitator or the team to help the team explore the obstacles and try to overcome them. Having a process observer is important because the team leader or group chairperson is usually focused on moving through the agenda and may ignore significant process issues. Sometimes if a team is really struggling, it is wise to call in an expert from the behavioral health specialty to bring a greater level of expertise to the situation.

Observers must be given something to observe. Developing a structured tool to be used by all process observers is a good strategy. The tool can contain open-ended questions, a checklist of team roles assumed by members, or diagrams of key interactions. An interesting application of this role is when the process observer teaches team members how to evaluate their own process by completing the tool as well. The members then discuss their effectiveness as a closing activity. Examples of open-ended questions follow[10]:

- What was the atmosphere of the team today: competitive, hostile, happy, relaxed, cooperative?
- At any point in the team's discussion, did the atmosphere change? What was being discussed? Who was doing the discussion?
- What was the level of participation? Did every member contribute? Did some members fail to contribute? Did some members contribute more than others?
- What behaviors fostered or blocked full participation?
- Did the team achieve its objective for this meeting? Why or why not?
- Did interest or energy ever lag? When and what was happening at the time?

Competency in facilitation requires an unparalleled honesty in interactions and an abandonment of some of the political tactics of the past. The facilitator does not let things slide for the sake of friendship or do whatever it takes to stay on good terms with someone on the team. The facilitator does not take the safe route in order to avoid confrontation. Risks are taken by refusing to indulge any person engaging in unacceptable behavior and by sharing necessary information, even when that information discloses someone else's poor performance. Honesty is evident as the facilitator refuses to criticize people behind their backs, turns down the opportunity to participate in the "meeting after the meeting," and confronts both silence and distortions of the truth. In addition, the facilitators must develop insight about how his or her behavior influences others and must work to keep personal issues out of the group's processes.

### Case Example

In a multidisciplinary project team charged with implementing a new care delivery system, there was obvious tension between the nursing clinical staff and other professional disciplines. The group was failing to develop a plan for work redesign. Members were beginning to miss meetings. They felt that the tension was impeding their work and asked the facilitator to focus on identifying process issues contributing to the tension and to help the group resolve them. The facilitator observed and reported several things to the group. Although the vice-president of nursing and the chief of operations were described as coleading the group, it was the nursing executive who sat at the head of the table. Members' interactions were largely with the nursing executive and were in a direct question-answer format. The nurse executive often felt like she had to force people to talk! The nursing members of the group referred to their colleagues as the "nonnursing" services. Staff from each discipline sat together in a cluster, unwilling to collaborate.

The facilitator used a process in which each member was asked to think about how they were feeling at the moment. Dialogue was initiated by handing the first person to speak a worry stone. Members agreed to only listen and ask questions for clarity and understanding. There would be no judging of what was said and no defensive reactions.

The two-hour dialogue that ensued led to the team's recognition that the term "nonnursing" was experienced as devaluing by the clinical and support department team members. They felt additionally belittled by the fact that their supervisor, the chief operating officer, remained largely silent. He was shocked by this feedback, since he had adopted a posture of silence in an effort to empower his clinical staff to participate more fully. Team members had accepted an informal norm to deal with conflict by avoiding the expression of negative feelings about the process.

The nurse executive, instead of confronting his silence, avoided bringing it up for fear that she would antagonize him and harm the relationship. However, she recognized that someone had to act as a leader in the group, so she assumed that role. The clinical and support staff indicated that her active leadership further insulted them. Therefore, they found themselves failing to accept any leadership roles in the spinoff work groups directed by the project team. Nursing members of the project team recognized with some embarrassment that they had all too happily assumed these roles. With the facilitator's assistance, they recognized that this was because they were worried about controlling the outcomes. Feelings of being controlled by nursing led to the clinical and support staff members becoming even angrier. Nursing team members mistakenly perceived this anger as generalized resistance to change.

By recognizing their process issues and owning up to their behaviors, the members of this project team avoided the certain disaster that comes when people are not trusting of each other, are unable to learn from each other, and are unswervingly committed to their own agendas. First, the team members made a commitment to refer to the lab, pharmacy, and housekeeping departments as clinical and support departments in their remarks. The chief operating officer and the nurse executive agreed to take turns chairing meetings and to evaluate the effectiveness of each meeting with the facilitator at its end. The leadership of spinoff work groups was realigned to include multidisciplinary representation. To this day, a multidisciplinary group from the project team makes presentations to the board of directors, clinical staff groups in the organization, and the professional community.

The conditions for effective social systems can be created by applying a variety of tools. The development of a team adds a sense of purpose to the everyday work

> *Our work should be exciting and vital to us. If it is not, maybe we are in the wrong place.*

of the members because they are motivated by a collective mission. There is equity and unity in their relationships. The experience of being a member in a well-facilitated group increases one's capacity for self-organization and self-management because of the focus on the content and the processes of decision making. New connections in thought and action are made because members feel secure enough to suspend judgment. There is recognition that the team is greater than the sum of the individuals who make it up. The facilitator makes sure that the members engaged in consensus building in the group are the ones who must carry out the decisions made, thereby avoiding power imbalances and paralysis of action. There are several dynamics that commonly arise and must be addressed by facilitators in developing capable work teams (see Exhibit 9-2).

## Performance Coaching

### *The Leader as Coach*

Coaching is one of the more difficult interpersonal competencies to master, for it demands a rejection of the discipline and control methods of performance improvement. The degree to which an organization operates based on discipline rather than commitment to mastery is evidenced by the number of "mandatory activities." Another indicator is the amount of time between the identification of a new behavior as important and a mandate requiring it. The disciplinary model of performance improvement is flawed because it assumes that if leaders establish enough rules, the right systems, and strong incentives and punishments, people

**Exhibit 9-2** Key Team Processes

- Cohesion
- Interpersonal behaviors of members
- Norm-setting dynamics
- Building of commitment
- Power imbalances
- Communication deficits

will perform satisfactorily. In fact, many organizations are struggling with the validity of their performance measures, particularly "overinflated" performance ratings. It is interesting that there seems to be little concern being expressed over underinflated ratings.

The fact is that people perform at a level of excellence because they choose to perform that way. People comply with minimum accepted standards of performance because that is what the rules require of them. People decide where to direct their energy and how they will prioritize their work on a daily and sometimes an hourly basis. Why does one nurse choose to ignore a troubled family member in the ICU whereas another juggles multiple demands in a way that allows her to listen, support, or inform that family member? Why does a laboratory technician choose to let his actions be driven by requisitions and turn-around times? He fails to report to a nurse that the last patient he saw was having trouble breathing whereas another technician never fails to communicate problems patients are having. In each case, it is clear that the person had discretionary time and energy. They made deliberate choices to work a little bit harder or a little less, to perform at a satisfactory level or a level of excellence. What was the difference? Commitment! Imagine the quality of patient outcomes if everyone delivering care elected to devote their discretionary time and energy to the patients. This is the goal of coaching.[11]

> *Rules, systems, and incentives or rewards do not produce either excellent or poor patient outcomes, people do.*

Coaching sets the stage for the increased involvement of clinical staff by creating conditions in which they can fully apply their knowledge and skills as well as develop their full potential as caregivers. When people are competently coached, they are empowered to assume greater accountability in their work and will make better decisions, to the benefit of customers and the organization as a whole. The most important coaching task is to tap the breathtaking potential of every team member, which can only be accomplished when the managers embrace a whole different philosophy of operation. Uncovering the bureaucracy within will lead to uncovering management practices that were aimed at compliance and replacing them with practices aimed at commitment. Examples of these differences in leadership practices are presented in Table 9-1.

Leaders can help staff make good use of their discretionary time and energy by creating the conditions for their release. Four elements characterize an environment that stimulates and sustains commitment: clarity, competence, influence,

**Table 9-1** Compliance Behaviors versus Commitment Behaviors

| Compliance Behaviors | Commitment Behaviors |
| --- | --- |
| Manager sets schedules, makes adjustments | Self-scheduling systems enable clinical staff to set schedules and make adjustments |
| Clinical staff perform work assigned by manager, who is also accountable for the outcomes | Clinical staff make judgments and have control of their work |
| Manager monitors quality improvement | Quality improvement is part of clinical staff accountability |
| Manager plans, organizes, and directs operations and production | Managers coach, coordinate, support, teach, clarify, listen, and facilitate |

and self-appreciation.[12] Clarity results from the application of communication and facilitation skills to create real understanding of the organization's mission and strategic plan. Leaders must seize on opportunities to dialogue rather than debate the merits or organizational plans. They must work hard to listen to real concerns and to clarify misperceptions rather than to tell staff how they need to think about the organization's goals. To have real dialogue, leaders must first be sure that they are acting in ways that support the goals of the organization. Nothing does more damage to clarity than failing to "walk the talk." For example, some managers may recognize and espouse the value of participation but consistently cancel clinical staff meetings or move forward with decisions without clinical staff participation because the census is too high or the clinical staffing is too low. All leaders will recognize that the demands of patient care and of participation must be met in a balanced manner and must collaborate with clinical staff in constructing unique solutions to conflicts of demand.

Creating the condition for commitment means developing staff so that they can contribute and meet the requirements of their accountability. Staff will naturally do those things they can succeed at and avoid work that is difficult for them. Coaching is focused on making sure that staff not only have the skills that they need to succeed but also have the confidence to use them. Some managers reject the notion that staff development is included in leadership accountability, claiming that staff are responsible for developing themselves. This is the same as saying that computer systems should revise themselves because changes in the environment have altered what is required of the systems.

Unfortunately, leaders and clinical staff only sit down annually to discuss goals unless there is a problem. In a world of unrelenting change, this simply is not often enough. Leaders acting as coaches regularly engage clinical staff in conversations about professional development needs, the skills likely to be needed in five years, and possible future demands of technology. Such conversations have the effect of replacing the outdated concept of lifetime employment with the concept of maximal employability. Through individual coaching, leaders help the clinical staff to recognize the direction that health care is going and how to maximize their employability in the new marketplace. Leaders will identify and encourage the pursuit of opportunities for staff to work in different roles or departments in order to develop new skills even if it means losing good workers for a while.[13]

Creating the opportunity for real influence is necessary for commitment. Leaders cannot expect commitment if the clinical staff are expected to follow their orders without question. When questions are not allowed, underground sabotage, passive resistance, or restricting activities to what is actually written in the job description will be the end result. Creating the conditions for self-appreciation are just as important. People do not feel that they have influence if they are not able to appreciate their unique gifts. We develop self-appreciation through the feedback of others, particularly those whom we respect.

One way to determine if staff feel valued is to see if they exhibit self-appreciation in the way that they treat themselves. Are team members quick to criticize anyone or anything? What does the employee lounge look like? Is it dirty and disorganized, with cartoons depicting negative or victimization situations posted on the walls? Capable coaching includes the application of strategies that convey real rather than insincere appreciation. Managers have to have taken the time to know individuals' unique strengths in order to know the difference.

Coaching is basically a conversation with a person or with a group aimed at developing potential and assuming accountability for the outcomes of one's choices. Examples of coaching versus controlling communication are given below.

> *Coaching:* "What is happening that is keeping you from meeting your accountability in this area?" Here, the coach is conveying confidence in the individual's ability to ascertain what the problem is as well as reinforcing accountability for performance.
> *Controlling:* "You are having trouble doing this work. Let me review the steps for you again." The leader is directing the person to follow the rules.
> *Coaching:* "What strategies have you considered using to improve the quality of your performance in this area?" The coaching focus is on the individual taking action in the future as well as reinforcing accountability for taking action rather than being told what to do.

*Controlling:* "My suggestion is for you to do these things in order to solve this problem. . . ." The manager is telling the person the right way to do something.

*Coaching:* "What do you suppose the implications of that particular decision will be for you?" By asking this question, the coach assists the individual in exploring options and thinking about new solutions. It sets the tone for the mutual exploration of both parties' knowledge and experience.

*Controlling:* "Watch out. If you choose to do it this way, here's what I think will happen. . . ." By starting this way, the leader has assumed the task of telling the person what not to do.

More than likely, leaders will struggle to find the time to engage in coaching. Sometimes leadership work feels like being inside of a percussion instrument. As adrenaline rises, leaders are tempted to take actions that relieve the tension but fail to produce effective decisions. Let's face it, it is much easier to tell people what needs to be done than to guide them toward discovering it for themselves. It is less stressful to redo substandard work than to confront the obstacles to excellence. Demands on leaders' time will continue to exceed capacity, producing niggling guilt or a sense of insecurity.

Unfortunately, accountability-based organizations will not develop without consistent eyeball-to-eyeball contact between leaders and clinical staff. The creation of self-directed teams means that managers and clinical staff must spend quality time engaging in coaching conversations. Without good coaching, self-managing teams will be just an excuse to eliminate some management layers and shift the authority for decisions to another level. Those in leadership positions will themselves need coaching in order to revise how and where they set their priorities. Managers will need help in examining how they are spending their time and in learning better ways of delegating work. In order to find the time for productive coaching conversations, leaders will have to be challenged and authentically supported to stop doing some work. Finally, leaders in the process of becoming coaches will need to learn how to empower certain individuals and groups to accept the accountability for work that belongs to them in the first place.

> *When leaders become coaches, they can stop spending their time deciding whose problems they will accept accountability for.*

Where to begin? Clinical staff and colleagues alike will need to be oriented to the managers' acting as coaches, because the personal touch is missing in so many organizations. When senior managers make rounds, for example, the clinical staff know that during these visits they are not to bring up real issues of concern and to act pleased about the visit. They also know that the difficult problems they encounter in doing their work will probably not be resolved as the result of the visit but senior management might leave them alone for a while. Unfortunately, many staff members try to hide when they see managers coming because the only time they see them is when there is a patient complaint or a budget problem or some new task to do.

Coaching conversations have many focuses. They can be used to counsel staff about obstacles to excellent performance, educate staff about the politics of getting a certain job done, teach new skills or convey knowledge, and confront substandard performance. Coaching is successful when it results in increased self-sufficiency, the integration of organizational goals with personal meaning, and improved performance.[14]

Clearly, facilitation skills are critical to successful coaching. Reflecting, clarifying, listening, affirming, and dropping the agenda to deal with emergent emotions are some of the key facilitation behaviors used by coaches.

> *Management by walking around will not be successful unless those who are doing the walking around are coaches.*

Without the competent use of facilitation skills, the relationship between managers and clinical staff can be compromised. When facilitation skills are successfully applied, then the interactions are characterized by mutual respect and are problem focused, future oriented, and logical.

Coaching is not something a leader can do in a hallway or in a ten-minute meeting. It demands a quiet environment free from distractions. The leader should have already decided on the goals of the conversation and should follow a process that is logical and psychologically satisfying.[15] This means that the discussion has a beginning, a middle, and an end (at which point actions for the future are identified). It is psychologically satisfying because it makes sense. If the leader works hard to convey his or her meaning clearly and presents verifiable information, then the discussion will be mutually satisfying. As leaders become increasingly competent in

> *Accountability-based organizations require eyeball-to-eyeball contact between managers and clinical staff.*

their coaching activities, clinical staff will begin to initiate the coaching for themselves as a part of self-management.

## *Case Example*

A manager recognized that an evening assistant manager was having difficulty meeting clinical staffing standards for clinical staff assigned to the critical care department. She had two conversations with the staff member in which she reviewed clinical staffing policies and the steps to use in staffing to standards. Although things improved for a while, the problem continued. When the manager shifted her focus from directing to coaching, the results were entirely different. The conversation went something like this:

> *Manager:* Tell me what is getting in the way of your meeting the clinical staffing standards for this unit?
>
> *Assistant Manager:* I really do not know. I am trying to do a good job.
>
> *Manager:* I am confident that this is true. I would not have hired you for this position if I did not respect your knowledge and skills. Tell me, what strategies have you applied to address your difficulties in staffing to standards?
>
> The assistant manager reviews what he has done.
>
> *Manager:* It sounds like you have tried a lot of things but none of them are working well. You sound pretty upset by this. Is that what I am hearing here?
>
> *Assistant Manager:* You have no idea how I dread clinical staffing decisions. I did not want to tell you this because I did not want you to think that I was incapable of doing this job. You know, I am younger than many of the clinical staff and this job is really new to me. I really worry about making a bad decision and having people mad at me or causing mistakes in patient care to be made.
>
> *Manager:* Let me see if I understand you correctly. You dread making clinical staffing decisions because the clinical staff are not acting as your colleagues, and since you are a good nurse, you really worry about patient care?
>
> *Assistant Manager:* That is right! I guess I never thought about the fact that the clinical staff's pressuring me is not collegial behavior. I don't think I spend a lot of time thinking about what it means to be a colleague. I haven't been feeling like a very good nurse lately.
>
> *Manager:* Well, what do you think you could do to address these pressures and to regain your feelings of being a good nurse?

In this scenario, the manager's use of coaching led to an entirely different outcome than simple compliance with clinical staffing standards. Both parties had a better understanding of the real obstacles to meeting clinical staffing requirements. In addition, the assistant manager was able to overcome feelings of inadequacy and guilt and became refocused on action. The affirming nature of the interaction laid the ground work for more coaching conversations aimed at developing the leadership potential of the new manager.

### Creating Coalitions

The boundaries between competitors and partners is increasingly becoming blurred as health care enterprises seek to share scarce resources, achieve the economies of scale needed in times of crisis, and network in the delivery of care. Another interpersonal competency lies in understanding the dynamics of coalitions (or alliances). The effective application of this understanding is central to the development and the maintenance of such relationships.

A coalition can be defined as a temporary partnership in which two or more groups join together for the purpose of achieving a common outcome. In a coalition, both parties keep their own identity. Often, the leader will seek to establish a coalition in order to provide a framework for handling conflict or sorting out power imbalances. Coalition building requires both facilitation and coaching skills to assist the parties in identifying the objectives they want to achieve, helpful and hindering behaviors they may be engaging in, and the payoffs for parties at the time.[16] The key tasks of the leader in the development of the coalition are to facilitate the combining of diverse viewpoints and to assist the parties in managing their conflicts.

> *The wonderful thing about real conversation is that it stimulates one to new insights.*

Cohesion can be enhanced if the leader helps the parties explore and develop a set of shared ideals and principles. It can be further strengthened by planning activities, because the parties will begin to see they can have a greater influence acting jointly than if they were acting alone. The leader will be successful in creating cohesion and shared viewpoints by making sure that the parties have frequent contact with each other. Another strategy in coalition building is to have some members of the two groups act as integrators by assuming overlapping membership and working in both groups' area of accountability. Leaders will also need to make sure that there exists equal influence and an equal share of rewards for both parties.

Coalitions fall apart for many reasons, including the lack of facilitation and coaching. When each party is not kept informed, trust can decline. It is important to meet regularly, even when there is no decision to be made. Some outcomes take a long time to be achieved and people can lose interest and therefore commitment. Loss of commitment can be avoided by planning for purposeful contact and keeping communication flowing. In the case of a coalition, absence does not make the heart grow fonder but instead entrenches the parties in their divisive viewpoints. Sometimes the leader of a coalition is so dominant that collaboration between members of the groups is not possible. If the leader should leave, the coalition falls apart because the accountability for the coalition was not shared by the members.[17]

The actions of the leader in building a coalition should be purposeful and reflect the following principles:

1. *Do not make coalitions any larger than they need to be in order to achieve their goals.* Carefully examine who are natural allies and who are the peripheral contacts.

2. *Through dialogue with both parties, find a common goal or central rallying point.* This enables both groups to leave behind their conflicts with each other in order to achieve a greater common goal.

3. *Lead the groups in clarifying, affirming, and then committing to provide the resources needed for the coalition to reach its objectives.*

4. *Facilitate the development of the coalition's ability to manage its own process, particularly in the areas of conflict resolution and win-win negotiation.*

## THE LEADERSHIP EMPOWERMENT CYCLE

### The Manager as Integrator

The health care marketplace in the twenty-first century will cross the boundary into the interior of each health care organization. In the past, information about the vagaries of the health care marketplace was considered the special property of the management team. Leadership inside the marketplace will only occur when managers provide staff with access to everything they know about the market's ups and downs, including disturbing financial indicators. When staff understand the implication of this kind of information, certain changes in attitudes and behaviors are sure to follow. They will feel more uncertain, which in turn will lead them to examine and reflect on their work and professional accountability. Groups will become more tightly knit as individuals seek to share understandings and anticipate the future.[18]

Astute managers will seize the opportunity to *integrate* a focus on continuous improvement and flexibility in work in order to meet the demands of the health

> **Management occurs by consent, not coercion.**

care marketplace. Integration activities are an essential part of empowerment. Managers must accept responsibility for participating as a partner in the workplace community. Understanding the when, how, and where of integration becomes a central participative competence.

When individuals are empowered, they have an open channel to supplies, support, and information. Clinical staff possess the capacity to bring the resources that they need to their jobs. They have access to strategic formal and informal information. In meeting their professional accountability, empowered clinical staff exercise judgment about how to perform their work, engage in risk-taking behaviors, and apply innovative strategies without going through multiple layers of approval. In addition, all managers in the organization tacitly encourage and approve of such behaviors.[19] The cycle of empowerment enacted by managers acting as integrators is represented in Figure 9-1. As integrators, managers connect individual meaning and individual actions to the organizational mission. A unifying shared vision pervades communication activities, decision making, and the performance of work. Can the clinical staff articulate how the patient care mission is achieved through their individual practices? Is the shared vision for

**Figure 9-1** The Cycle of Empowerment

patient care services evident in *every* decision-making situation and in every group membership? Does the patient care mission get set aside for the sake of expediency or because of financial pressure?

When a shared vision has been crafted in a shared manner, with all of the players at the table, a powerful theme for commitment and action is established. The intrinsic motivation of a shared vision creates a unity of purpose, which in turn leads to a strong commitment to that vision on the part of the work team and to increased opportunities for collaboration because of their recognition of the unity of purpose.

When the managers engage in empowerment activities, the clinical staff are connected to other parts of the system. Through the application of facilitation and coaching skills, the managers help work teams to develop peer networks for gaining access to informal strategic information and support. In a similar manner, staff are assisted in developing advocate networks composed of top leaders who can confer approval, prestige, and visibility. Staff are recognized for freely participating in the decision-making process and for innovation. There are well-defined methods for local problem solving as a result of manager coaching. Cross-functional cooperation and information sharing is evident and linked to the shared vision for patient care.

> *A multiplicity of relationships is an avenue for growth.*

## Bold Strategies for Letting Go

Empowerment is virtually guaranteed if leaders do the following[20]:

- Develop a set of core values that can never be compromised in response to short-term financial pressures or for purposes of expediency.
- Coach the staff to connect their reason for working to the core values and challenge them to evaluate regularly the contribution that they make and the reason they are still working.
- Give staff the room they need to act, adjust, move, and learn from their failures.
- Describe a whole picture of the patient care delivery system using a variety of signals and actions that reinforce the core values.
- Pay attention to those little things that leave big impressions and obliterate structures and processes that interfere with adherence to the core values.

## When Empowerment Is Dangerous

There are some pitfalls that may endanger empowerment programs if they are left unaddressed. The first has to do with the relative empowerment of first-line managers. People cannot learn to share power if they have none or create access to information when they are information deficient themselves. It is critical to examine the layers of the management structure and to flatten it as much as possible so that first-line managers have clear authority, visible influence, and discretion as to how they perform their work.

Managers need to recognize symptoms of dysfunctional reactions to empowerment in both staff and managers and to intervene as necessary. Sometimes peers will exert pressure on those pioneering staff who would engage in new partnerships with managers. This type of response is usually driven by the perception that collusion with managers will result in a threat to staff interests. It will be important to address these concerns directly with the parties involved as well as provide support systems for the staff pioneers. Empowerment is also obstructed when managers either coerce staff to participate or retaliate for poor decisions rather than foster learning. These behaviors can be minimized through coaching managers in the methods of empowerment. It is also important to act on feedback about retaliation or coercion as soon as possible so that trust is not eroded to a point where it can never be restored.

> *True leaders fulfill their destinies by helping others to fulfill theirs.*

Managers must monitor power and status to see whether people are trying to maintain past differences and also watch for traditional trappings of power, such as "management only" meetings or a special parking lot designated for managers. Another issue involving power arises when staff who have had leadership roles in empowerment activities, such as shared governance, return to their former roles. The transition is difficult and confusing for many. Clinical staff often find that their participation in empowerment activities was far more satisfying to them than their clinical work. The result can be significant dissatisfaction, demotivation, and negativity. An unintended consequence of a clinician's assumption of a leadership role in empowerment activities is that relationships with members of the clinician's clinical peer group are disrupted and replaced by relationships with other staff leaders. The work of re-entry to the former clinical role also involves a disengagement from the leadership group and a reconnection with the old clinical peer group. The staff leader will need to be eased through this very difficult transition in order to be able to continue making a positive contribution.

When it comes to empowerment, uncovering the bureaucracy within means understanding that clinical staff have traditionally had to sell their ideas to staff and bargain for resources with precious little to trade. As a result, health care organizations are filled with many distinct islands. People group together in order to achieve some semblance of visibility and influence. The problem is that such groups set themselves up as guardians of the right way of working—their way. They create false distinctions between themselves and others that interfere with the collaboration that is so desperately needed today. These barriers can be seen in turf battles between work shifts, departments, or subgroups within the same department.

Empowerment is about restructuring or redefining the boundaries of influence in manager–clinical staff relationships. The outcome of empowering practices is the redistribution of intelligence to all parts of the organization and an increased capacity for local problem solving without information distortion and interference by powerful others. Empowerment is not a dispassionate process. Managers must coach and assist individuals and groups through emotional struggles over the control of resources, definitions of health, how to design care delivery, and the appropriate tactics of empowerment. As in all leadership practices, there will be significant constraints on the managers' time and resources. Empowerment requires that individuals and groups are capable of assuming accountability for their actions and for acting in a self-managing manner. Since not all staff have the necessary competencies, managers will need to coach some in the development of certain skills, such as role negotiation or political skills.[21]

## SYSTEMS THINKING: LEAVING BEHIND THE MACHINE MENTALITY

### Systems Thinking Skills

Heralded by learning organization theorists, systems thinking is described as the process by which leaders can facilitate leaving behind outdated, inaccurate, or irrelevant connections between ideas, experiences, and emotions. When one engages in systems thinking, interconnected parts rather than discrete elements are the focus of inquiry. Each situation is examined to determine its elements and how they interact with other parts of the system. Factors do possess unique characteristics but do not represent the essence of the whole system. No single element can produce the outcomes of the system. As organizations reconfigure and become even more complex and confusing, managers will be challenged to uncover bureaucratic mindsets and the habit of analyzing wholes into parts. By developing systems thinking skills, managers and staff will be ready to engage in synthesis instead of just analysis. Synthesis is integrated thinking, which produces knowledge of the whole system. Analysis assists in understanding the parts of the system. Integrated systems thinking is characterized by the set of skills summarized in Exhibit 9-3.

**Exhibit 9-3** Systems Thinking Skills

- Recognizing jumps from observations to generalizations
- Articulating mental models of past and present realities (mind-mapping)
- Balancing inquiry and advocacy
- Seeing differences in what is said and what is done
- Recognizing the unintended consequences of certain actions (causal loops)

The leader who develops competency in systems thinking will achieve certain important outcomes. The first is success in dealing with complexity or "managing the mess." The problems requiring solutions in today's health care enterprises are neither simple nor easily understood. Not only that but most professionals have not been taught to solve problems outside of their own discipline. In order to make messy situations manageable, systems thinking must be applied. When the impact of one action upon a larger system is understood, then leverage points for greater impact can be readily identified. Managers no longer have the luxury of testing solutions that, from the beginning, have a minimal promise of success.

As systems thinkers, managers become theory builders within their own organization. They insist, in order to keep pace with change, that individuals and groups refrain from problem solving through the use of predefined applications or frameworks. They apply systems thinking methodologies in order to assist groups to develop an intimate understanding of the whole. Reflection, inquiry, mind-mapping, advocacy, causal looping, and archetypes are examples of the methodologies presently available for application. However, systems thinkers avoid the traps sometimes encountered by quality improvement practitioners in that they recognize there is no golden formula or technique. Inquiry is not done as an academic exercise but as a process that is at all times grounded in reality.

As stated previously, the predominant worldview of reductionism resulted in managers who solved problems from a cause and effect perspective, often ignoring the environment or hidden consequences of action. Uncovering the bureaucracy within one's own thinking means recognizing when thinking is self-contained or hermetically sealed in closed boxes. The object is to break open the boxes and connect people's thinking. Managers in the twenty-first century will be managing knowledge, not people. This means they will have to view intelligence as a capital resource. Intelligence, of course, is like no other object. It cannot be left to one's children, redistributed differently, measured, or quantified. Yet what people know will make the difference in how well care is delivered.

Leaders can stimulate systems thinking in work teams by fostering the understanding that the organization is not a machine consisting of interdependent parts but a complex social system. In

> ## Where are you on the information highway?

leading a group through a systems-focused, problem-solving process, a manager might ask questions such as these:

- What larger system is this problem a part of?
- How would we describe this larger system?
- How do the parts that we have identified connect and integrate?
- How does knowing their connections help us to understand why we are having this problem?
- What is the purpose of this element in the larger system?
- Have we really explained why this is happening?

Leaders need to encourage reflection and inquiry so that people slow down their thinking in order to become aware of connections. The process of inquiry should be a nondefensive exploration of issues and questions. Pert charts, Gaant charts, and fishboning will not produce appropriate solutions to problems. Inquiry and advocacy should be stimulated instead, expanding understanding and leading to more effective solutions. The greater the systems we comprehend, the greater will be our knowledge and the more potent the solutions.

## Mindmapping

Mindmapping is a systems thinking tool that can be easily taught to team members as a problem-solving methodology. Rooted in cognitive psychology, mindmapping has been used for many years to assist children with certain learning needs. The process is designed to reflect the structure and the processes of the human brain. Brain cells receive numerous impulses from thousands of connecting points. Messages, perceptions, and thoughts pass from brain cell to brain cell. Memory traces are established and stored as familiar ways of thinking in long-term memory. When people are challenged to make these maps explicit, the process allows for an external mirroring of thinking.

Mindmaps improve learning and clarify thinking. They can be used by leaders to check the accuracy of perceptions that guide behavior. They can also be used to develop and test new mental models, redirect learning, and identify the trade-offs of various actions. For example, a work team may be in conflict over who is responsible for discharge planning. The social worker's mindmaps result from the long-term stored connections of social worker theory and practice. Likewise, the mindmaps of the utilization review professional and the professional nurse are determined by their professional backgrounds. Mindmaps are always flawed in some way, subtly distorting what is experienced and understood. They exist largely at an unconscious level, although they can be made explicit. Professionals are at a major disadvantage because we each believe that our own profession's model is the one true model, and this prevents us from seeing the advantages, possibilities, and deeper implications of other mindmaps. By making mental models explicit, conflict resolution is fostered. Each person is required to make his or her mindmaps explicit and to understand what is outdated or inaccurate as well as the similarities and connections between mindmaps. Characteristics of mindmaps are listed in Exhibit 9-4.

The novice mindmapper may experience certain difficulties that will limit the effectiveness of this methodology at first. Sometimes mindmaps fail because they are a reflection of reductionistic thinking. It is necessary to examine a mindmap diagram very carefully. Is it really a fishbone consisting of discrete parts or does it describe a whole system? Are all of the associations and connections among subjects indicated?

Written down sentences or phrases on mindmaps should be avoided. Their use limits understanding because a sentence often combines connections or maps of several ideas and may cause important associations or connections to larger systems to be missed. For example, "leadership roles in this organization" is a phrase that encompasses many different kinds of leadership located at many different points within multiple systems.

Leaders who use mindmaps must learn to be comfortable with messiness. Pert charts are so clean. It is a wonderful feeling to organize everything into a flow sheet. Mindmaps, if done correctly, will represent the messiness of exploratory thinking and confusion.

**Exhibit 9-4**  Characteristics of Mindmaps

- The subject of concern is located in the center as the focal image.
- The main themes or connecting systems of the subject of concern radiate as branches of the focal image.
- Branches contain key images or descriptors that are symbolic of the system. (Smaller branches may flow from larger branches in order of importance.)
- A completed mindmap looks like a web or a nodal system.

Finally, individuals and groups may react negatively once a mindmap is made explicit. It is uncomfortable and embarrassing for people to realize that they have been operating from inaccurate information or outdated ideas, and leaders should be ready to guide emotions so they do not become obstructive.

## CONCLUSION

Major organizational transformation does not occur simply because a group of people decide to transform themselves. It takes the grueling work of leaders who combine and apply interpersonal, participative, and technical competencies in order to sustain a concerted long-term effort. The political nature of change in combination with the current unstable marketplace make organizational change even more difficult to achieve.[22] What is needed is the development of a new organizational ethic. Through the leaders' purposeful application of facilitation, coaching, empowerment, coalition-building, and systems thinking methodologies, work teams will be able to negotiate the messy terrain of the health care workplace with a sustaining confidence in their own skills, an acknowledged pessimism about the future, and a driving need for connection.[23]

### REFERENCES

1. R.W. Hallstein, *Memoirs of a Recovering Autocrat* (San Francisco: Berrett-Koehler, 1992).
2. J.D. Beck and N.M. Yeager, *The Leader's Window* (New York: Wiley, 1994), 210.
3. E.L. Trist, *The Evolution of Socio-Technical Systems: A Conceptual Framework and an Action Research Program;* Occasional Paper No. 2 (Toronto: Ontario Quality of Working Life Centre, 1981).
4. M. Weisbord, *Designing Productive Workplaces* (San Francisco: Jossey-Bass, 1987), 296–311.
5. Hallstein, *Memoirs of a Recovering Autocrat,* 69–75.
6. I. Yalom, *The Theory and the Practice of Team Psychotherapy* (New York: Basic Books, 1975), 3–105.
7. C.E. Wheeler and P.L. Chinn, *Peace and Power* (New York: National League for Nursing, 1991), 90–96.
8. Ibid., 92.
9. L.B. Hart, *Faultless Facilitation* (Amherst, Mass.: HRD Press, 1992), 20–45.
10. Ibid., 186.
11. D.C. Kinlaw, *Coaching for Commitment* (San Diego: Pfeiffer and Co., 1989), 9.
12. Ibid., 10–20.
13. R.H. Waterman, J. Waterman, and B.A. Collard, "Toward a Career Resilient Workforce," *Harvard Business Review* 72, no. 4 (1994): 87–104.

14. Kinlaw, *Coaching for Commitment*, 21–33.

15. P.R. Garber, *Coaching Self-Directed Work Teams* (King of Prussia, Pa.: Organizational Design and Development, 1993).

16. E. Levin and R.V. Deneberg, *Alliances and Coalitions* (New York: McGraw-Hill, 1984).

17. Ibid., 27–103.

18. E. Locke and D. Schweiger, "Participation in Decision Making: One More Time," in *Research in Organizational Behavior*, ed. Barry Straw (Greenville, Conn.: JAI Press, 1989), 265–339.

19. R.M. Kanter, "Power Failures in Management Circuits," in *Life in Organizations*, ed. R.M. Kanter and B.A. Stein (New York: Basic Books, 1979), 43–59.

20. J.I. Porras and J.C. Collins, *Built to Last* (New York: Harper Business, 1994), 1–99.

21. R. Skelton, "Nursing and Empowerment: Concepts and Strategies," *Journal of Advanced Nursing* 19 (1994): 415–423.

22. M. Nichols, "Does New Age Business Have a Message for Managers?" *Harvard Business Review* 74, no. 2 (1994): 52–62.

23. Ibid., 59.

# Chapter 10

# How Do You Know When You're There?

Exactly like the nuclear family, the school, the mass media and other key institutions of the industrial age, the corporation is being hurled about, shaken and transformed by the Third Wave of change. And a good many managers do not know what has hit them.

Alvin Toffler
*The Third Wave*

As described in earlier chapters, a new health care reality is radically changing the way we work, compete for resources, relate to each other, and gather influence. The entire framework that stabilized how health care was delivered is coming apart. Traditional divisions of labor, professional role boundaries, contracts between employers and health care providers, the role of the consumer, and even traditionally accepted protocols of care are under attack as never before. Health care is in the midst of a full-blown identity crisis, creating incredibly volatile workplaces in which to manage.

Some leaders are actually trying to suppress the turbulence that comes with radical change, hoping to ride out the storm until they retire or make a comfortable lateral career move. Still others are so terrified that they are actively searching for ways to return to the stability of the health care past. These are not the people who will guide our health care enterprises through the reconceptualization and restructuring of health care delivery. By nature "survivors," these individuals will continue to do battle over who will squeeze the last benefits out of the dying delivery system. Mired in the past, they will be unable to function as leaders in the creative restructuring of integrated, seamless delivery systems or as managers in the context of partnership and the continuum of care. Early retirement or a different kind of work are no longer options but mandates for those who would seek to hold onto the status quo. Fewer managers will be needed in the future. Those who remain will not be able to make the needed changes in organizational relationships, structures, and operations without moving beyond their current management practices.

What is needed are leaders who are finely attuned to the patterns of emerging change and are willing to ride the waves into the future. They will be self-reflective and self-examining, looking to themselves and others to find the courage, trust, and knowledge to lead their organizations into the future. They will courageously scrutinize their long-held assumptions, sacred beliefs, and cherished practices. This will help them to acquire the ability to develop teams who are not afraid to explore the assumptions behind their own practices. They will continually ask "Why?" "What for?" and "What are we doing here?" Examination will extend to processes and performance: "How do we get the performance we want?" "How will we set new leadership practice norms and standards?" "How will we measure the outcomes?" "What kind of people do we want to lead with?"[1] Decisions based solely on spreadsheets and economic analyses will be rejected because of their inability to capture the unquantifiable outcomes of change. A holistic framework will guide leadership actions.

The momentous challenge faced by leaders in health care demands a singular and significant investment in professional and personal development. It must be recognized that this investment will produce an identifiable change in the content and the context of leadership practices. There is not a ready and able group of leaders waiting in the wings who fully possess the skills to lead organizations into the twenty-first century. Individuals within management teams differ in their repertoire of practices, comfort with risk taking, and pursuit of knowledge. Institutions of higher education are just barely changing their curriculums to fit the new reality. You will have to grow your own new leaders.

How will you determine whether the investment in personal and professional development is yielding a return? What will the return look like? What indicates whether someone has made the transition or is stuck in old paradigms? And what will indicate to you whether the content and the context in which leadership is operationalized within your organization has indeed shifted?

> *Assisting managers to deal with the new realities of health care will place a greater demand on an organization's capacities than was ever imagined.*

Any model of leadership development must be linked to operational results. How is the linkage made? This chapter addresses the organizational practices, indicators of cognitive and behavioral change, and performance evaluation activities that can be applied in identifying the benchmarks along the manager's transformational journey. It has been observed by many organizational theorists that the manner in which people describe their organization is directly related to the organization's leadership practices. Clearly, the pursuit of leadership development activities designed to change management performance will be a culture-changing process from which there is no turning back.

**WILL YOU SURF THE THIRD WAVE OR FALL INTO THE SWELL?**

Toffler coined a term for this era of profound and explosive change: *The Third Wave.* An enormous upheaval is occurring as the paradigms of the Second Wave (the industrial age) are replaced by high-technology, anti-industrial, network relationship prototypes. We constitute both the final generation of the industrial age and the first generation of the new age.[2] Health care managers are caught in the middle between the old and the new. Newfangled partnerships are being formed that blur the distinction between competitor and ally. Contemporary work groups delivering health care are made up of people committed to maintaining the crumbling order as well as those who are ready and even eager to construct something new. The paradoxes that must be understood and managed are numerous and complex, and the health care environment is filled with conflicting ideologies and an undercurrent of discontent.

*The fundamental accountability of twenty-first century leaders is to ease their enterprises through the transformation to a Third Wave of health care delivery.*

A perfect example is the battle in health care reform. One has only to turn on a TV news show to hear one group or another demanding a limit to government activities. Government agencies are viewed by many as preventing a simpler and more streamlined form of care delivery from emerging. The paradox is evident when one examines the health care enterprises in which these same people work or receive care. Many continue to hold on to cumbersome bureaucratic structures and processes that have the same overall effect as government activities, although on a smaller scale. In a similar vein, some pioneering health care enterprises have courageously dismantled their bureaucratic structures only to find themselves attacked by the rhetoric of Second Wave professionals and labor unions possessed by a self-serving syndrome.

Effective leadership programs include formal classroom instruction, personal development training, and systems of accountability for new leadership practices. They must provide the opportunity for participants to shift from the industrial model assumptions of the Second Wave to the principles of Third Wave thinking. This collective mental shifting in the leadership group will enable organizations to change the context in which leadership occurs and thereby impact the dominant coalition that determines who is represented, the structure of the organization, and the mechanism for governance. In the absence of a powerful leadership development program, managers will continue to use traditional tactics, since they are familiar and comforting, instead of trying out something new. It is as important to concentrate on what managers are *thinking* as on what they are *doing*. There are some specific cognitive indicators to watch for that signify the management team is abandoning Second Wave mindsets:

- There is an identifiable search for the connections between things that on the surface seem unconnected rather than attempts to reduce problems to their lowest common denominator.
- The future is viewed as a journey, not a destination. Even a major restructuring effort is seen as only the beginning of many changes to come.
- Individuals see themselves as constructing their own future through self-examination and self-design.

> *There are no answers to be found in minutia, only more minutia, which tell you less and less about nothing.*

- There is evidence of synthesis and breakthrough thinking in operational decision making. Broad theories about the relationships inherent in the delivery of care are reconceptualized and the pieces are put back together again in a new way.
- The obsessive quest for the right answer employing useless databanks filled with quantified minutia is a thing of the past. Instead, the underground connections of events, ideas, people, and experiences are applied to management work.

Leaders must try to determine whether their actions are designed to keep the industrial model of work intact or ease the transition of their enterprises into the Third Wave of health care delivery.[3] Table 10-1 provides a way to evaluate the thinking underlying a manager's actions.

**Table 10-1** Comparison of Second Wave and Third Wave Solutions

| Second Wave Solutions | Third Wave Solutions |
| --- | --- |
| Resembles a factory | Has semiautonomous units with little standardization of work |
| Lumps people into interchangeable masses or groups | Favors individuality, self-design, and self-management |
| Supports centralized decision making | Reflects a decentrist philosophy (local is better) |
| Evidences vertical integration, exceeds economies of scale, and administers everything impacting care delivery | Evidences virtual integration, outsourcing, contracting, and distribution of work among different people at different locations |

*Source:* Adapted from A. Toffler and H. Toffler, "Getting Set for the Coming Millenium," *The Futurist,* March–April 1995, pp. 13–14, with permission of the World Future Society, © 1995.

## EXAMINING THE CONTEXT FOR REAL LEARNING

The business literature is filled with references to the new success behaviors of contemporary managers. However, most of the time the complexity of the necessary personal and professional transformation is grossly underplayed. It is not easy to shift from directing and controlling all situations to working behind the scenes as a coach in the complicated world of a health care organization. Some would have managers believe that all they need to do is follow a set of team-building steps with good intentions. Others argue that managers should never give up authority—to do this would be tantamount to abdication of the management role. Still others attribute failure to learn new managerial practices to deficiencies in the individual. In truth, the literature on organizational behavior describes the process of actual change in a manager's work behavior as extremely complex. To understand why some managers are able to transition and adopt new skills whereas others stand still, more conceptualization is necessary.

An environment conducive to learning effectively is the single most important factor contributing to the success of health care enterprises. The twenty-first century will continue to demand that managers deal with abstractions, new types of problems, paradoxes, and routine challenges to their creativity. *Slow learning by the leadership team dooms an organization to certain failure.* Leaders must develop and master the new core competencies that will enable them to create the context for partnership at every level, equality between the players, and accountability in every role. If this occurs, the organization will find itself learning from its environment more quickly than its competitors.

There are specific characteristics of the workplace that will change if leadership development activities have been successful. *Contextual factors* are factors that are always present in every management situation. They are one focus of managers' thoughts and actions. The organizational context for leadership practices allows managers to see work events as connected to a larger whole rather than as isolated incidents. It is the "meaning" behind one's work as a manager. *Structural arrangements* are organizational configurations that either promote or limit the acquisition of shared leadership behaviors. *Process factors* include organizationally sanctioned operations, methods, and procedures employed by managers in the course of their work.

## ORGANIZATIONAL LIFE CYCLES

Context encompasses the organizational and personal conditions that can drive the decision to change management practices. Such conditions influence managers' beliefs and actions. Depending upon the situation, a manager may appear to change while really maintaining the status quo, may work hard to acquire new skills, or may actively resist the adoption of new management practices. Where an organization is in its life cycle and how its leaders choose to confront the future are important contextual factors, for they dictate the organizationally sanctioned norms for appropriate manager behavior. These norms may either foster or impede the adoption of shared leadership practices.

Consider the following scenario. The members of the leadership team of a tertiary care hospital in the aging stage of its life cycle are in a panic as the number of empty beds continues to grow month after month and resources decline. Survival and maintenance behaviors become typical. Although the system's leaders utter frequent exhortations to pursue excellence, they show little real tolerance for experimentation. They view technology as a cost rather than an investment, and they consider "good" managers to be the ones who meet their monthly variance targets while keeping down the "noise" in their departments. The members of the team share the belief that there is not enough money or enough time to shift to new manager behaviors, much less develop self-management among the staff. Although shared leadership is espoused as the right strategy

> *A morose view of the future creates dead-end hopelessness and saps all energy for learning.*

for the organization, there is collusion among those on the leadership team to continue to practice in the traditional manner. The leaders do not confront each other about substandard management practices because job security is a paramount issue for everyone.

The leaders' beliefs about the organization and its future obstruct the acquisition of shared leadership behaviors. Because of fears about declining resources and possible job loss, the leaders are simply not willing to make the necessary investment. Those managers who ignore the contextual cues in such a scenario and attempt to develop shared leadership practices find themselves with little support and leave themselves open for rebuke.

> *Having high expectations for the future is risky but can motivate those interested in real change.*

Imagine now an organization that is in an extremely competitive stage of its life cycle. Energy is high, in spite of anxiety about market share. Although resources are stretched thin, there is hope and positive motivation. The development of managers and staff is seen as a most efficient use of resources, since development activities will expand the organization's capacity to meet market demand. Good managers are considered to be those who come up with new ways to solve problems and who facilitate the participation of staff in decision making. They lead groups through effective decision-making and conflict resolution processes, and they share the belief that they should practice in a manner that reinforces people's control over their own destinies.

In this scenario, the set of beliefs held by managers about the organization and its future supports the acquisition of new manager behaviors. Management practices are able to be critically evaluated for their relevance to current issues. Some are able to be discarded because there is hope about the future and faith in the organization's capacity to meet challenges effectively. *You will know you are there when the life cycle of the organization is understood by the leadership team and this understanding guides action rather than causes paralysis.*

## MANAGER-STAFF RELATIONSHIPS

Manager-staff relationships flow directly from the human resource practices embraced by the organization and are important contextual factors to consider since they affect the degree to which managers are able to operationalize the new facilitator, integrator, and coaching roles.

Human resource practices descend from early movements to give employees voice. Administrators needed individuals who would see to it that the organization fulfilled its obligations to the employees as defined by contracts and labor law. Conditions of employment, pay, and benefits were the initial concern of human resource professionals. As the roles of the manager and the employee became increasingly governed by regulation, human resource professionals took on more of the interpersonal component of the employer-employee relationship.

Unfortunately, this Second Wave labor template still guides the practice of many human resource professionals working in health care organizations. In fact, human resource professionals occasionally have aggressively inserted themselves between managers and staff, and in some organizations the staff view human resource professionals, not managers, as the "neutral" persons to go to with problems. In such organizations, managers will not be able to develop full coaching relationships with the clinical staff because coaching is believed to fall within the domain of another department. Other managers, who are deficient in interpersonal competencies, will be able to go on undetected because someone else is managing their relationships with staff. In addition, manager-staff relationships may be severely limited by rigid and sometimes inaccurate definitions of what is or is not appropriate behavior.

> *Only when managers and the clinical staff take back the accountability for defining their relationships will authenticity be guaranteed. Period.*

Consider the organization where the noise that accompanies any change is seen as indicative of poor management practices. The human resource professionals may work actively to keep conflict of any kind from surfacing and chastise those managers who have noisy departments. Or consider the large human resource department that exerts significant control over operations by limiting managers in their implementation of partnership structures, dictating recruitment and staff scheduling practices, and controlling the resources for ongoing manager and staff development.

When a human resource department has been allowed to define manager-staff relationships, new management practices that alter the balance of power or accountability in these relationships will be very difficult to institute. The patriarchal nature of the industrial model and the accompanying fear of giving employees too much control will stifle prospects for growth and maturity in the manager-staff relationships. *You will know that you are there when the managers and the staff*

*own the accountability for the quality of their relationships and human resource*
*professionals see themselves as consultants to this most central of all dyads.*

## INTERPERSONAL DYNAMICS IN THE MANAGEMENT TEAM

The leadership group can be an agent of change. To the degree that the norms of
the leadership group fit with the new practices being learned, there will be successful transfer of that learning to management practices. Three dynamics within
management groups create powerful conditions that either encourage or deter individuals from engaging in the risks
necessary for personal and role change:
subgrouping, victim behaviors, and
power struggles.

### Subgrouping

Are there identifiable factions in the
leadership team? Subgrouping occurs
in leadership teams because of shared
beliefs about access to recognition, rewards, and resources. The degree of
subgrouping is a direct reflection of the
current level of cooperation and trust in

> *The mind accustomed to factionalism anticipates a knife in the back whereas the mind accustomed to inclusion is comfortable with vulnerability and anticipates growth.*

the group. The more that subgrouping occurs, the lower the trust and the fewer the
opportunities to collaborate. If left unaddressed, lack of trust and lack of collaboration eventually become part of the overall culture of the organization.

There are many forms of subgrouping evident in health care organizations.
Sometimes the top leadership creates subgroups by demanding unfailing loyalty,
thereby creating distinct groups of loyal and disloyal followers. If new practices
are tested at all, they are tested as trial balloons, with careful observation of the top
leaders' reactions. Subgroups can also be divided along departmental lines, such
as in the nursing versus the "other departments" scenario. Competition rather than
collaboration becomes the norm because it is believed that recognition, rewards,
and resources are distributed unequally. A win-lose philosophy is evident. New practices are evaluated based on how well they allow departments to pursue their individual agendas rather than how much they foster the achievement of outcomes. The
shared leadership practices described in this book will fail the test because they are
derived from the principles of partnership, equality, and integration.

Another powerful form of subgrouping is seen when an alliance is created
among poorly performing managers. There is a tremendous inertia in today's

health care organizations when it comes to dealing with inadequate leader role achievement. If there are several poor performers on a leadership team, they will stick close together and let no new members in for fear of being exposed. This group can be counted on to resist change, fan the flames of gossip, and approach learning in a cynical, defensive manner. Their collective actions can breed significant distrust, which in turn prevents the application of new learning for fear of mistakes, criticism, or lack of support from peers. Precious time is spent both inside and outside the classroom dealing with their defensive smokescreens, and time is taken away from coaching the rest of the group in the application of new skills.

*You will know you are there when an atmosphere of security and collaboration exists within the leadership group.* This type of atmosphere encourages dialogue, peer learning, and peer support. Feedback loops are plentiful and, even more importantly, are used to transmit specific and verifiable information about the outcomes of new managerial competencies. There is greater flexibility in roles, since people recognize and value each other's expertise. Finally, the absence of subgroups in a leadership team indicates the existence of a unified belief system that will impact management decision making.

## INADEQUATE ACCOUNTABILITY SYSTEMS AND VICTIM BEHAVIORS

Declining resources, rising discontent, loss of professional credibility, and a shrinking job market are only a few of the more disquieting issues currently facing health care managers. They can be confronted with an optimistic attitude or with the pessimism typical of victims. Inadequate leadership accountability systems reinforce a tendency toward pessimism and dependence, impeding real behavior change.

The commitment to take on new leadership practices naturally leads to new job descriptions and alters accountability. If there is no way to hold managers accountable for the new practices, then some individuals will not commit the time, energy, and resources necessary for acquiring them. Four behaviors commonly occur when individuals are not accountable for their own learning[4]:

*Maintaining ignorance* is one strategy for evading accountability for developing new practices. Managers sometimes studiously avoid occasions where new expectations are discussed or taught. They have many excuses for avoiding training and often are summoned out of the room to answer pages or phone calls. They may eventually become isolated from the rest of the group as their peers begin to change their management practices.

There are specific solutions for this behavior. It is very important to require, in the context of supervision, that each manager articulate verbally and in writing what he or she see as areas of potential growth. It is also important for managers and their supervisors to meet regularly between training sessions to continue discussing areas of potential growth, thus reinforcing ownership and self-direction in the learning process.

In addition, leadership development programs must be designed from a performance outcome perspective. Action methodologies should be carefully selected and participants challenged regularly to articulate and demonstrate what they are learning in front of their peers.

*Shifting the blame* is an effective strategy for not meeting accountability because one cannot be held accountable for something believed to be owned by someone else. In the course of leadership development, individuals practiced in this technique will blame the trainer, the work group, a specific practice exercise . . . anyone or anything else for their failure to learn and apply a new skill.

The best approach for dealing with this behavior is to note the individual's pattern of blaming others for failure to transfer what is being learned and then confront the individual. For example, sometimes blame is shifted to the staff for a failure to develop shared decision making. The staff "do not come to meetings" or they "fail to follow through." Physicians can also be used as scapegoats. For example, managers may describe them as incapable of accepting "the equality of doctors and clinical staff." In both situations, the managers need assistance in recognizing that the stumbling blocks in shared decision making are due to them. They must accept that they have not been successful in developing effective tools for assisting the clinical staff in their shared decision making or helping the physicians view the clinical staff as partners in care.

*CYA (Cover Your Actions)* is an accountability avoidance method that works well because it gives the individual using it time to create a defense before an action has even occurred. The individual fashions well-crafted rationale explaining why new practices will be difficult to implement long before training ever begins. This strategy is easy to spot and also requires confronting the individual.

*Confusion* can be cited as an excuse in the same way that ignorance can. One cannot be held accountable for practices one does not understand. Managers might justify their failure to use new practices by claiming they missed a certain program or could not understand what was being taught. The solution is to indicate to these managers that they are expected to fill in the gaps in their knowledge. This can be done by asking coaching questions such as "What is getting in the way of your learning how to facilitate conflict resolution in groups?" "What is your plan for acquiring the knowledge about conflict resolution strategies that was taught in the program you missed last week?" or "How will you go about getting your questions about this new practice answered?" *You will know that you are there when the leaders see barriers to their learning, own the accountability for doing something*

> **Enlightened leadership development activities benefit managers, staff, and the organization.**

*about it, act to secure what is needed to apply the learning, and work to surmount the obstacles to that application.*[5]

## Power Relationships

What are the dynamics of power in the leadership group? Are the relationships between the levels of leadership in the organization authoritative, parental, consultative, or partnering in nature? The dynamics of power in a leadership team can impede the application of new leadership competencies because so many of the new practices are based on the philosophy that there is no limit to power. This is Third Wave thinking at its best. If managers are to break the artificial barriers between managers and staff, reject parental relationships, and ensure equality between players, then the power relationships in the leadership team must be scrutinized to see that they support these goals.

For example, in the industrial model, the rise of the general manager was accompanied by a loss of faith in the capacity of staff to make good decisions. This became a self-fulfilling prophecy, since staff began to believe that making decisions was not their job and managers were then able to point to the mediocrity of staff decisions. Authoritative and parental styles of management were adopted, accountability for organizational outcomes was looked for at the top, communication was downward, upward communication was distrusted, and there was little participation. Managers in an industrial model organization unsurprisingly resist adopting the shared leadership competencies necessary for the future out of fear of losing the little managerial authority that they have left.

*You will know that you are there when a commitment to engage in new leadership practices is made by each and every person in a leadership position.* When the top leaders are involved in examining their own practices, support and resources for the application of new skills and the removal of barriers to their application are sure to follow. People have to understand that there are no more secrets and that the undiscussables of every management practice are now going to be discussed.

## WHEN THE PERSONAL BECOMES THE PROFESSIONAL

There is no way to separate the personal context from the professional when it comes to a role change as far reaching as the one being proposed here. There are certain very private and personal issues that must be considered in evaluating an individual manager's propensity to apply new leadership competencies. First, what is the individual's definition of success? This definition will stem from the individual's personality needs, work experiences, and formal education. The challenge comes as the application of new competencies increasingly places managers as facilitators in the background instead of in the foreground, where once they operated. This may be an unacceptable shift, particularly when it is accompanied by a change of titles, such as from vice-president to team integrator. *You will know you are there when managers accept as one of their tasks the skillful acquisition of resources for others to disperse as they need them rather than the acquisition and the control of these resources.* Managers should view it as a major accomplishment if staff need them only as consultants.

A second set of issues has to do with where people are in their careers. Novices do not have enough experience to be entrenched in ways of doing things. In fact, they will be the easiest to develop because their potential is waiting to be released. Those at the end of their careers will do what they have to in order to hold on until the golden day of retirement. It is the group in the middle who present the greatest challenge. This group have enough experience to have formed entrenched habits and enough personal or family responsibility to worry about job security. They are the most ambivalent about changing leadership practices because of the risks to their future. How will they get another job at a higher level if they are saddled with the "dumb title" of team integrator? If they do not embrace the revisions in leadership accountability, will they lose their job? *You will know you are there when there is open dialogue about the real risks inherent in personal and professional change and the results of that dialogue are incorporated into professional development plans.*

The complexity of each manager's life will influence the rate of behavioral change. For example, many leadership teams have single parents who occupy leadership positions. They may be raising children, caring for parents, and trying to attend school—all at the same time. The degree of complexity in an individual's life must be examined as part of the assessment of the goodness of fit of the individual to the new role demands. For some managers, the complexity of their personal life simply means change at a different pace. Investment in these individuals is essential, particularly if they show a real willingness to grow.

However, if the complexity of someone's personal life drastically interferes with the performance of new role demands, it might be a time to transition that person into another kind of role with different expectations. The desire to learn is not enough. Real limitations in flexibility and time because of life circumstances must be acknowledged or both the individual and the organization will suffer a great deal. There is nothing sadder than losing a person with a strong potential to make a difference. *You will know you are there when the career paths within your organization have been changed to consider the whole person.* The wise organization will hold on to good people by replacing the more linear model of career advancement with a more flexible and pluralistic career advancement philosophy that recognizes multiple paths for making contributions and developing competence.

Finally, the pre-existing management skill set and the credibility possessed by a manager will influence the rate of transfer of learning to the workplace. Some individuals will have a base or foundation to build upon while others will have to radically retool their practices. Those who have a strong foundation already will begin to produce the expected outcomes sooner than their peers and can be tapped as coaches or role models for those who have a way to go yet. The issue of credibility is important to consider when evaluating the transfer of learning. If a manager is respected; viewed as trustworthy and honest; seen as walking the talk, consistent, caring, and a resource for problem solving, then he or she can provide support during the struggle to adopt new practices. On the other hand, if the manager lacks credibility, staff will suspect there are ulterior motives for the manager's behavior and will refuse to get involved at any level. *You will know you are there when issues of level of skill and credibility are confronted in the process of individual performance planning.*

Clearly, the context in which new leadership competencies are learned and then applied is very important to the actual adoption of new behaviors. Indicators of a context in which new leadership practices can successfully unfold are listed in Exhibit 10-1.

**Exhibit 10-1** Context That Supports New Practices

- The life cycle of the organization is understood and the organization's current stage is taken into account in determining policy.
- There are new definitions of managerial success.
- Definitions, beliefs, and the quality of the manager-staff relationship are owned by the manager and the staff.
- There is no subgrouping in the leadership team.
- There are effective accountability systems and an absence of victim behaviors.
- Power relationships are based on partnership, with each partner working for equity.
- Personal definitions of success fit new leadership roles.
- There are multifaceted career paths for leaders in the organization.
- Individual differences in life circumstances, skill set, credibility, and stage of career are acknowledged and addressed in performance planning.

## STRUCTURES THAT SUPPORT THE TRANSFER OF LEARNING

Organizational structures impact the actions of the people who work in organizations. For example, certain structures and structural features encourage the adoption of new management practices because they provide access to power and create opportunities for exerting influence. In particular, the number of layers in the management structure and the degree of bureaucratization in the organization can have a substantial effect on the adoption of new practices. Bureaucracy is about activity, not outcomes, and as the management layers increase, the opportunities for influence decrease, except at the very top. Each layer strives to hold onto its influence, prestige, and power.

In a many layered management structure, the freedom to design one's work as well as access to resources, information, and support systems vary from level to level. For example, communication barriers down the line can prevent the management team from reaching a shared understanding regarding the need to change leadership practices. Individuals at each level control just what is and is not communicated to the level below, and as a matter of habit they often censor information. Power is located in boxes on the organizational chart. People located in one box are not privy to the vision of people in the next box over.

*How can we do this faster? Is there a less expensive way? What happens if we do not do this anymore? What is the market? Who is the customer? What are we aiming at? What will happen if we do not control it?*

New leadership practices require the leadership team to engage in face-to-face dialogue in which each person's ideas are heard and understood. Power in the new age basically consists of the capacity of leaders using their own skills and abilities to facilitate and integrate the activities of the clinical staff for the purpose of achieving specific outcomes.

Consider what occurred in one organization, where position cuts were identified as necessary by the executive level of the organization. First-line managers were not involved in any of the discussions. They were informed of the cuts 24 hours before they were implemented. It was no surprise that they did not manage the noise that accompanied the layoffs and in fact distanced themselves from the decision.

In another organization, it was recognized that traditional systems of communication were inadequate to support the management team's work in moving to a shared governance model. Regular four-hour retreats were held for each acute care division, attended by vice-president for patient care services, representatives from every level of leadership in the organization, and members of the shared governance steering committee. The purpose was to dialogue and reach a shared understanding about expectations for the manager role in shared governance and the needs of leaders in making the transition to shared governance.

*You will know that you are there when in the course of leadership development programs those systems, policies, habits, and rituals that interfere with the application of new leadership practices are identified and ameliorated.* For example, are the chairpersons of task forces always managers? Are house supervisors routinely left out of important discussions about leadership work? Do all managers have equal access to secretarial support, adequate space to think and work in, and computers or other labor-saving technologies? Is conflict kept underground, denied, or ignored? Are systemwide recommendations for action developed by a select few or by a multilevel, cross-disciplinary group containing staff and managers?

## CHANGE MANAGEMENT

How change is typically managed in an organization can impede or support the adoption of new behaviors because of the impact that change processes have on people's time, energy, and capacities. The pace of change, the resources available for assimilating change, and the architecture in place to implement change need to be examined and understood for their impact upon the transfer of learning.[6]

*What is the pace of change in the organization?* How many changes are being attempted at one time? Are there efforts to connect the different change programs so as to lessen stress factors? Do managers experience the adoption of new leadership practices as connected or unconnected to other major change initiatives?

*What are the resources available in the organization for assimilating change?* Multiple changes can cause information overload, excessive stimulation, distraction from daily operational demands, and burnout in leadership groups. What strategies are being actively pursued to ensure change initiatives do not rob managers of the vitality necessary for successful behavior change?

*Are there sufficient structures, processes, and resources in place to ensure that intended changes are actually implemented?* Do leaders of change projects have strong project management skills? Are there relevant resources available, such as project management software, standardized implementation guidelines, and change management experts? Without the support of implementation architecture, changes will not be sustained over the long term, will have unanticipated negative outcomes, or will sometimes fail altogether. The result will be distrust in regard to any kind of change. People will simply avoid involvement in change initiatives because of the negative outcomes of such initiatives in the past.

*You will know you are there when leaders attend to the pace of change, the need for the assimilation of change, and the selection of appropriate means for the implementation of change.* Managers involved in leadership development activities should be able to describe the relevance of their practice changes to the other major change initiatives in the organization.

## PERFORMANCE EVALUATION

Job descriptions and performance appraisal processes guide the manner in which managers prioritize the tasks they are accountable for. In order for new leadership behaviors to be adopted in practice, performance appraisal must be based on outcomes rather than extent of activity. The multiple-page performance review narrative must be discarded in favor of an interactive review process. In this model, manager job descriptions and evaluation tools are based on the core leadership skills defined as strategically important to the organization. People who know and work closely with the manager whose performance is to be evaluated form a review team. This team includes two staff members, a peer, a supervisor, and someone from another department with whom the manager interacts regularly in the course of daily work. The team discusses the strengths and weaknesses of the manager and writes the review. The manager later meets with the team and discusses the review. Information is presented in a coaching manner, conveying a strong belief in the potential of the person.[7]

> *Not only the managers but those who are managed must understand why the enterprise needs something different from managers.*

## WHAT LEADERSHIP DEVELOPMENT CAN AND CANNOT DO

A central thesis of this book is that leaders in the future must be accountable for designing structures and processes that will enable people at all organizational levels to realize their potential for commitment, competence, and learning. Such structures and processes will allow health care organizations to continually expand their capacity to create their own future rather than fall victim to circumstance. The first step is authentic commitment to the nurturance of new leadership competencies through formal training programs and informal leadership development activities. Such commitment will be manifested in active work by everyone to sustain the application of new practices, the self-conscious deployment of interventions to remove barriers to the application of learning, and the creation of processes for communicating the effects of new practices.

However, no matter how the development programs and activities are presented, leaders will be deeply concerned about the potential impact of their participation upon performance. Their worries can be mitigated by making evident the risks inherent in not engaging in the learning process and not altering their practices. The need for something different from managers must be understood as a strategic necessity by everyone in the organization. If everyone recognizes the importance of reforming traditional practices, open communication about the effects of manager practices is more likely to occur, along with open and informal evaluations of the outcomes resulting from new practices. In addition, the manager–clinical staff relationship will be opened for renegotiation.

The organizational message that managerial practices need to change will foster support for managers to really change the way they perform their role. The oppressive mantle of being expected to always have the right answer is replaced with an acceptance for a wide range of manager behaviors, accompanied by the realignment of accountability between managers and staff. A more open environment will also make it increasingly difficult for individual managers to hide or to resist performance change.

As was mentioned in Chapter 8, leadership development programs of any sort will not be successful if they are not integrated into the corporate priorities of the organization. Learning programs must be developed strategically in order to support the service, fiscal, and environment tactics identified by the health care organization as necessary to success. Just as importantly, the main focus of all activities must be on improving performance. The point of convergence for all leadership development activities inside and outside the classroom has to be on-the-job application and real behavior change. Note that the application of learning in the real world is no easy accomplishment. It requires a considerable commitment of time, energy, and material resources by the organization, the trainers, and the participants of the training programs.

## A FUNDAMENTAL APPRECIATION FOR CLARITY

It is important at the outset to be clear about what leadership development programs can and cannot do. Unfortunately, the literature contains scant informa-

> *Our past and our future are small things compared to the potential inside of us.*

tion upon which to base an assessment of the potential of such programs. Studies of the effectiveness of leadership development usually fall into one of three categories: (1) descriptive evaluations of trends, content, and benefits from participant perspectives; (2) testimonials (subjective reactions toward or assessments of the learning experience); and (3) statistical analyses of behavior or attitude changes.

In fact, a recent attempt to examine management development evaluation studies found that the majority of the studies located were of the descriptive or testimonial type and that the few identified behavioral studies were conducted almost fifteen years ago. Two case studies of long-term behavioral assessment programs uncovered the fact that evaluation was discontinued because participants feared for their jobs.[8] These findings suggest that those interested in documenting a real return on their investment in management development activities will struggle with identifying which behaviors and outcomes can be attributed to the activities and which cannot.

How does one begin to identify the appropriate indicators of successful leadership development programs and processes? The first step is to identify the *underlying assumptions* about leadership development. Is participation expected of everyone in a leadership position? Some assumptions can negatively affect the participant selection process. For example, one assumption may be that it makes sense to invest "only in the best and the brightest." The elitist approach likely to result from this assumption can demotivate some people who have the potential for real growth but are not performing at a level of excellence for a variety of reasons. Also, participants may heave a sigh of relief once they have "made it" to the development program, believing that acceptance into the program by itself represents a measure of organizational success and recognition. When this assumption underlies participant selection, the motivation for real behavior change is severely compromised.

> *Consider how hard it is to change something in yourself and you will appreciate what little chance you have of changing anyone else.*

For example, in one large health care system, an internal management development school was based on an elitist philosophy. Every spring managers from all the member hospitals eagerly waited to see who was on the list to be sent to the school, taking acceptance as evidence of an imminent move one step up the ladder. Since many of the top executives of the system also taught at the school, participants also viewed their classroom time as an opportunity to impress decision makers and avoid career-breaking mistakes rather than engage in real learning.

Another questionable assumption is that the more knowledgeable people are, the better leaders they will be. A selection process based on this assumption will indiscriminately select every manager to participate in training so as to gain knowledge of trends in delivery system configuration, new leadership practices, the financing of health care services, and a host of other topics. However, the problem comes in trying to tie the acquisition of new knowledge to operational outcomes. A deeper understanding of the health care environment is often an inconsequential outcome of leadership development programs. The goal should be to give managers not only an increased knowledge of the health care environment but also the skills to effectively manage it.

A third problematic assumption has to do with the sometimes reactive nature of program planning and execution. It may happen that critical mistakes are being made in a certain area of performance, in which case the knee-jerk response will be to institute remedial training immediately. One unhappy consequence of this response is that people will come to the training angry, feeling singled out for criticism, and fearful of making mistakes, which in turn will inhibit real learning.

Finally, it behooves everyone involved to be realistic about what training can and cannot do regarding a manager's actual performance. Improved performance is primarily in the hands of the participant of a leadership development program. It is the participant who must apply new knowledge in the workplace and act to improve the context in which new management skills are practiced. The motivation and willingness to do something with the feedback received cannot come from the trainer or the learning activities but from within the learner.

How do leaders decide to apply what they have learned? Four questions guide the making of this decision:

1. What do I know that I, as a leader in this organization, must do?
2. What do I know how to do and what do I not know how to do?
3. What resources do I have to do what I must do?
4. Why should I practice in this manner?[9]

In order to apply learning, managers must understand clearly what the new role expectations are and, even more important, how they differ from past expectations. The new role expectations need to be defined by the executive leadership in conjunction with the managers at the outset of a development program to ensure that actual manager performance changes are indeed outcomes of the learning experience. What leadership development can or cannot do is summarized in Exhibit 10-2.

As mentioned in Chapter 8, managers must continually assess their management practices in order to identify which practices to keep and which to discard. Feedback is the basis for any true performance change. Feedback can be provided through a formal self-assessment along with ongoing dialogue during the course of training. Executive leaders can facilitate this process through their own actions.

> *Don't be afraid to go out on a limb. That's where the fruit is.*
>
> **Arthur F. Lenehan**

For example, a nurse executive in one organization applied the concepts being taught in leadership development classes by leading discussions of real case examples in her biweekly operational meetings. There was no doubt in anyone's mind that she expected changes in leadership practices as the result of participation in training.

Observation and feedback during training can be extremely powerful. For example, participants can be assessed and receive feedback in the classroom on the patterns of informal leadership that they exhibit in training exercises, their demonstration of critical thinking as evidenced in linking new concepts, their comfort with risk-taking behaviors, and their attempts to deal with intergroup power or conflict issues.

**Exhibit 10-2** What Leadership Development Can and Cannot Do

Can Do
- Facilitate understanding of skills through practice
- Provide self-assessment opportunities
- Develop understanding of new role demands
- Improve team relationships and feedback skills

Cannot Do
- Make practical use of knowledge
- Improve the context necessary for application of new skills
- Provide motivation to sustain behavior change over the long term
- Replace relationship management

## THE COMPETENCE-MASTERY CONNECTION

Clearly, the transfer of learning to the daily operations of a health care organization is a complex process. The elements of this process and their relationships are shown in Figure 10-1.

Every manager has a unique combination of predispositions, talents, abilities, and developed skill sets. The challenge for the organization is to create the conditions that will release the manager's potential and support the manager in the exploration and adoption of changes in both self and role.

Regardless of the organizational context (i.e., the structures and processes in place), the individual manager must commit to real behavior change. Commitment to change is present when there is a pursuit of honesty in the self-assessment

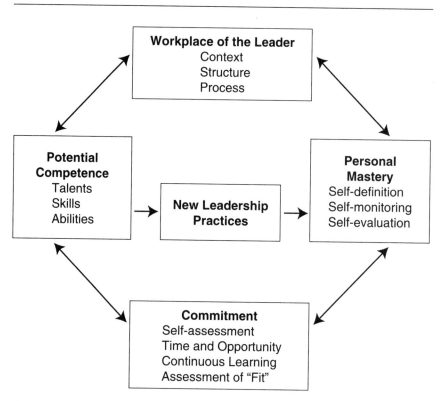

**Figure 10-1** The Competence-Mastery Connection

process, enough time and energy is devoted to leadership development activities, and the manager continually seeks opportunities to learn and apply what is learned and continually assesses the "fit" of new role demands.

New competencies will be used by managers when they have the potential to build upon existing skills, when they have a genuine affinity for the new managerial work, and when they have the opportunity and motivation to change. It is important for managers to like the kind of work that the new leadership role affords them the chance to perform. Some people may not be able to handle the strain of increased interpersonal interactions, as in the case of the accountant who was promoted but became stressed and depressed for lack of good people skills. The new leadership role demands an ability to accomplish objectives through others. There is a basic disconnect if managers, when confronted with substandard staff performance, continue in spite of training to take over the work themselves. The characteristics of the workplace and managers' personal commitment hopefully will combine to release their potential for new leadership practices and the pursuit of mastery. The pursuance of mastery is evidenced in the self-design of leadership roles, which in turn enhances the capacity for competence. This process is circular and self-reinforcing.

> *Partnership, integrator, and technical competencies of the manager add value to the delivery of care, rather than increase rank and status*

The competence-mastery connection helps explain why there are differences in how leadership groups adopt new management practices. Some people may possess the potential for competence, but the characteristics of the workplace made it impossible for them to succeed in the application of new skills. Some people simply avoid commitment, responding to exhortations for a change with a shrug of the shoulder. More dangerous are those individuals who have a high level of confidence but do not have the potential to succeed in the new leadership role. They erroneously believe that they can perform in new ways and are masters at politics. If not detected, they can undermine accurate definitions of new practices.

## PLANNING FOR RE-ENTRY

Leadership development does not end once formal classes have ended. Following completion of classes, the focus of leadership development activities is on smoothing the transition from the classroom to the workplace and setting expectations for the application of what has been learned to daily operations. The organization, the program participants, and the trainer each have a different accountability in regard to this effort.

### Ensuring an Effective Re-entry Process

There needs to be an organizational plan to debrief the participants of the program. Discussions need to occur about the quality of the training, the nature of the content, and what objectives were or were not reached. The managers will need assistance in exploring what learning is most applicable to their particular area long and short term. The discussions can either be small-group discussions or discussions between each manager and his or her immediate supervisor and the trainer. Each manager must be assisted in identifying critical goals for re-entry. Exhibit 10-3 contains sample questions to guide the development of a manager's re-entry strategy.

The top leaders also need to show their support for the leadership practices by attending to the culture in which leadership is exercised. This means creating an environment that facilitates the identification and removal of barriers to new ways of thinking and doing.

### What To Expect from Trainers

The trainer's accountability for the re-entry phase is twofold: to design training activities in the phases of formal training that raise the level and the intensity of feedback and to create a mechanism that makes future training more efficient and

**Exhibit 10-3**  Questions To Guide Re-entry

1. What have I learned that I can use right away in my work?
2. What have I learned that I can use long term in my work?
3. What have I learned that I will need significant support to apply?
4. What will I do differently as a result of my training?
5. What is the potential impact on my peers, the staff, or my boss if I change my leadership practices?
6. What are my strategies for dealing with reactions to changes in the way that I operate?
7. What are my incentives and my motives for changing at this time?

internally driven. In the last months of training, courses must be designed around actual application exercises. This can be accomplished by having participants bring major workplace issues to the training sessions for solution. The intensity of feedback is increased by combining peer, superior, and trainer feedback about performance. Creating conditions to ensure feedback is essential for the transfer of learning to performance. Feedback must be specific, direct, reliable, and useful. It is specific when it is exact and verifiable; direct when it comes from individuals or systems that originated it rather than secondhand; reliable when it is accurate and presented in the form expected; and most useful when it is objective and nonjudgmental.

Commitment to formal leadership development programs will cause demands to extend the workshops to new groups of participants, such as new hires, newly promoted managers, clinical staff leaders, or the leaders of newly formed partnerships. A good trainer will see to it that the leadership development programs improve in efficiency and eventually become internally driven. This is best accomplished by ongoing examination of the methodologies used for teaching new concepts, discarding those that do not produce the optimum outcomes in the least amount of time. The trainer can assist the organization in the ongoing development of new leadership groups by creating and implementing a "train the trainer" methodology. This approach calls for the selection and certification of a core group of peer trainers charged with spreading selected leadership competencies across the system. The trainer develops these individuals and certifies that they are able to teach the requisite content and thus eliminates the organization's need for his or her own services.

It is reasonable to expect certain behaviors from the trainer right from the beginning. The trainer should provide the life-cycle cost of the leadership program being delivered. This helps in setting defined beginning, end, and re-entry training phases and in allocating adequate resources to support the program.

The trainer will systematically analyze, design, and develop a customized program for the leadership team. The executive leaders will ask for descriptions of the methodologies to be used as well as the rationale for their inclusion in the program. They will also meet with the trainer quarterly to discuss the progress of training and any modifications that may be necessary. Also, the trainer will work with the organization to make the training increasingly efficient. For example, the trainer must participate in the evaluation of the training.

The trainer must be a skilled facilitator. Competence as a facilitator will allow the trainer to maximize interaction, challenges to thinking, and peer feedback. In the model used by the authors, participants in a development program are assigned to "learning labs" consisting of peers with whom they stay for the course of the program. Care is taken to ensure that the groupings are cross-disciplinary and multilevel so as to maximize peer feedback and support. This strategy not only keeps subgroups from forming but facilitates education about other people's work. Furthermore, each group becomes a minilab, where participants are continually challenged to apply their partnership, interactive, and administrative competencies in practice exercises.

## EXPANDING NEW LEADERSHIP COMPETENCIES

The health care environment demands that leaders develop the capacity to take people and move them to different places. This will not happen without the clear delineation of manager performance expectations, a recognition of the organization's need for something new from managers, the responsibility, authority, and freedom of individuals to design the management role as needed, and an expectation that leaders develop and execute personal development plans. All too often advocates of organizational change have focused on staff development but have ignored the needs of managers, leaving them hanging by their fingernails in an uncertain environment. Some managers may be given new titles, along with a good dose of Theory Y leadership philosophy, but few adequately understand the tasks of their new role or what it takes to do them well. It is our belief that at least one year of leadership development activities must be directed toward educating the management group. Anything less will be doing those in leadership positions a great disservice as well as reducing the potential for new organizational configurations. The invisible assets of any organization are the core competencies of its leadership group. What can you do to ensure that leadership development activities really do produce the intended results? The following strategies are highly recommended:

- Always seek maximum performance improvement. Keep this objective out in front and visible at all times.
- Take a strategic approach to the planning and designing of the program. Resist the temptation to invest in costly "bandwagon" concepts and select leadership competencies that will really make a difference.
- Set your aim high. Expect leaders not only to develop competency in new leadership practices but also to stretch to greater levels of competence through the pursuit of personal mastery.
- Make sure that the training makes use of the full range of educational technologies. Avoid using technology for technology's sake.
- Build in peer training programs to assist the leadership group in eventually taking ownership of the leadership development process.

- Set goals that ensure that a certain percentage of each manager's time every year is dedicated to the development and application of new leadership practices.
- Make leadership development one of the top tactical strategies for your organization.
- Shift from short-term to long-term thinking. One of the greatest threats to effective leadership development programs is the demand for short-term outcome from a long-term developmental process. It is reasonable to expect to see changes in actual practice six months after formal classes end.

Robert Reich, the Secretary of Labor and one of the foremost experts on the American workplace, made an interesting observation that points up the importance of investing in leadership development. He noted that what corporations are doing to meet the unique demands of their marketplace is "profoundly less relevant than the skills, training and knowledge commanded by American workers."[10]

If health care organizations have any hope of revitalizing their competitiveness in the managed care marketplace, they must invest in their leaders and ensure that the investment produces the intended results. Leadership development activities must teach new principles, values, and behaviors and also how to apply them in the health care workplace. A truly potent leadership development

*If knowledge is power, how do I get some?*

program will include formal educational opportunities, peer feedback and support, and the constructive feedback of those who are being managed. During this time of painful transformation, some will not make it. Along the journey, it will be important to remember the broad accountability entailed by our mandate to serve. Only the sum of what everyone in the organization knows and applies, the intellectual resources of the organization, will enable the attainment of a proper balance among the difficult issues of access, quality, and cost in the delivery of health care services.

## REFERENCES

1. J. Champy, *Reengineering Management* (New York: Harper Business, 1995), 6–8.
2. Ibid., 12.
3. A. Toffler and H. Toffler, "Getting Set for the Coming Millennium." *The Futurist*, March–April 1995, pp. 10–15.
4. R. Connors, T. Smith, and C. Hickman, *The Oz Principle* (San Francisco: Jossey-Bass, 1994).

5. Ibid.

6. D. Collins, R.A. Ross, and T.L. Ross, "Who Wants Participative Management?" *Group and Organizational Studies*, December 1989, pp. 422–445.

7. Champy, *Reengineering Management*, 141–142.

8. H.W. Moulton and A. Fichel, *Executive Development* (New York: Oxford University Press, 1993), 124–169.

9. C. Carr, *Smart Training* (New York: McGraw-Hill, 1992), 14.

10. R. Reich, "Who Is Us?" *Harvard Business Review*, January–February 1990, p. 54.

# Appendix A

# Management Performance Evaluation Process

## THE NEW PARADIGM

> Definition: *Paradigm* **A new model of how a system operates that comes about because of new knowledge. A true paradigm shift results when the new knowledge is so contradictory that it requires major (as opposed to incremental) changes in the approach one takes to that system.**

The implication of the paradigm shift that is occurring in the business world today is that change is a given and our ability to adapt to change is what will lead to our success as an organization. The new paradigm for adaptability is development of an involvement culture, one that emphasizes the partnering of employees with the organization at large and implies that many instead of few will participate in decision making and in the responsibility for and rewards of success. This partnering will result in creation of synergy, the so-called "energy of success."

For managers, this means a move away from the "command and control" style born out of the industrial revolution to a style characterized by facilitation, integration, and coordination. This change is occurring as a result of forces external to our organization. The goal of this task force is to develop a product and a process that will support and facilitate these cultural shifts. Our attitudes, plans, and approaches to work must change—and the change must begin with us. It is time to learn to see the world anew.

---

*Source:* Courtesy of Community Hospitals of Central California, Fresno, California.

## OBJECTIVES

- To provide clarity and consistency in performance expectations and in organizational direction for all managers.
- To serve as a "script" for managers in developing a more intimate understanding of their role and the relationship that it has to the success of the organization.
- To support and reinforce the desired organizational culture by moving to a performance management process that is collaborative, constructive, and continuous.
- To shift from evaluation of management activities to an emphasis on management results (or outcomes).
- To develop a generic job description that will enable us to eliminate job codes.

## DEVELOPMENTAL PROCESS

### 1. Discussion of Underlying Organizational Values

Creation of a culture characterized by

- development of "partnerships" with employees at all levels
- empowerment of employees at all levels
- alignment of employees with key business goals
- development of self-directed work teams
- treatment of the customer as the boss and provision of superior customer service
- continual and ongoing cost-benefit and risk-reward assessments to ensure that we are doing the "right things right" (CQI)

Only by creating an organization guided by this type of culture do we feel our vision can truly become reality.

### 2. Development of Accountabilities

Recognized and briefly defined are the five major areas of management accountability:

Human—having the right people, in the right place, at the right time, doing the right things.

Fiscal—having the right number and the right kind of resources.
Material—having the right supplies, equipment, etc.
Support—having the right work environment and people relationships.
Systems—having the right linkages and systems relationships.

We further identified the three functional accountabilities of management, which are coordinating, integrating, and facilitating.

## 3. Development of Outcome Statements

Once the accountabilities were defined, we began developing statements of outcomes that form the basis of the management role and encompass each of the five areas of accountability. Written in outcome format, the statements of outcomes become the standards; the activities and processes that lead to these outcomes and the measures used as evidence require development by the manager and are individual to the unit/area of responsibility.

The implications of this format are these:

- The tool is generic and can be used for all management.
- Accountability is driven at the individual level.
- The evaluation process is continual and ongoing.
- Performance rating comes as no surprise at year end!

## 4. Development of Evaluation Rating

Two evaluation rating options will exist in this plan. They are "Achieves Outcomes" and "Achieves Exceptional Outcomes." This implies that achieving the stated outcomes is the minimal expectation. Any performance deficiencies will need to be addressed in a performance improvement process.

The evaluation and rating will be "unhooked" from any pay increase. This will allow for a process unencumbered by a focus on pay. In addition, it supports a strategy for paying for measures directly linked to organizational performance.

## 5. Development of Implementation Plan

We have acknowledged that buy-in, commitment, and understanding cannot be gained simply through listening but that reality develops only through an interactive process. For this reason, we recommend that management work in groups to discuss this product and to develop the evidence specific to their individual area and role. Our vision is to divide management into groups of 8 to 12. These groups will include management from all facilities and will be multidisciplinary in nature.

This process will support a partnership culture through development of

- buy-in and commitment
- across-facility and across-unit linkages
- shared understanding and consistency in interpretation
- a team-based approach
- a performance management process

# Appendix B

# Areas of Management Accountability

## HUMAN RESOURCES

- There is a unit staffing plan that effectively addresses staffing guidelines, productivity measures, and the hospital plan of care.
- There is a staffing system that meets customer/service needs utilizing available resources.
- There is a mechanism for selecting human resources that meets the identified needs of the unit.
- There is a mechanism for removing human resources that do not meet the identified needs of the unit.
- There is compliance with all applicable policies, regulations, and laws.

## FISCAL

- There is a unit business plan based on products and services provided that is in alignment with the overall goals of the organization.
- There is a system for effective management of the business plan based on monitoring and modification of operations.
- There is a process in place for communicating the business plan to all involved parties.

## MATERIAL

- There is an ongoing mechanism for assessing material and capital needs.
- There is an effective plan for meeting material and capital needs utilizing available resources that is consistent with the goals of the organization.

*Source:* Courtesy of Community Hospitals of Central California, Fresno, California.

329

- There is an ongoing system for effectively managing material/supply usage on the unit.

## SUPPORT

- There is a work environment that effectively achieves the desired outcomes of the organization.
- There is a process in place that empowers employees through the relocation of decision making.
- There is a mechanism in place to measure quality and to ensure that quality relates to desired outcomes.
- There is a system in place that facilitates staff development, including the performance appraisal process.
- There is an approach to problem solving that utilizes facilitation skills/tools to achieve unit objectives.
- There is a plan that assesses and meets the ongoing developmental needs of the manager.

## SYSTEMS

- There is an approach to work systems that is multifocal, multidisciplinary, and patient based.
- There is an approach to operational systems that ensures effective interdepartmental linkages.
- There is an approach to technological systems that ensures support for work and operational systems.
- There is a mechanism in place for integrating and evaluating systems within and across units to support partnerships.

# Appendix C

# Shared Leadership Survey Items

**SAMPLE SELF-ASSESSMENT ITEMS**

- I carefully observe the various roles that staff play in groups, the methods they use in decision making, and their communication patterns. I freely share this information with the group to help them work better.
- I work hard to gain support for my own ideas. I do not manipulate or withhold information in order to advance my own ideas.
- I free the staff to collaborate and share in decision making. I get staff personally involved in the work to be done. I accept the staff's control of the content and the pace of the work.
- I create an environment where the staff feel connected to me and feel great working with and relating to me.

**SAMPLE LEADER-ASSESSMENT ITEMS**

- The leader clearly spells out her/his own facilitator roles and responsibilities to shared leadership groups.
- Spends little time worrying what the "higher ups" are thinking. Bravely represents people and groups, even if the issue is unpopular with senior management.
- Communicates a leadership vision that inspires others to act. Has a strong sense of purpose. Can describe how her/his work and the work of others contribute to the achievement of the organization's mission.
- Frees staff to collaborate and share in decision making. Gets staff personally involved in the work to be done. Accepts staff's control of the content and the pace of their own work.
- Creates an environment where the staff feel connected to their leader/manager and feel great working with and relating to them.

# Appendix D

# Sample Training Activities

*Cathleen Krueger Wilson*

## ACTIVITY 1

### FACILITATION EXERCISE

This exercise teaches use of problem-solving tools in shared leadership groups (facilitator and maximum of 40 participants).

### Objectives

1. To amplify understanding about when to use nominal group technique, brainstorming, and force field analysis.
2. To provide experience in the application of group problem-solving methods to an emotion-laden problem. (You may use this problem or have groups bring to the workshop an emotion-laden problem from their own setting.)
3. To demonstrate that there are many different solutions to one problem or "more than one way to skin a cat."

### Supplies Needed

1. Handouts on the steps of each problem-solving method
2. Exercise instructions and a copy of the scenario for each participant
3. A blank force field analysis chart
4. Flip charts, markers, and tape for each group

### Time

2½–3 hours

**Steps**

1. Provide lecturette on the four methods of group problem solving, with hand-outs for use later on in the exercise.
2. Tell participants they now have the opportunity to apply these tools in a simulated problem-solving activity. If not already in groups, divide in groups of no more than 8–10 people.
3. Ask each group to appoint a facilitator and a recorder (5 minutes).
4. Hand out scenario. Instruct group to silently read this scenario (5 minutes):

> Your organization is in the throes of work redesign, including the exploration of a stronger professional RN role. It has been proposed that the BSN be the entry-level degree for the new nursing role (probably some version of case management). In addition, it has been recommended that you implement the TEXAS model of pay differentiation according to level of education and that each nurse be counseled to pursue a bachelor's degree, with a goal of an 80 percent BSN-prepared staff by the year 2000. This recommendation has been brought to your council for discussion, recommendations, and an implementation plan that, among other things, addresses ways to overcome problems in implementation.
>
> The board of nursing is considering two levels of license, and several of your managed care contracts are requiring a BSN-prepared nurse to act as a case manager.

*Questioning and Listening (30 minutes)*

In this first step, your group is to collectively identify and summarize the feelings, opinions, values, concerns, and attitudes of each member regarding the proposal. **Do not role-play. Be yourself and honestly express your thoughts.**

*Nominal Group Technique (30 minutes)*

In this step, you will clarify this particular problem and decide which aspects of it your group is able to address. Use the following steps to make this decision in your small group:

**Step 1** Silent Generation of Ideas (Worksheet)
**Step 2** Reporting
**Step 3** Discussion for Clarification
**Step 4** Ranking
**Step 5** Problem Statement

Consult your handout if you are unsure how to proceed. Use the flip chart to record your discussions, ranking, and summaries of your conclusions for presentation to the larger group later on.

### Brainstorming (20 minutes)

In this step, you will generate as many solutions as possible to the problem identified in the previous activity. Follow the steps outlined on your brainstorming handout to identify your top two solutions. Use the flip chart to keep a record of your discussions and conclusions for sharing with the larger group.

### Force Field Analysis (30 minutes)

In this step, your group will analyze one of the solutions identified in the previous step. Use the force field analysis handout and blank worksheet. Use the following questions to guide your discussion:

- Which forces can you influence?
- How can the effects of the helping forces be reduced?
- What additional forces might be listed to carry out the solution?

### Debriefing

Reconvene the groups into a large group for debriefing. Have each group present their conclusions for each step. Lead the group in a discussion of the following key points (30 minutes):

- How did the application of problem-solving techniques limit the emotionality of the situation?
- Are there certain points in a problem-solving process where a technique is more useful than others?
- What was most difficult about using the tools? Easy?
- What did you observe about the solutions presented by each of the groups?
- What will you take from this activity?

# ACTIVITY 2

**FOCUSING ON CONFLICT MANAGEMENT**

This exercise is intended to be used in preparing groups for conflict management training.

A workshop on conflict management causes us to think about our roles, ourselves, our relationships and interactions, and our organization. The statements below should help us get started on this work. You will use your reflections in an early group exercise. Please answer the following questions and bring the completed survey with you to the workshop. Be as candid as you can in completing the answers.

1. Check the most common kinds of conflicts that you encounter in your workplace. Select as many as apply:

   ❑ Conflict with a peer over resource allocation or utilization

   ❑ Conflict with a peer over my role responsibilities or theirs

   ❑ Conflict about the best way to resolve a problem

   ❑ Conflict with my boss

   ❑ Conflict with physicians

   ❑ Inter- or intracouncil conflict

   ❑ Conflict with other departments

   ❑ Conflict with the direction of this organization at this time

   ❑ Conflict with how we go about implementing change

   ❑ Conflict with persons who report to me

2. Select the two most frustrating kinds of conflict you encounter at work. Describe the most recent situations in which you encountered this kind of conflict.

**Situation 1**

**Situation 2**

3. Complete the following sentence: My definition of a work-related conflict is when _____

_____

_____

_____

4. If I could redo one aspect of my position, I would:

5. If I had to state what the two most important things about conflict management are, I would say:

6. My biggest irritation when dealing with conflict is:

7. My greatest satisfaction when it comes to dealing with conflict is:

8. My boss would describe my conflict style as:

9. If my peers could change my approach to conflict management, they would recommend that I:

10. If I could change the organization's response to conflict, I would:

11. The hardest thing about conflict resolution in shared leadership groups is:

# ACTIVITY 3

## ACCOUNTABILITY BEHAVIOR ASSESSMENT TOOL

This tool can be used in training after simulated role-playing in which participants act out a scenario involving an accountability failure. The trainer can either
provide the scenario or ask each small group to write their own and perform it for
the larger group.

**Observation Tool**

1. What did you see happening in the role-playing? (Describe)

2. Is this a common accountability failure in your organization?

3. Check any and all behaviors that were displayed by either of the role players:

| | | Role A | Role B |
|---|---|---|---|
| a. | Pretending not to know that there is a problem | ❑ | ❑ |
| b. | Choosing to deny the problem altogether | ❑ | ❑ |
| c. | Excusing oneself or the other for failure to take action | ❑ | ❑ |
| d. | Asking for direction from the other | ❑ | ❑ |
| e. | Recognizing the need to intervene and taking that risk | ❑ | ❑ |
| f. | Expressing confusion | ❑ | ❑ |
| g. | Redirecting blame to the other | ❑ | ❑ |
| h. | Avoiding the need to involve oneself in the problem | ❑ | ❑ |
| i. | Coaching the other in negotiation strategies | ❑ | ❑ |
| j. | Being unaware that the problem affects oneself | ❑ | ❑ |
| k. | Focusing more upon the uncontrollable aspects of the situation | ❑ | ❑ |

|  | Role A | Role B |
|---|:---:|:---:|
| l. Expressing why one could not possibly be to blame for any aspect of the problem | ❏ | ❏ |
| m. Taking a "wait and see" approach to possible problem resolution | ❏ | ❏ |
| n. Facilitating joint accountability for problem resolution | ❏ | ❏ |

# Appendix E

# Group Guidelines

*Cathleen Krueger Wilson*

S hared leadership groups differ from traditional committees in that individuals do more than give their input and sit back to receive direction from the leader. Dialogue is central to decision making. This means that each member truly understands the perspectives of the others and that these perspectives are then carefully incorporated into a shared decision. In order to set the expectations for dialogue and to differentiate shared leadership group work from past experiences, it is helpful to spend the very first meeting discussing not only what the work is but how the work will be accomplished. The following set of steps can assist you in facilitating the reaching of agreement on a shared leadership group's work process. The agreement reflects a shared commitment to the work of the group and assists in conflict resolution when group problems arise in the course of doing their work.

*Step 1:* Distribute a copy of the sample guidelines (provided below) to group members prior to the meeting. Encourage them to think about each item, modify items if needed, and add any items that may be missing.

*Step 2:* Discuss each item in the group until there is consensus.

*Step 3:* Write up a final list of guidelines and have each member sign them.

*Step 4:* Review guidelines with new members and use them as an assessment tool to determine how well you are working together.

*Step 5:* Review guidelines at least annually and modify them if necessary.

## SAMPLE GUIDELINES

- We respect each member's right to privacy; however, we will strive to be as open as possible in our discussions.

- We will be supportive of each other and refrain from judgment or criticisms.
- We will respect our individual differences and work to bring these to the table. We will not devalue viewpoints that differ from our own.
- Feedback will be given in an open, timely, and direct manner. Feedback will be objective, specific, and related to the work at hand.
- We will not make phone calls or interrupt the group. We will leave our pagers on vibrate during our meetings.
- We will all be contributors to our work because we recognize that within our group we have the expertise to solve any problem we may encounter.
- We are accountable for the work we produce. We agree to ask for what we need in order to be successful and to ask for help when we are confused.
- We will work to know each other better so we can dialogue with greater comfort.
- We will use our time effectively by starting and stopping on time.
- When members miss a meeting, they are accountable for bringing themselves up to date, so as not to require time in our meetings be spent in review.
- We will avoid hidden agendas, personality conflicts, and power struggles. When we encounter a problem in our group, we will deal with it and with each other as soon as possible.

Group Member Signatures

_____    _____

_____    _____

_____    _____

_____    _____

_____
Date

# Appendix F

# Vision and Mission Statement

MISSION
TO IMPROVE THE HEALTH
STATUS OF OUR COMMUNITY

VISION
• TO MANAGE A PATIENT POPULATION TO A
VALUE STANDARD
• TO EMPOWER STAFF TO GROW PERSONALLY AND PROFESSIONALLY

COMMUNICATION

COLLABORATION

PERSONALIZED CARE

EMPOWERMENT

CONTINUOUS IMPROVEMENT

WE PUT OUR PATIENTS FIRST

*Source:* Courtesy of Community Hospitals of Central California, Fresno, California.

# Appendix G

---

# The Flying Starship Factory

## BACKGROUND

This is an all-day simulation exercise, facilitated by the authors, for health care organizations contemplating work redesign. This work redesign program was devised by William O. Lytle and Associates and is published by Block and Petrella and Weisbord, Associates. Materials must be purchased from the publishers in Plainfield, New Jersey, in order to conduct the simulation (tel. 908/754-5100). It is helpful for those facilitating the simulation to be knowledgeable about principles of sociotechnical design as well as to have participated in an actual simulation themselves.

## HOW IT WORKS

In the simulation, participants actually experience the problems and dilemmas encountered in enterprises where work is organized and managed in a traditional manner.

Participants assume roles and are given job descriptions and the tools and blueprints, product samples, and so on, necessary to produce a folded and colored starship. They are given a chance to practice their roles and then they perform an actual product run and measure cost, quality, and satisfaction results.

## OUTCOMES

The discussion of the outcomes is a major part of the simulation, since the limiting effects of traditional structures on work productivity, quality, and satisfaction become evident. This sets the stage for the facilitators to discuss how work is structured in the participants' organization, how the experience that participants

342

just have had mirrors those problems, what alternatives might be considered, and so on. Principles of sociotechnical design are applied here.

Finally the participants reconvene and are given the opportunity to redesign their work in any way that they wish. The results are usually astounding! The simulation clarifies the limitations of the present system of care delivery as well as providing a low-risk, nonblaming environment where people can experience what is not working and understand why.

# Appendix H

# Core Workshops for a One-Year Leadership Development Program

| | |
|---|---|
| **Month 1** | The Manager as Facilitator |
| **Month 2** | The Faultless Facilitation of Groups |
| **Month 3** | The Leader/Manager as Coach |
| **Month 4** | Learning from Conflict |
| **Month 5** | The Empowered Manager: The Personal Journey |
| **Month 6** | Developing Empowered Work Groups |
| **Month 7** | Negotiating the Messy Terrain of Change |
| **Month 8** | Making Change Happen and Making It Work |
| **Month 9** | Organizing Professional Work Systems (the Flying Starship Factory) |
| **Month 10** | Mastering Systems Thinking |
| **Month 11** | Developing Accountability in Organizations |
| **Month 12** | A New Day Is Dawning: Planning Your Career in the New Paradigm |

# Index

## A

Accountability, 28–31
  basic concepts related to, 30
  of board, 95–98
  clarification of, steps in, 79
  and delegation, 29
  and dialogue, 234–236
  as dynamic process, 211
  factors in effectiveness of, 213
  and goals of organization, 73
  in health care reform, 19–22
  impact of, 29–31
  inadequate, signs of, 306–308
  of individual, 216
  and leadership, 58, 215–222
  leadership development program
    related to, 266–267
  and management, 78–79, 80, 81,
    91–94, 220
  of managers, 78–79, 159, 216–221
  of operations council, 168–169
  and organizational structure, 75
  and outcomes, 233–234
  and partnerships, 30, 82
  of patient care council, 164–165
  versus responsibility, 205–207,
    210–212
  and roles, 29, 77
  and service, 85–86
  and shared governance, 158–159
  of teams, 227–228
  and whole systems shared
    governance, 79–82
  of workers, 80–81, 85–86, 209–210
Accountability-based system
  implementation obstacles, 230–234
  locus of control in, 226
  partnerships in, 226–227
  roles in, 224–225
  shift to, 213–215, 223–230
  teams in, 227–228, 232–234
Administrative structure, reduction,
  reasons for, 166–167
Aging population, and health care, 10
AIDS, and health care, 11–12
Association, nature of, 244
Automobile accidents, and health
  care, 11